**What's Left?**

# What's Left? Radical Politics in the Postcommunist Era

**Charles Derber**

with
Karen Marie Ferroggiaro
Jacqueline A. Ortiz
Cassie Schwerner
James A. Vela-McConnell

AMHERST · UNIVERSITY OF MASSACHUSETTS PRESS

Copyright © 1995 by
The University of Massachusetts Press
All rights reserved
Printed in the United States of America
LC 94–36925
ISBN 0–87023–953–8 (cloth); 954–6 (pbk.)
Designed by David Ford
Set in Adobe Stone Serif and Adobe Kabel by Keystone
Typesetting, Inc.
Printed and bound by Thomson-Shore, Inc.

Library of Congress Cataloging-in-Publication Data
Derber, Charles.
    What's left? : radical politics in the postcommunist
era / Charles Derber ; with Karen Marie Ferroggiaro ...
[et al.].
    p. cm.
   Includes bibliographical references.
   ISBN 0–87023–953–8. —
ISBN 0–87023–954–6 (pbk. : alk. paper)
   1. Socialism.  2. Radicalism.  3. Right and left
(Political science).  4. Post-communism.
I. Ferroggiaro, Karen Marie, 1964–  .  II. Title.
HX73.D46   1995
320.5'31—dc20                     94–36925
                                      CIP

British Library Cataloguing in Publication data are
available.
This book is published with the support and
cooperation of the University of Massachusetts Boston.

To activists and scholars
working for social justice

# Contents

|  |  |
|---|---|
| Preface | ix |
| Introduction | 1 |

## Part I. On the Death of the Left

| | | |
|---|---|---|
| 1 | Deconstructing the Death of the Left: The End of Ideology Revisited | 17 |
| 2 | Beyond Socialism and Identity Politics: The U.S. Left after the Fall | 32 |
| 3 | Reflections on the Death of Marxism: A Paradigm in Crisis | 46 |
| 4 | Reframing Revolution: The Rebirth of the Latin American Left | 86 |

## Part II. A Postcommunist Left Agenda

| | | |
|---|---|---|
| 5 | Four Futures of the Left: Defining the Next Stage | 109 |
| 6 | Beloved Comrades: A History of the Left as Community | 120 |
| 7 | The Value(s) of the Left: Toward a Democratic Community | 145 |
| 8 | If Not Socialism, What? The Social Market and Economic Democracy | 168 |
| 9 | Coming Glued: Left Communitarianism vs. Communitarianism of the Professional Middle Class | 196 |
| | Notes | 215 |

# Preface

This book grew out of a Boston College graduate seminar on civil society and progressive politics led by Charles Derber. The contributors to this volume worked collectively to help frame the book's argument, meeting over almost two years to discuss our ideas, data, and writing. Each contributor researched and wrote her or his own chapter, although drafts were discussed and edited by other contributors, with Derber taking the lead. Derber wrote the introduction and the five chapters in part 2, while the other contributors each wrote one chapter in part 1. This volume thus reflects the spirit of community that we advocate for the Left and the nation.

We owe a special debt to S. M. Miller and Patricia Bergin, both of whom participated regularly in the discussions in which this book took shape. Miller's lifelong concern with questions of political vision and strategy informed all of our thinking, and his insights are sprinkled generously throughout the volume. Bergin contributed extensively to our discussions, helping us develop our thinking about civil society, particularly in the context of political developments in Eastern Europe. She also provided systematic, detailed, and valuable feedback on much of the manuscript, especially part 1.

We also want to thank Richard Flacks, Stanley Aronowitz, and Alan Wolfe for reading and offering comments and suggestions on the manuscript. In addition, we thank Dan Feeney for his contributions to our early discussions, and Bill Gamson, David Karp, Eve Spangler, John Williamson, and Diane Vaughn for their encouragement. A special thanks to Elena Kolesnikova for reading and commenting on the manuscript and patiently sustaining the principal author.

## Preface

Finally, this project reflects our goal to be activist-scholars, which is to say that we hope academics will use their talents and skills toward the betterment of society. In this spirit, we are assigning the royalties of this book to Resist, an organization that helps fund grassroots community groups fighting for justice throughout the United States.

# What's Left?

# Introduction

Western leaders have triumphantly proclaimed the "death of the Left." "We won!" exulted President George Bush in 1990, after the collapse of communism in Eastern Europe and the Soviet Union. The president was declaring the final victory of the "free market" over "big government," savoring the delicious notion that the ideas of the Left, not only in the Eastern bloc but around the globe, were history.

Bill Clinton seems to agree that the Left's day is done. While denouncing Bush's free market as the victory of "the inside traders, quick-buck artists and savings and loan kingpins," Clinton is quick to join Bush in declaring big government a nonstarter in the post–Cold War era. Clinton says he has "moved beyond" the old left-right divisions, viewing both Left and Right as Cold War anachronisms and the idea of socialism as a charming relic.[1]

As East and West Germans ripped down the Berlin Wall, both liberal and conservative intellectuals were laying the groundwork for this bipartisan burial of the Left. Ralf Dahrendorf, a liberal and one of the most eminent writers about the 1989 "revolution" in Eastern Europe, announces that every form of socialism and "the hundreds of byways of Marxism" are now "all ending in the sewers of discarded history." He derides the leftists who now speak of the possibility of finding a more humane socialism. To speak of "socialism with a human face," he writes, is "pathetic," as is the effort by some leftists to construct a "third way" between capitalism and socialism, which Dahrendorf calls "a mirage." After the "double nightmare of Stalin and Brezhnev," and the disenchantment with social democracy in Scandinavia, symbolized by Swedish voters in 1991 throwing out their labor government, the Left is "spent."[2]

Many commentators have written that the Left has already self-destructed. Neoconservative sociologist Seymour Martin Lipset writes that "in country after country, socialist and other left leaning parties

## Introduction

have taken the ideological road back to capitalism." The Left is dissolving itself, Lipset suggests, because it is obvious that leftist economics is a disaster and that the electorate will no longer put leftists in power.[3]

Indeed, as the dust clears after the collapse of the Berlin Wall, it is no longer obvious who or what the Left is. Fifty years ago, socialist and communist groups constituted a clear "left," as did civil rights and antiwar activists in the 1960s. But today, while there are lots of "progressive" and dissenting groups, from radical feminists to "deep ecologists," who makes up the Left? Even self-identified leftists are not sure. As one radical intellectual we interviewed said, "I don't know what it means to be a leftist. . . . when I was a child—a red-diaper baby in the fifties—the Left meant the communist and fellow-traveling Left. . . . Another Left that was coherent to me was the New Left of the 1960s and early 1970s." But today, he laments, "Who the hell knows what it is?"

The only people in the United States publicly challenging the idea of "the death of the Left" have been a small number of radical or Marxist intellectuals who have published their own interpretations of the events in Eastern Europe. Their view is unambiguous: that Eastern Europe is no death warrant for the Left. As Michael Lowy wrote in the Marxist journal *Monthly Review,* "One cannot die before being born. Communism is not dead, it is not yet born. The same applies to socialism."[4]

Lowy believes, like many Western radicals, that Eastern European socialism was "far from socialism. . . . What the conservative or liberal media call 'the death of communism' is in fact the crisis of the authoritarian and bureaucratic system of development first established in the USSR in the 1920s and 1930s on the ashes of the Russian revolution. . . . What is moribund and dying in Eastern Europe," Lowy concludes, "is not 'Communism' but its bureaucratic caricature: the monopoly of power by the nomenklatura."[5]

If Eastern Europe was not really socialist and was run by authoritarians posing as socialists, its disgrace and fall should not cast shame on the Left, let alone kill it. Lowy suggests that, more than ever, the Left today has a burning mission: to create democratic socialism. The collapse of the Eastern European political and economic system only makes clearer its sham socialism and the need for the real thing. That, he writes, has always been and remains the Left's agenda.

In reviewing about thirty articles by radicals or Marxists on the "fall" of Eastern Europe, we found Lowy's argument echoed over and over again. "Reports of [our] death," writes Marxist Victor Wallis, "are greatly exaggerated." Most Left activists, he writes, "have for a long time understood the Soviet regime and its offshoots to embody a clear departure from the democratic vision of working class rule that Marx expressed, for example, in his essay on the Paris commune." This was never a reason, Wallis continues, "to abandon the socialist project from which the Russian Revolution had sprung. Why should the final unraveling of a 'false start' prove more debilitating than its earlier institutionalization in a repressive bureaucratic regime?"[6]

Marxist historian Eric Hobsbawm also writes that there remains a compelling case for a "socialist agenda of the 21st century" and that socialism will arise again "from the ashes." An influential U.S. Marxist, Manning Marable, agrees that, far from making a funeral, it is a ripe time for American radicals to "remake American Marxism." And it is not only the Left in the United States, Marable believes, but people all over the world, including the Eastern Europeans themselves, who will join in the new anticapitalist struggle. "The Eastern European and Soviet working classes will be bitterly disillusioned when they see exactly how market economics really works." If we "have historical imagination and dare to be Marxists," Marable concludes, "the so-called death of socialism in 1989–1990 will one day transform itself, Phoenix-like, into a new birth."[7]

Perhaps. But there is a knee-jerk quality here, something as ideologically predictable in these Marxists' responses as the mainstream writers who repeat the "death of socialism" like a mantra. The defensiveness of the Marxists is tangible, and their almost reflexive call to struggle on for the "real" socialism bespeaks the angst of the true believer. A Left not able to contemplate the possibility of its own death may be a Left whose survival in the end will not make much difference.

The authors of this volume all share a commitment to progressive social change, and some of us have been active all our lives in Left politics. We believe this is a pivotal moment to think anew about what the Left is and where it is going. In a seminar at Boston College, we read everything we could find in the public debate over the "death of the Left" and came away disappointed. The mainstream is too eager to bid a hasty and final farewell to the Left, too grandiose in its proclamations of the "end of history," and too smugly complacent about the triumph of capitalism. Marxist writers are too quick to gloss over the significance of what has happened in Eastern Europe, too premature in announcing business as usual for the Left, and too facile in their calls for democratic socialism. One finds on both sides some brilliant argumentation and stylish writing, but not great wisdom.

## Introduction

It is scarcely surprising that the debate, which has had much of the quality of instant analysis and spin doctoring, would be predictable and stereotyped. Neither side took the time to find out how ordinary Left activists or sympathizers are actually thinking about Eastern Europe and its implications for Left politics. One would think that any diagnosis of the Left's condition would involve listening carefully to the patient. One would want to know how people on the left are now thinking about their movement, whether they see a crisis in the wake of the collapse of communism, whether they hold on to some vision of socialism, whether they remain committed and politically active, who they now see as their companions in struggle, and where they see the Left headed. Knowing the answers to these questions cannot resolve the question of the "death of the Left," but it certainly seems an important starting point.

We decided to move forward with two aims. One was to carry out a fresh study of the Left—more accurately of several different "lefts" in the United States and other parts of the world—to find out how the events in Eastern Europe and the Soviet Union are actually being experienced by people on the left and are affecting how they think and act. But the Left self-diagnosis that we heard, as well as our own year-long seminar discussions, also led us to new questions and interpretations. So a second objective was to approach the question about "the death of the Left" from the perspective that was emerging from our work and offer our own assessments about the Left's prospects and agenda. Our hope is both to engage fellow members of the Left community in a dialogue about change and simultaneously to speak to the great majority of people who do not identify with the Left about why the whole debate is relevant to their lives and the future of their societies.

We believe that both sides of the "death of the Left" debate are seriously in error. Contrary to the mainstream, we shall show that the Left has a role, potentially of surprising importance, in the reconstruction of Western capitalist societies as well as the beleaguered nations of the Third World. But contrary to the Marxists who have been heard in the debate, we suggest that the Left cannot realize that role without fundamental transformation, including possibly a shift away from the socialist project itself.

## The West after Communism: Civil Society at the Brink

The West is sliding into a period of social breakdown that neither conservatives nor liberals can forestall. To see the prospects for the Left in this

## Introduction

new era in the United States and other Western societies requires a clear diagnosis of the malady. After twelve years of a conservative regime committed to a free-market revolution, Western capitalism, particularly in the United States, is in its worst crisis since the Great Depression and civil society—the set of moral and social ties that bind people into a community and constrain individuals from acting purely out of self-interest—is dangerously eroding.

Remarkably, the "death of the Left" writers, who have written instructively about the decay of civil society in the East, say almost nothing about the crisis in the West. The implicit view is that the collapse of communism proves our own troubles to be pedestrian. In fact, by enthralling themselves and the public with the spectacle of communism's grand collapse, they have obscured the gravity of the West's ills and the need for a new transformative voice.

Western capitalism may have "won," but its problems, as the public has begun to recognize, are not those of ordinary recession nor of traditional political apathy or routine social upheaval. By the early 1990s, a large majority of U.S. citizens told pollsters that they believed the country was fundamentally "off course" and moving "in the wrong direction." Alarmed by urban decay, poverty, crime, homelessness, low wages and high unemployment, high medical costs, crumbling public education, and many other problems, those polled feared that things would only get worse and sensed that the crisis has a systemic character. Most were pessimistic that any form of mainstream politics could solve the problems.

Indeed, there is a surprising similarity between the problems of Western societies and the disorders of the failed socialist countries. Western economies are not in the same terminal condition as the Eastern ones, but there are overwhelming economic difficulties, even in the most prosperous countries such as the United States. Wages in the United States have declined since 1973, and for the first time in U.S. history, children can no longer expect to enjoy a standard of living better than their parents. Productivity and global market share have tumbled in one industry after another. Despite President Clinton's deficit-cutting zeal, the total federal government debt, by 1994, had reached a record $4.6 trillion. None of the conventional fiscal or monetary tools seem to solve the problem—suggesting, as in the East, the need for systemic change.[8]

But perhaps the most serious problem facing the West is not economic but social, again suggesting surprising parallels with the Eastern bloc failure. Dahrendorf argues that the collapse of civil society—that is, a

## Introduction

rotting of the social fabric and the moral order—is the most poisonous legacy of communist rule. We are only now learning, Dahrendorf writes, of the extent of the "social and moral degradation of the countries of Communist Europe." He does not wildly exaggerate in claiming that Eastern "socialism" constituted a "pretty pure form of what it pretends to have overcome, exploitation, except that the regime is sufficiently incompetent in economic matters to make sure that there is not a great deal to exploit." In the name of socialism, centers of power independent of the state were crushed, disempowering people and producing a level of distrust, manipulation, and alienation in everyday life that many leftists had assumed could only be produced by the market. One Czech leftist intellectual told this author that morality had broken down so completely under the communists that she no longer trusted anyone, even her mother and sister. The prevailing ethos in the twilight of communism: trust no one and do whatever is necessary to survive.[9]

In the United States and other Western countries, similar social and moral cancers, although of quite different origins, are spreading. There are endless social statistics that suggest a serious weakening of civil society. We have the highest murder rate in our history, between five and ten times that of other industrial countries such as Japan or Germany. Over fifty million households stock guns to protect themselves. By one estimate, 135,000 kids bring guns to school on any given day.[10]

The social infrastructure is eroding. As affordable housing shrinks, the homeless are multiplying. At least thirty-five million have no health insurance, and 10 percent of the country uses food stamps. Over thirty million are poor, including one out of every five children. Life expectancy of our black urban youth is lower than that of children of the same age in Bangladesh.

Americans of every class are discovering forms of insecurity formerly reserved for the poor. Over one-third of the labor force are "temps" or other disposable workers; these include accountants and middle managers as well as janitors, supermarket cashiers, and factory laborers. As jobs become more contingent for everyone, so do families. Over 50 percent of all marriages break up (75 percent among young marrieds), about 70 percent of children will experience a change, loss, or absence of one parent before age eighteen, and, by the year 2000, over 50 percent of adults are projected to be single or divorced, all suggesting an atomization and family ungluing unprecedented in modern times.[11]

The erosion of civil society is the dark side of what some are calling "postmodern capitalism." Ever since the British enclosures threw the peasantry off the land, as Karl Polanyi described in his epochal book *The Great Transformation*, the history of capitalism has meant never-ending social dislocation, leaving a trail of broken communities and uprooted workers. But as multinational corporations now shift capital and technology with lightning speed around the globe, they have upped the ante, shredding the fragile social contract that had permitted a modicum of stability in jobs, families, and neighborhoods.[12]

A healthy civil society is marked by a robust sense of solidarity, in which intact families, neighborhoods, work communities, and other voluntary associations cooperate for common ends. A leftist concept of civil society envisions democratic communities that meet needs for belonging and meaning while struggling against injustice in all social spheres. This implies, we shall see, that the Left has not only to pursue a robust agenda of economic democracy but help reshape familial, sexual, ethnic, racial, religious, and other communities so that they create "habits of the heart" consistent with universal ideals of equality and solidarity.

## The Left's Opening: Postcommunism and New Opportunities

While the Left could, indeed, fade away in the postcommunist era, we believe that the erosion of the social fabric presents a new opening for the Left. Buried deep in the Left's tradition is a vision of community and of a "social market" that can help heal the sickness afflicting the United States and many other societies that are beginning to unravel. We argue in this book that a Left politics of democratic community, or Left communitarianism, has the potential to speak powerfully to Western publics haunted by the fear of social breakdown and can help guide the reconstruction of a national community characterized by democracy and justice.

The possibilities of the Left are rooted in two political realities. First, both conservatism and liberalism are wedded to forms of individualism that render them incapable of envisioning a new positive form of community. This creates a vacuum at the center of political discourse in an era focused on the task of social reconstruction.

Second, the concept of social solidarity, indispensable to any project of social reconstruction, is close to the heart of Left politics. Socialism was originally conceived as an alternative to individualism, not capitalism. Its evolving critique of capitalism is often mistaken for a simple defense of equality, but the defense of community is no less fundamental.

The Left in the United States has a historical communitarian legacy, one emphasizing the possibilities of solidarity and cooperation, that we

## Introduction

seek to reclaim in this volume. That tradition, while largely forgotten today, is rooted in the concerns of the earliest Left thinkers, who contemplated with awe the rise of industrial capitalism and its shattering impact on human connections. While not nostalgic for the communal order of tradition, the early critics of capitalism struggled for a vision of a new solidaristic society, recognizing that humans are deeply social and need community both to belong and to develop their own individuality. Their idea of a politics of community speaks viscerally to a society in which the sense of shared fate is disappearing; it should echo powerfully down all the mean streets of the United States in which passersby meet indifference and violence.

Since community can mean all things to all people, we should be clear at the outset about what Left communitarianism is not. It is not a romantic return to a precapitalist golden age, which created communities based on deep economic, racial, and sexual inequalities, nor an embrace of postmodernist futures, which envision only partial, fragmented, and particularistic communities of protean individuals with no enduring commitments. And it is not the vision of the self-proclaimed "communitarian movement" advanced by academic advisers and "new Democrats" closely associated with President Bill Clinton. That movement, as we show in the last chapter, has reactionary overtones on matters of crime and "family values" and imagines restoring morality and social responsibility while aiding and abetting the very market forces that are turning communities into shuttered ghost towns and large sectors of the work force into rootless migrants.

Left communitarianism views morality, family, and community—themes until recently monopolized by conservatives—as close to the heart of the current political challenge. It looks to the rebuilding of family, neighborhood, ethnic, and other ties—along with the strengthening of the new communities that have mushroomed among women, gays, and minorities of color—to create a new civility and morality. It is a struggle in favor of multiple and rich forms of human association and solidarity, recognizing that the preservation of society is at stake.

But Left communitarianism rejects the now-fashionable view that the crisis of community is a moral rather than economic question, unrelated to capitalism and the structures of social power. At the heart of Left communitarianism is a new economics that embraces markets but seeks to tame and regulate their relentless tendency to uproot and dislocate. The crisis of values begins among elites who preach community but undermine it in the service of power and money, and Left communitarianism recognizes that revitalizing family values and community morality depends on a new economy that takes stock of the social consequences of business decisions.

While it seeks to build connections among all struggles for justice in a fight for a new economic order, the new vision does not subordinate, as did the Old Left of the communist era, all social struggles to those against capitalism. Finding community in resistance to many different forms of shared oppression, Left communitarianism recognizes the crucial importance of new gender, race, and other communities of resistance whose struggle is only partly economic. Nonetheless, it points to the interpenetration of economic, racial, and gender-based systems of power and seeks to unite widely diverse groups in common struggle.

While the challenge is formidable, we see unique opportunities. For one thing, as it goes about the business of honing its vision of community and civil society, the Left is now liberated from its ambiguous relation with Eastern bloc or Soviet communism. As noted earlier, most Western leftists long ago disassociated themselves from what they variously called "state capitalism" or "*nomenklatura* [or apparatchik] communism," but they never fully cut the umbilical cord, many continuing to feel that Eastern European existing socialism was deeply flawed but still important proof that alternatives to capitalism could survive in the modern era. A kind of misty romanticism about the social planning and programs of the Eastern bloc persisted in many sectors of the Left. Perhaps the majority of leftists, fearful of reinforcing the crude anticommunism of Western leaders, never fully came to terms with the hypocrisy of class rule by the nomenklatura, the disaster of bureaucratic central planning, the ecological catastrophe of the Eastern bloc, and the efforts to suppress civil society in the Soviet Union and its satellites.

A leftist reappraisal of Eastern Europe is an enormously important opportunity to refine the Left's vision; it will help inspire new thinking about Left values, principles, and future directions. As we try to suggest in this volume, the tragedy of authoritarian statism and civil society in Eastern Europe should ignite a new debate on the left about community, the state, and public life. Likewise, Eastern European economic failures offer an opportunity to reconsider the Left economic agenda, with many leftists in Eastern Europe itself having already drawn the lesson that certain forms of private property and market arrangements are vital to freedom and prosperity.

The postcommunist era opens up other opportunities linked to political credibility. Common wisdom suggests that the collapse of communism has destroyed whatever credibility the Left once had, and no doubt there is some truth to this. But, conversely, the disappearance of the bogeyman of Soviet communism will unburden the Left of external baggage that saddled it for many years. When it can no longer be caricatured as the agent or dupe of a foreign enemy, the Western Left will experience a great liberation. The Right is now deprived of its most potent weapons of slander, and the Left will not be vulnerable to repeated episodes of McCarthyism or J. Edgar Hooverism.

Tactically, the Left in the 1990s may be in a surprisingly advantageous position not unlike that of the far Right in the mid- to late 1970s. Apparently marginalized as a fringe group, Ronald Reagan and his fundamentalist and neoconservative cohorts in one short decade catapulted themselves into the mainstream. They skillfully capitalized on the existing economic and social malaise of the Carter years, partly by convincing the U.S. public that their problems could be traced to the liberal and Left movements of the 1960s.

Twelve years of Reagan-Bush and the Republican landslide of the 1994 mid-term elections seemed to make the Left as hopelessly marginal as the early Reaganites. Speaker of the House Newt Gingrich proclaimed he would bury any remnants of the "Great Society, counterculture, McGovernick" legacy. It is "virtually impossible," Gingrich said, for the Left now to be part of the national political conversation, a verdict many Leftists themselves glumly accepted.

But the Republican "Contract With America"—and Gingrich's vision of capital gains cuts, school prayer, and orphanages—will not solve the problems of jobs, violence, and family breakdown afflicting the nation. Conservatives now bear the onus of responsibility; as the new Republican program—which columnist Sandy Grady called "warmed-over Reaganomics with a dash of Pat Robertson Bible-thumping"—fails, the country will be receptive to radically different visions. In the final wreckage of Reaganism lies fertile ground for a transformed Left offering genuinely democratic and communitarian remedies.

## Where We Go from Here

Will the Left seize the opportunities we describe? This obviously depends most on the Left itself, which is now confronted with major choices about survival, identity, and new directions.

The first part of this book is a fresh study of the Left, in which we let

## Introduction

Left activists and intellectuals speak for themselves. Our objective is to give voice to a wide variety of Left communities through a series of conversations, interviews, and analyses of written documents. We have been most interested in Left activists and intellectuals in the United States, but we also have attempted to learn about the Left in the Third World.

But who exactly constitutes the "Left" that we were trying to understand? As noted earlier, nobody seems quite sure who the Left is anymore, and the political and ideological bases of definition seem increasingly muddied. Many define the Left as those seeking a greater role for national government in the economy. But many leftists, including a significant percentage of socialists today, are antistatist and think of themselves as anarchistic, localist, or populist.

A more sophisticated definition has been advanced by Richard Flacks, who defines the Left as "that body of thought and action that favors the democratization of history making, that seeks to expand the capacity of the people themselves to make the decisions that affect the conditions and terms of everyday life." But Flacks acknowledges that his own definition is flawed in practice, since left-leaning New Dealers of the 1930s and state socialists through much of this century have favored top-down rather than bottom-up decision making. While holding to his view that the Left is that tradition which seeks to empower ordinary people as the primary shapers of history, Flacks argues that the Left in practice is a proliferation of relatively autonomous social movements that are not and should not be linked to a single vision or agenda, a view highly contested by other theorists.[13]

The problem of defining the Left today reflects two remarkable developments that together form the context for this book: the collapse of communism in the East and simultaneously the rise in the West of feminism, the gay and lesbian movements, antiracist struggles, and other new social movements that do not share a focus on the transformation of capitalism or any other common vision. Communism's collapse has helped shatter the socialist vision that unified an earlier Left, while the rise of identity politics has appeared to divide the Left into inherently segregated struggles for racial, sexual, and gender equality.

The problem of defining the Left is, then, ultimately part of the very problem we seek to understand and remedy. As currently constituted, the Left has no singular identity and no clear definition. Rebuilding and redefining a coherent Left ultimately means conceiving an alternative economic vision to socialism while finding a way to meld the new iden-

## Introduction

tity movements in common cause. This emphatically does not mean subordinating the new movements to a new economic agenda, although an alternative economic vision is discussed here. Instead, it means finding a new universalistic vision, rooted in the Left's own traditions and the multiple liberation struggles of its current splintered movements, that can help bring both the Left itself and the larger society together.

We started our study without a fixed theoretical definition of "the Left," since our problem was partly to learn empirically how the term is now being defined by both activists and ordinary citizens. We thus selected groups who tended either to self-identify with the Left or to be classified as "on the left" by others. This led us to social movements such as the peace movement and Third World solidarity groups, the labor movement, feminism of many varieties, movements of racial minorities, gay movements, citizen action groups, and environmentalists, as well as radical intellectuals and writers.

In chapter 1, Jacqueline Ortiz frames part 1 by analyzing three of the most influential theorists of the "death of the Left." Ortiz argues that while their analysis is deeply flawed, the Left cannot afford to ignore it and that, ironically, it can help inform a new Left politics.

In chapter 2, Cassie Schwerner writes about Left activists in the United States, focusing on their views about the collapse of communism and the prospects for socialism and the Left at home. Drawing on interviews with activists from a wide range of movements, Schwerner concludes that the fall of communism marks the beginning of a third stage in the American Left, founded on neither the socialist agenda of the 1930s Left nor the "identity politics" of the 1970s and 1980s.

In chapter 3, James Vela-McConnell writes about the crisis in Marxism, based on his interviews with Marxist academics in the United States. Vela-McConnell argues that Marxism is entering a stage of "paradigm crisis" and that Eastern Europe may constitute one of those decisive anomalies in the old paradigm that leads to intellectual revolution and a potential revitalization of the Left.

In chapter 4, Karen Ferroggiaro shifts our focus from the United States to the Third World. Focusing on the impact of events in Eastern Europe on the Left movements of Central America, she argues that the "death of the Left" thesis is fatally "Eurocentric"—that is, inappropriate for understanding the unique circumstances of the Third World. In an intensive case study of El Salvador, she concludes that a new political space may be opening up in the Third World for a transformed, democratic Left.

In the second part of the book, we expand on our perspective about

Introduction

where we believe the promise of the Left lies. The social movements that make up the Left have yet to discover the common ground on which a postcommunist era of Left politics can be launched. Richard Flacks and others have argued that such ideological diversity and organizational decentralization actually serve the Left well, helping ensure that it does not succumb to a monolithic doctrine or to a stifling hierarchical structure. While we are sympathetic to these concerns, we believe the Left is now characterized by an excessive and destructive fragmentation that threatens to subvert any possibility of concerted, unified Left politics beyond the limited agenda of particular identity movements. In our view, this threatens the very essence of what has constituted the best tradition of the Left, that capacity to advance a universal vision of solidarity and justice that builds and depends on pluralistic social movements but transcends their own particularistic agendas. We thus propose a dialogue about a common agenda that might unite all sectors of the Left and about the directions of change necessary not only in the larger society but in the Left itself.

In chapter 5, an introduction to part 2, we review four different visions of the Left in its next stage. We discuss the limitations of socialism, identity politics, and radical democracy, and then make a case for Left democratic communitarianism.

In chapter 6, we look at the history of the Left in the United States, drawing on both the old and new Lefts. We show the Left has rich communitarian roots to draw on but that it has to learn from its mistakes and grow beyond the limits of its old and comfortable modes of thought.

In chapter 7, we argue that in a period of breakdown, the issue of values moves close to the center of politics. Publics haunted by the specter of social disintegration sense a moral crisis and seek a revitalization of values. The Left has for too long allowed the Right to represent itself as the defender of social values, permitting conservatives to obscure their central role in weakening the moral fabric. We argue that the time is ripe for the Left to offer its own interpretation of the current crisis in values and to present a new public and moral philosophy based on its historic embrace of democracy, justice, and solidarity.

In chapter 8, drawing on lessons of Eastern Europe, we suggest that the Left should not wed itself to socialist economics in the coming stage. Instead, it needs to envision a "social market order" that integrates the Left's cooperativist and social democratic traditions and embraces the vision of economic democracy that Left thinkers in the United States have proposed as an alternative to both capitalism and socialism.

## Introduction

Many may conclude that we are advocating that the Left join forces with the new communitarian movement that some prominent intellectuals and policy analysts in the United States have founded. While there are affinities between their agenda and our own vision, we show in chapter 9 that our conception of Left communitarianism departs radically from that of mainstream communitarian thinkers.

Can the Left save itself from the premature death now being widely predicted for it and help save society by doing so? We believe it can, and we hope this book will help inspire the new thinking necessary for the task.

# Part I

## On the Death of the Left

Jacqueline A. Ortiz

# 1

## Deconstructing the Death of the Left:

THE END OF IDEOLOGY REVISITED

Two years following the German reunification, an article in *Newsweek* magazine reported the sighting, on an office wall in one East German high school, of a cartoon depicting Karl Marx addressing a legion of followers. The caption read, "Sorry, guys, it was just an idea."[1] If life seemed difficult for the Left in the past, things have recently taken a turn for the worse. The collapse of the Soviet and Eastern European nations casts a long shadow of doubt on the traditional socialist project. Both in the West and in the East, journalists and academics alike trumpet the triumph of liberal democracy and the death of socialism.

The same nostrums were offered by liberals and right-wingers during the Cold War days. What has changed is the global political atmosphere and loss of the tacit support provided by the existence of alternative systems, however flawed. Even for those who continue their quest for a more humane socialist alternative, the implosion of one communist state after another in the span of one short year poses difficult questions. The move away from social democracy in nations like France and Sweden adds to the evidence that socialism and the Left are in an unprecedented crisis.

The tone of many post–Cold War writings reflects what E. P. Thompson has appropriately coined "liberal complacence." Although deep social and economic problems in the West are acknowledged, the resounding message conveyed in these pieces is that liberal democracy has triumphed and that solutions to these problems can be found within its framework. The rationales provided to support these claims vary considerably, yet the final message encourages the abandonment of the socialist project and any "idealistic" notion of fusing the best elements of socialism and liberalism. The Left is advised to join the ranks of those who search for solutions within the bounds of liberal democracy. Within this body of literature, three of the most influential interpreters of the events in Eastern Europe, Paul Starr, Ralf Dahrendorf, and Francis Fukuyama, provide important arguments to support the "death of socialism" perspective.[2]

The aim of this chapter is twofold. In the first half I take a close and critical look at the "death of socialism" proponents and their resistance to searching for alternatives. In the second part, I suggest that even though these three authors offer persuasive reasons to abandon some of the ends and means of socialism, their arguments for an exclusive reliance on liberal democracy are both premature and incomplete. All three of the works examined in this chapter fail to recognize adequately the challenges presented to liberal democracy by the deterioration of civil society. It is this deficiency in liberalism that points to the need for a new leftist agenda.

## Humming Socialism's Requiem

Pulitzer prize–winning sociologist Paul Starr presents his endorsement of liberalism in his 1991 article entitled "Liberalism after Socialism." Starr relies heavily on the evidence of the economic collapse of socialist models to condemn both socialism and the search for a "third way." In his view, any search for a middle road between socialism and liberalism in the United States is misdirected and should be abandoned.[3]

According to Starr, the traditional leftist assumption that socialism would succeed liberalism is false. He suggests that the speed and breadth of the transformations in the former USSR and in the Soviet bloc point to fatal flaws of centrally planned economies. The track record of socialist politics in Latin America and Africa also points to drastic problems with the model, as do the shifts in European leftist political parties away from centralized economies. In essence, socialism has failed to provide either the economic equality or the communitarian ethos that it had initially been intended to ensure.

Socialism, according to Starr, is defined as "a party or program that gives highest priority to equality of economic condition and calls for replacing private ownership in the sphere of production and substituting some form of public control for the market as the principal mechanism for allocating investment." Discussing the inefficiency and inflexibility of state bureaucracy, Starr argues that "the burden of the socialist experience" dooms prospects for successful central planning.[4]

Along with his familiar critique of the Eastern models of central planning, Starr also denounces the Western tradition of democratic socialism:

> The theory comes to grief on the hard rock of specifying political arrangements. To condemn bureaucracy is easy; to find means that will actually avoid it is the trick. . . . Oscar Wilde's famous remark that the problem with socialism is that it takes too many meetings is not just the view of the ironic aesthete: it is the basic problem with a theory that is unrealistic about human interests and energies.[5]

Because none of the different varieties of socialist experiments has yielded much in the way of successful alternatives to capitalist economics or democratic politics, it follows that no combination or "third way" between the two systems could contribute solutions to American problems. He warns:

> Liberals ought to continue striving to reform capitalism—to eradicate poverty, to overcome racism, to protect the integrity of the environment, in short to achieve a wide variety of humane and democratic objectives. But it is time, I will argue, to give up on the idea of a grand synthesis or a third way, if by that is meant some system mid-way between capitalism and socialism or an alternative altogether "beyond" them. Reform capitalism, yes; replace it, no.[6]

Starr resolutely advises, "while the house of liberalism in America has many rooms, it should not be allowed to become the last refuge of a defeated and disappointed socialism . . . the romance should be over once and for all."[7]

Starr's recommendation is that the Left continue to fight the pathologies of capitalism but not strive to construct a systemic alternative to liberal democracy. He advises the Left that,

> democratic liberalism rests on a foundation of constitutionalism and guarantees of individual and political civil liberty. These rights are primary; they take priority over property rights where they come into conflict . . . the realistic democratic alternative to socialist planning lies primarily in the design of markets and other institutions: the shaping of the rules of the game . . . liberalism has a conception of equality that is more restricted, but less likely to be perennially disappointed.[8]

For Starr, capitalism is the only viable form of economic organization that permits both needed economic growth and social stability. Even though capitalism is not problem-free, it has provided what he judges

## On the Death of the Left

to be a minimal standard of justice and equality. Poverty, racism, and environmental degradation are all problems that can be satisfactorily solved within a liberal democratic framework.

Starr brushes under the rug a substantial body of literature suggesting that class conflict and its accompanying social degradation will always be part of capitalism. He insists that the eradication of poverty and racism will be possible in liberal democracies but fails to provide any plausible explanation why this has never happened. Starr ultimately suffers from the same affliction as the socialists who rely on theory instead of the burden of reality. If liberalism were also judged on the burden of its history, the search for an alternative beyond capitalism would seem more urgent.

Ralf Dahrendorf, another highly influential exponent of the "death of socialism" argument, presents a variant of Starr's call for liberal democracy in his book *Reflections on the Revolution in Europe*. In a lengthy essay intended to be a letter to a Polish colleague seeking advice concerning the political future of his country, Dahrendorf presents his thoughts on the demise of communism and the future of Eastern Europe. Even though his work is written to address the issues confronting the Eastern bloc nations, Dahrendorf very clearly includes a series of prescriptions for leftists and intellectuals around the world. Like Starr, Dahrendorf declares the death of socialism, encourages its abandonment, and advises his Polish friend to accept the framework of liberal democracy, or what he calls the "open society."[9]

Also like Starr, Dahrendorf points to the many economic deficiencies of centralized bureaucratic authoritarianism, or "really existing socialism." Its failure to produce its own version of a Protestant ethic led state socialism to make "exploitation and suppression as inevitable as scarcity and pretense." Dahrendorf suggests that "market-oriented economies based on incentives rather than planning and force represent the advanced stage of modern development. In this sense, capitalism succeeds socialism."[10]

Dahrendorf also highlights political reasons for socialism's failure in Eastern Europe. In his view the totalitarian and nondemocratic nature of socialism never permitted a stable and sustainable political arrangement. In his words, "Communism never worked. In Central Europe, at least, it was an imposed regime of suppression which from the beginning gave rise to resistance and violent conflict." He adds, "suppression defeats its own ends: totalitarian governments are in 'danger' of being violently overthrown to the extent to which they resort to suppression as a means of dealing with conflict." In the end, it was socialism's illiberalism that destroyed it.[11]

Like Starr, Dahrendorf urges the abandonment of any attempt at fusion between capitalism and socialism and declares that any search for this systemic "third way" will not improve the chances of the new democracies to ensure freedom and prosperity. " 'No' is the simple answer to this demand. We should not engage in this 'inter-cultural dialogue,' and more, the very idea needs to be quashed. It is wrong because it is another version of system thinking, and thinking in terms of systems lies at the bottom of illiberalism in all its varieties."[12]

Instead of searching for the "third way" or futilely attempting to revive socialism, Dahrendorf strongly encourages the pursuit of what he calls the "open society." In general terms, the open society is based on constitutional guarantees of civil and political rights. He explains that, "In constitutional terms, there are only two ways: we have to choose between systems and the open society. In terms of normal politics there are a hundred ways, and we can forever learn from one another framing our own." In other words, civic and political freedom must be constitutionally guaranteed in order for the open society to remain as such. While he does not define the open society as a capitalist system, many of the elements of capitalism are included. Private property, legalized rules for proper market function, competition, and a certain level of economic growth must all be present.[13]

Dahrendorf's observations about open and closed societies are somewhat misleading. Despite his refusal to endorse any system, his descriptions of the open society bears a remarkable resemblance to capitalist liberal democracy. He may not endorse any particular system for Eastern Europe, but his recommendations include the classic ingredients of Western-type liberal democracy and capitalism. This argument, much like Starr's, has the same blind spot: a total devotion to the principle of liberalism without an honest analysis of the pathologies present in the classic liberal democracies of the West. By relying only on the repudiation of totalistic systems without seriously searching for the causes of the crisis in Western liberal societies, Dahrendorf takes the easy way out.

Francis Fukuyama, former analyst for the Rand Corporation and former U.S. State Department official, offers a third view that diverges somewhat from Starr's and Dahrendorf's analyses, yet he also hails the undisputed victory of Western liberalism over all other forms of political organization. Going even further than the other two authors, Fukuyama argues that liberal democracy is humanity's political destiny and that no other form of political organization could be better suited to human needs. He states,

> Western liberal democracy seems at its close to be returning full circle to where it started: not to an "end of ideology" or a convergence between capitalism and socialism, as earlier predicted, but to an unabashed victory of economic and political liberalism.

He continues

> what we may be witnessing is not just the end of the Cold War, or the passing of a particular period of postwar history, but the end of history as such: that is, the end point of mankind's ideological evolution and the universalization of western liberal democracy as the final form of human government.[14]

Fukuyama's thinking is in large part based on Hegel's conceptualization of history as a coherent process leading toward higher states of consciousness. For Fukuyama, Hegel's ideas on the primacy of human consciousness are exactly what accounts for the widespread acceptance of liberal democracy. Since history is driven by contradictions in human consciousness, the most important question to answer in the post–Cold War era is whether there are "any fundamental 'contradictions' in human life that cannot be resolved in the context of modern liberalism, that would be resolvable by an alternative political-economic structure?" If none can be found, history has ended and liberal democracy has been declared the victor.[15]

Two of the most serious challenges to the liberal idea were presented by communism and fascism. According to Fukuyama, fascism's threat to liberalism was destroyed by its own failure to deliver on its promises and by the defeats of World War II. The other great threat, communism, posed a more realistic challenge to liberalism but this alternative, Fukuyama argues, was also discarded because of its inability to deliver more equality or prosperity than liberal democracies. Western liberal democracy had transcended its own potential contradictions.

> [T]he class issue has actually been successfully resolved in the West. As Kojove noted, the egalitarianism of modern America represents the essential achievement of the classless society envisioned by Marx. This is not to say that there are not rich people and poor people in the United States or that the gap between them has not grown in recent years. But the root causes of economic inequality do not have to do with the underlying legal and social structure of society, which remains fundamentally egalitarian and moderately redistributionist, so much as with the cultural and social characteristics of the groups that make it up, which are in turn the historical legacy of pre-modern conditions. Thus black poverty in the United

States is not the inherent product of liberalism, but is rather the "legacy of slavery and racism" which persisted linger after the formal abolition of slavery.[16]

It is important to note that Fukuyama's work centers around issues of global ideological evolution. Gorbachev's attempts to decentralize and democratize, whether successful or not, signaled a move away from communist ideology to the liberal ideas first espoused during the French and U.S. revolutions. Serious political discourse all over the world now incorporates democracy and market economics as the most realistic combination. As Fukuyama explains, "at the end of history it is not necessary that all societies become successful liberal societies, merely that they end their ideological pretensions of representing different and higher forms of human society."[17]

Fukuyama's liberal state is quite similar to Starr's and Dahrendorf's. He explains that "the state that emerges at the end of history is liberal insofar as it recognizes and protects through a system of law man's [sic] universal right to freedom, and democratic insofar as it exists only with the consent of the governed." Contradictions inherent in other systems would be obsolete in the "universal homogeneous state" (liberal democracy) because of its achievement of universal suffrage, the abolition of slavery, and even the resolution of the proletarian-capitalist tension. What we are left with is "the content of the universal homogeneous state as liberal democracy in the political sphere combined with easy access to VCR's and stereos in the economic." What was before a world caught in the grip of history is now a world involved in the never-ending search for solutions to "technical problems, environmental concerns, and the satisfaction of sophisticated consumer demand."[18]

Despite Dahrendorf's criticism of Fukuyama's ideas as "a caricature" of a serious argument, all three pieces convey a remarkably similar evaluation of the political panorama of the twenty-first century. Socialism must be abandoned as should any social democratic variant that relies excessively on the state to redistribute or regulate. No amalgam of the best elements of liberal democracy and socialism should be pursued because of the inadequate results that socialism has yielded in the past. By default, liberal democracy constitutes the system of choice, providing the greatest amount of equality that can be realistically expected without being "perennially disappointed" and the greatest amount of economic freedom and prosperity. For all three authors, the reasons for the wholesale adoption of liberalism are different, yet the outcome is the same: in the post–Cold War era, no systemic alternatives exist to liberal democracy, the search for any "third way" should be abandoned, and the Left's only alternative is to emerge from the socialist trenches to join in the search for liberal solutions.

It is true that liberal democracy enjoys more legitimacy today than at any other time in its history. But despite the apparent victory of Western ideas, there still remains an unsettling feeling that liberalism may itself be profoundly flawed. Many of the potentially devastating social currents appearing in the West point to the inability of liberalism to provide satisfactory solutions to a crumbling social structure. As our values erode and our communities yield to the effects of hyperindividualism and obsessive material pursuit, the dark side of liberal capitalism suddenly appears more menacing.

Liberalism, like socialism, must be subjected to the burden of its own history. If we take a close look at our modern democracies, it becomes apparent that key issues center around issues of community and the disintegration of civil society. It is true that the West has been more effective in the provision of economic benefits and political freedom. It is also true that most of the Eastern European socialist experiments, for a variety of reasons, failed to deliver on their promises. However, the conclusion that liberalism constitutes the ultimate form of human government is misdirected.

Ample evidence suggests that serious social ills exist in the West that are not attributable only to historical residue or to the incomplete implementation of liberal principles, as Fukuyama suggests. The skyrocketing incidences of child abuse, violent crime, drug addiction, and corruption all point to serious flaws in the way in which modern liberal democrats handle issues of morality, solidarity, and responsibility. Liberal democracy hides an invisible contradiction: the role of civil society within liberalism. This important consideration ignored by our three theorists may outline an important part of a future agenda for the Left.

## The Hidden Contradiction: Liberalism and Civil Society

In one of the most controversial sections of his work, Fukuyama makes the claim that not only was Marxism incapable of producing a "better" society than liberalism, but that the United States boasts the "achievement of the classless society envisioned by Marx."[19] This bold claim is based on his belief that despite the existence of poor and rich people, the legal and social organization of the United States is "fundamentally egalitarian." Therefore, no real contradiction exists in liberal democracy.

Even though Dahrendorf and Starr do not overtly claim this much, they do not offer any indication that they believe differently. In fact, their insistence that solutions to our social problems should be sought only within the framework of liberal democracy suggests that they also find no inherent contradiction within liberal democracy that would call into question the feasibility of a liberal democratic answer to such problems as racism, economic inequality, homophobia, or environmental degradation.

What all three authors fail to acknowledge is the contradiction between liberal economic and political principles and civil society. This conflict is the key to understanding the limits of their arguments and points to a possible direction for a new agenda that now confronts the Left.

Michael Walzer defines civil society as the "space of uncoerced human association and also the set of relational networks—formed for the sake of family, faith, interest, and ideology—that fill this space."[20] Civil society refers to those purely social relationships outside the economy and state formed by families, neighbors, members of parent-teacher associations, strangers in public places, service association members, and others. Such associations are the fabric that binds members of a society not only with other persons but also with the market and the state. It is in civil society that voluntary associations are formed not because they are legally ordained, nor because it is profitable to do so, but because persons consider these relationships to be important in and of themselves. Civic organizations formed around charity and service and other groups with purely altruistic purposes arise from the bonds of civil society. It is within the framework of civil society that we are taught and put into practice the unwritten moral and social rules that guide our daily interaction with others.

Alan Wolfe offers a definition that not only describes which types of relationships are included in civil society but also provides an explanation of their function. "There is, however, another meaning to civil society that, instead of embodying some nostalgic hope for a passing order, is more relevant than ever to modern liberal democrats.... We learn how to act toward others because civil society brings us into contact with people in such a way that we are forced to recognize our dependence on them. We ourselves have to take responsibility for our moral obligations, and we do so through this gift called society that we make for ourselves."[21] Civil society is not only the realm in which we conduct our daily affairs, but it is also where we learn to be social beings and to realize that we depend on others for our social and material survival. It is a locus for the production of morality and obligation. Civil society permits us to empathize, trust, feel responsibility, and experience solidarity.

Because civil society delimits those relationships that produce the positive bonds of solidarity, those relationships become critically important to modern liberal democracy. Civil society functions as an anchor for both the state and the market. As Wolfe suggests, "neither the market nor the state was ever meant to operate without the moral ties found in civil society."[22] Both of these mechanisms are based on an established solidarity that is presumed already to exist. Without even the weakened sense of solidarity characteristic of modern societies, markets could not function and constitutional politics would be impossible to implement.

The market is based on what Emile Durkheim called precontractual solidarity. Despite the existence of laws that sanction violations of contracts, the most important regulatory mechanism is the sense of morality and trust underlying market transactions. In Durkheim's words, "it is not enough for the public authority to ensure that undertakings entered into are kept. It must also, at least in roughly the average number of cases, see that they are spontaneously kept. If contracts were observed only by force or the fear of force, contractual solidarity would be in an extremely parlous state. A wholly external order would ill conceal a state of contestation too general to be contained indefinitely."[23] In other words, repressive measures are not enough to ensure that market contracts be honored. There necessarily has to be a level of solidarity that, by itself, permits contracts to be kept without legal enforcement.

Wolfe shows that market exchanges or capitalism "required noncapitalist moral values in society as a whole . . . capitalism lived its first hundred years off the pre-capitalist morality it inherited from traditional religion and social structure, just as it lived its second hundred years off the moral capital of social democracy." Markets depend on the moral solidarity in civil society to regulate self-interest and to establish the trust that permits the use of contracts. Without these, capitalism could not function. The utilitarian morality characteristic of market exchanges, is incomplete by itself because it is incapable of producing positive social ties. In an all-against-all competitive market scenario, no solidarity could be produced. Even though Adam Smith believed that self-interest would drive the exchange in the market, he recommended that this mechanism not be used to produce the "morality that made economic self-interest possible in the first place."[24]

By the same token the liberal state also depends on civil society for the production of the morality that it cannot produce effectively itself. Democratic politics require that citizens acknowledge that the common project of governing depends on the respect of individual rights and the execution of responsibilities like voting and paying taxes. In order for citizens to agree to the democratic recognition of others' rights, there must first exist a solidarity that allows them to consider each other as part of the same society. Civil society is the arena in which these relationships are produced. As Durkheim noted, "for a man to acknowledge that others have rights, not only as a matter of logic, but as one of daily living, he must have agreed to limit his own. Consequently this mutual limitation was only realizable in a spirit of understanding and harmony. Now if we assume a host of individuals with no previous ties binding them to one another, what reason might have impelled them to make these reciprocal sacrifices?"[25] Democratic responsibility and a respect for the political equality of others is learned through our daily interactions with other persons who enjoy those same rights. When those common ties break down, it becomes increasingly difficult to recognize one another's rights.

The central contradiction of liberalism, ignored by our three theorists, is that both the liberal state and market erode the ties of civil society. Just as the state depends on the solidarity produced by civil society, especially in social democratic nations, the state also assumes responsibility for functions that were previously the domain of either the family or the community. Traditional patterns of religious affiliation and hierarchical social arrangements that constituted the foundation for ties in civil society are giving way to the new forms of modern social organization. The welfare state in Scandinavia is a perfect example of how the state now performs the role of provider in matters that were previously the domain of the family or the community. Child care, care for the elderly, voluntary associations, and charitable work have all been made state responsibilities instead of personal responsibilities.[26] This is problematic, not only because the state is a less efficient and less effective provider for these services, but also because it removes these responsibilities from the realm of civil society to the state.

The extraction of moral duty from civil society by the state means that members of a society no longer participate in the duties that in premodern times were relegated to them. Not only is it difficult for people to understand the role of the state in their lives, but it is also difficult to undertake moral responsibility voluntarily when the state provides services to fill those obligations. Walzer argues that "the production and reproduction of loyalty, civility, political competence, and trust in authority are never the work of the state alone, and the effort to go it alone . . . is doomed to failure."[27] There is a necessary interdependence between the state and civil society, with the rise of the liberal state endangering forms of community.

Like the state, the market also erodes the social ties of civil society. But the market does so by replacing ties of social solidarity with utilitarian relationships that exist for the sake of economic profit. Slowly, the market has colonized civil society by replacing altruistic and trusting cooperation with rational decision making based on economic self-gain. When decisions are determined by market rationality, purely altruistic and cooperative motives begin to be replaced by utilitarian considerations, thus weakening civil society. As Alan Wolfe argues:

> People do not satisfy their responsibility to one another by thinking only of their responsibility to themselves. Economic man, so modern in his freedom is only quasi-modern in his obligations; he is responsible for his own fate but, to the degree that he follows economic models of economic choices, he has little sense of how to treat others. To create a society as modern as the individuals who compose it, we must look beyond the rules that emphasize self-interest to rules that enable people to take account of who they are and who they want to be.[28]

Civil society and liberalism stand in a paradoxical position with respect to one another. Liberal democracy cannot function without the social solidarity produced by civil society, yet both market forces and state forces penetrate civil society and erode the strength of its associations. The former accomplishes this through unchecked self-interest and the reliance on market forces for moral regulation and production. The latter does so by removing responsibility from the personal realm and allowing citizens to live relatively obligation free.

This paradox points to a profound contradiction between liberal economics, liberal politics, and civil society. If both the state and the market are relied upon excessively to produce the kind of solidarity that they assume exists a priori, then the deterioration of civil society is inevitable. Those very mechanisms that depend on civil society cannot produce the morality and solidarity which characterize it. Therefore, Starr's "design of markets" and Dahrendorf's "provision of citizenship," although necessary ingredients for a healthy democratic political system, do not provide any mechanism for the production and maintenance of a healthy civil society. Once the relations traditionally protected by the umbrella of civil society are met by the forces of the state and the market, both the market and the state are endangered.

Any serious discussion concerning the future of liberal democracy must take into account the role of civil society vis-à-vis the state and the market, yet our three liberal writers fail to incorporate any cogent analysis of the role of civil society. Starr briefly mentions that civil society is indeed an important part of liberal democracy but fails to acknowledge its vulnerability. He does indicate that "the cultivation and strengthening of civil society reflects a commitment, not to some mythical ideal of a single community, but to the many and various communities that must exist peaceably and tolerantly along with each other in a liberal society."[29] The problem lies with his failure to suggest how the reconstruction of civil society will take place under liberal democracy.

Dahrendorf includes a relatively longer discussion of the role of civil society in Eastern Europe. He acknowledges that civil society is crucial for the "anchorage of citizenship" but does not indicate how it can be created or sustained. He states, "Civil society in a certain sense sustains itself. It does not seem to need the state . . . this is why I prefer to think of civil society as providing the anchorage for the constitution of liberty, including its economic ingredients."[30] His view of civil society illustrates the common misconception that civil society thrives independently in liberal democracies and that civil society can be constructed merely through the establishment of citizenship and economic freedom.

Liberal democracy cannot provide a mechanism for the reproduction and strengthening of civil society. By definition liberalism provides freedom and rights but fails to produce solidarity and responsibilities. These latter elements have a different origin and can only be produced outside the boundaries of the state and market. We can gamble that communities will unite around common concerns and that the family will reappear in our societies in different yet more stable forms, but these scenarios are improbable. The evidence we now have points to trends in the opposite direction. We can believe with the Chicago school economists that utilitarian market logic will be capable of regulating our social and economic lives, but as we have seen, this will prove to be morally insufficient and eventually counterproductive. And we can wait for the government to start legislating morality and solidarity, but this strategy will surely fail.

There is, however, one possibility that none of our theorists considers in his writings. The production of solidarity, community, and morality clearly marks a new agenda for the Left. Without having to revert to an outdated socialism or to methods proven ineffective, the Left.now has the opportunity and responsibility to create civil society.

## Civil Society and the Left

The objective of this chapter is to show that despite the widespread declaration of victory for liberalism and the death of socialism, liberalism suffers from its own set of practical and theoretical problems. But, more important, the presentation of the problematic of civil society paves a new road for leftist forces. Socialism may be moribund, but the need for a Left to counteract the effect of the liberal state and market is now greater than ever.

What much of the new literature on civil society indicates is that social movements, which make up a large part of the Left, play a very important role in the generation of the solidarity and community that characterize civil society. As Cohen and Arato argue, "the revival of the discourse of civil society provides some hope in this regard. For the discourse reveals that collective actors and sympathetic theorists are still oriented by the utopian ideals of modernity—the ideas of basic rights, liberty, equality, democracy, solidarity, and justice—even if the fundamentalist, revolutionary rhetoric within which these ideals had once been articulated is on the wane." The challenge presented to liberalism by the weakening of civil society creates a role for a new Left capable of responding to these needs. The task of the Left is still centered around issues of economic inequality and political justice, but as Richard Flacks explains, activists need to begin to think of politics "as happening in ways and places that are not restricted to official arenas and governmental processes." In his opinion, "the fundamental work of those who identify with the left tradition is to show how 'private persons' are in fact implicated in history, to illuminate how private acts ramify through time and space, to nourish the spiritual resources that enable the 'powerless' to make History."[31]

The increased attention to issues of civil society does not imply that the Left will need to abandon efforts to reform the economy or politics. The Left will always be centrally involved in the fights against widening income gaps and political exclusion. But without a strong sense of social solidarity, there can be no economic or political reforms that increase justice, empowerment, and equality. The inclusion of all persons in a modern multi racial and inclusive civil society will help equip its members to view others as parts of a whole instead as separate individuals with different interests and goals. A critical task of the Left is to invigorate those institutions within civil society that produce the social glue of solidarity and to create new associations characteristic of our more modern societies. Throughout this volume, we shall point to new strategies that can carry this Left agenda.

Cassie Schwerner

# 2

# Beyond Socialism and Identity Politics:

THE U.S. LEFT AFTER THE FALL

On a chilly spring evening, hundreds of Boston's working people, political activists, and concerned citizens rally around the historical old South Meeting House. A demonstration has been called to protest the visit of David Duke. Duke, the former neo-Nazi and Imperial Wizard of the Ku Klux Klan, stands for a vision of the United States that the people at this gathering despise. The chanting at the rally represents a strong and unified rejection of Duke's vision. The identities and concerns of the protest participants, however, are not as easily unified. At this rally are people of color, Jews, lesbians and gays, feminists, members of the labor community, members of the Socialist Workers Party, AIDS activists, and others who don't readily identify with any social movement. This is a group unified in its disgust for Duke but not in its call for a political action.

This demonstration symbolizes a new identity crisis on the U.S. Left, which has become a multitude of fragmented social movements. At one time, a socialist vision loosely tied the Left together, but in the past several decades the Left has been undergoing a shift in its collective understanding of socialism. I shall argue in this chapter—based on interviews with Left activists in the United States—that with the recent collapse of the communist countries in Eastern Europe, a socialist identity can no longer define or unite the Left.

The "Old Left," which was composed of strongly conflicting constituencies (Communist Party members, anarchists, Wobblies), experienced some loose unity through a shared economic vision of various socialist arrangements. The New Left's identity around the concept of socialism (and that of movements which grew out of the New Left) has been weaker and more elusive.[1]

The Black liberation movement, the women's movement, the lesbian and gay movements, and others that emerged in the fifties, sixties, and seventies were part of a new tradition that embraced an "identity-oriented paradigm." The "new social movements," as scholars term them, had shifted from conflict with the state or economy to the arena of civil society.[2] At the grassroots level, they demanded new forms of cultural and institutional change against racist, patriarchal, heterosexist, militaristic, or environmentally unsound practices. In fact, many of the identity-oriented movements *did* mobilize around state and economic policy as well, but the role of socialism changed in the post-1950s Left movements. The socialist identity of the Left was by no means abandoned by the New Left, but its role became much more ambiguous.[3]

The transition to identity-oriented politics brought both advantages and disadvantages. By focusing on issues of civil society and participatory democracy, the New Left broadened the base of Left activism. But because these movements lacked a common vision and connection, they became isolated from each other as well as from the wider culture. By the 1980s the U.S. Left was thoroughly fragmented and increasingly voiceless.

This, of course, is a greatly simplified version of the Left's recent history in the United States. Although it is true that leftist movements turned to identity politics and cultural transformation, an ambiguous and somewhat schizophrenic relationship with socialism has remained. While the New Left turned its attention to movements pushing for cultural transformation, a sizeable portion of these movements was deeply committed to an anticapitalist agenda. A socialist vision was no longer at the forefront of these movements, yet a persistent and vague attachment to the concept of socialism remained.

In 1989 the revolutions in Eastern Europe began. The communist countries collapsed, one after the other; in December of 1991, the Soviet Union ceased to exist.

With the sudden "death of socialism," it is time for the Left to sort out its relationship with socialism. Although highly complex, this task may prove to be a crucial step in discovering what constitutes the Left's identity and may aid in the search for a unifying thread.

For the main body of this chapter I interviewed ten activists to explore two central questions: How do people who identify as leftists make sense

## On the Death of the Left

of the events that have taken place in Eastern Europe, and how do leftists currently understand the role of socialism in their own politics? In a concluding section I attempt to interpret these interviews and propose my own stage theory of the U.S. Left.

To carry out the empirical study several issues had to be considered. What is socialism? What is the Left's connection to socialism? Is a socialist vision essential to a leftist identity? If it is, what is this vision and what is the agenda to attain it? If not, how can leftists reframe the multiplicity of issues that fall within the tradition of the left into a coherent agenda without some vague reliance on socialism?

In an attempt to explore answers, I interviewed ten social-movement participants who identify themselves as leftists. These interviews were an attempt to understand how Left activists interpret the mainstream conclusions being drawn. After all, if the "death of socialism" is equated with the death of the Left it seemed appropriate to hear what leftists have to say on the subject. Have the revolutions of 1989 and the collapse of the Soviet Union affected the identity of the leftist community?

The activists I interviewed represent a broad range of contemporary movements typically considered to be within the tradition of the Left. Because the Left in this country is so fragmented, I wanted to discover to what degree there is commonality in the way activists from different movements make sense of the so-called death of socialism. The individuals I interviewed are people who identify themselves as leftists and furthermore identify the movement or organization they work with as leftist.[4]

Two of the people I spoke with were representatives of organizations working against U.S. intervention in Central America. I interviewed people involved with the labor movement—two organizers and one union member. Two interviewees are involved with the environmental movement. One of my interviews was with an African American involved with the Black liberation movement (although another respondent is African American). Four of the ten respondents were women, and two of them identify themselves as feminists. Two of my respondents speak as activists in the struggle for lesbian and gay rights.

My respondents do not casually identify themselves as leftists. Most have been active in Left politics for decades. All have made progressive politics their life work and are deeply committed to an alternative vision of U.S. politics. Warren Blumenfeld is in his forties and has been involved with a variety of progressive social movements including the civil rights movement, antiwar movement, and the gay, lesbian, and bisexual rights movement; most recently he has been involved in AIDS activism. Cheryl Gooding, forty, is most closely connected to issues concerning the labor and women's movements, both of which she has been involved with for the past two decades. When I interviewed Debora Gordon, in her thirties, she was a well-known figure in the Central American anti-intervention struggle in Boston. Mike Prokosch, forty-five, is also a well-known spokesperson from this movement, although he has been active in many other movements since his days as a member of Students for a Democratic Society (SDS). Alexander Lynn, in his forties, has been deeply involved in a variety of communist or socialist political movements since his youth; he has also been involved with various struggles for Black liberation. At the time of our interview he was the coordinator of an African American youth project in the Boston area. Annie Siegel, in her mid-twenties, has been involved with radical politics, identifying herself as an anarchist with strong environmental concerns, for several years. Cris Costello, in her early thirties, has been involved with a variety of Left social movements but spoke to me as an organizer for a progressive union in Boston. Greg Gigg, forty-three, is a progressive union member who has been active in union politics for decades. Michael Goldrosen, thirty-two, has been active in coalition politics since his college days, most visibly as a gay organizer. And Ron Robinson, in his mid thirties, has also been involved in a variety of movements—Black liberation, anti-intervention—and when I spoke with him it was as an organizer for a well-known environmentalist organization.[5]

## Interpreting "the Death of Socialism" in Eastern Europe

If socialism is defined as the economic and political systems that existed in Eastern Europe, socialism is clearly dead. If, however, the current claim of socialism's demise is a reference to any possible type of socialist project or organization, the socialist idea might still survive. The leftists I spoke with maintain that socialism is very much alive.

My respondents define socialism as a concept connected with human liberation. For them socialism is not merely an economic system but rather the description of a society in which human beings live full, creative, healthy lives free from oppression of any kind. Socialism, to many on the Left, is a "form of society where the associated producers are the masters of the process of production, a society based on the largest economic, social, and political democracy, a commonwealth liberated from all class, ethnic, and gender exploitation and oppression."[6]

## On the Death of the Left

According to the activists I spoke with, Eastern Europe did not represent their vision of socialism. Virtually all my interviewees said that these societies were brutal totalitarian dictatorships that were "wildly authoritarian" and thus in no way represented socialism. A just society can only be based on democracy. Eastern European societies were utterly lacking in both democracy and in respect for human liberation.

In my respondents' understanding of socialism, it is the people, the workers, who should have the power to make decisions that affect their lives. My respondents often echoed some version of the following: "I have a problem with the argument that socialism is dead—I don't think that socialism's been tried." Cheryl Gooding declared, "I don't think there was democratic control over the key decisions and the allocation of resources ... in the society." And Alexander Lynn said, "Socialism ... is created by the people, and it's the most creative thing on the earth." The reason the Soviet Union was not socialist, he went on, was because the people were forced into the lifestyle that the authorities demanded. "You can't have a revolution that is dropped down to you—given a revolutionary state by somebody?" he asked. "That's what the Red Army did. They placed in power communist parties that had not won over the mass of the people."

Providing resources for basic human needs is part of a leftist vision of socialism but certainly not all of it. Democracy is a necessary and critical component. For example, one activist speaking of socialism in Cuba argued, "Making a priority of certain social and human needs, I would say yes, that's certainly a big step in the right direction. But to what extent do people *really* have control over those decisions, I would say, no, it's not socialism—it's statism."

### Failure

> I think socialism is where the working people of our society take control and make decisions about all aspects of the society; and that certainly wasn't taking place in Eastern Europe.—Greg Gigg, union member

Mainstream observers of Eastern Europe argue that these societies collapsed because of the failure of socialism. But if these societies did not represent leftists' view of socialism, how is their failure explained?[7]

According to the leftists I spoke with, these societies failed for a number of reasons, principally massive internal contradictions, greed and the abuse of power, and an absolute lack of democracy. "A lot of the tactics and policies of the Eastern European governments were very similar to Nazis," maintained one respondent, "so in talking about the demise of socialism, I don't think socialism is dead. I think that the way it was corrupted in its practice, hopefully, is dead."

The socialist societies of Eastern Europe failed because of internal contradictions. "This is supposed to be a socialist society," said Ron Robinson, "yet I doubt that Riesa Gorbachev ever stood in line for bread. There were very definite elites." Many of my respondents believe there was a substantial gap between the ideology of the Soviet Union and the lived reality. When I asked Cheryl Gooding why these societies failed, she quickly laughed and, after a long pause, had this to say:

> There was a clear division around privilege. The lie between ideology and reality was very big. I think that does disturb people and makes them want to rebel. And for whatever combination of reasons . . . I think it is very compelling for people (like it is in this country) to see the lie between [ideology and reality]. People get upset when they've been raised to believe in democracy and justice and equal opportunity and they see it's not there. I think that's a big part of what sparked the sixties. People were furious.[8]

Moreover, there is always the potential for abuse. The greed of elites was often cited as another reason for failure. The utter lack of democracy allowed for the greed and corruption, not socialism. "You had careerists and opportunists who saw that they could advance their own goals and objectives through the party," maintained one activist.

Ultimately these concerns—internal contradictions, greed, and abuse of power—point to the dismal lack of democracy that existed in these societies. They restricted the decision-making capacity of the entire population. This is why mainstream commentators believe these societies failed, and this is why leftists believed they failed.

Well over half the people I talked to maintained that one of the greatest reasons for the failure of socialism in Eastern Europe was the effect of outside forces. That is, the economic pressures placed on these societies by the Cold War were ultimately devastating. If the Soviet Union had not had to put its money into a massive military build-up, my respondents believe, the distribution of goods and services might well have succeeded. "Outside influences played a major role," stated one woman. "I think the United States and Western Europe and the ongoing pressures have definitely put pressure that allows something that isn't perfect to cave in."

On the Death of the Left

*Lessons*

Leftists I spoke with agreed that the fall of socialism in Eastern Europe offers important lessons for the Left. Mike Prokosch says the lessons concern the dangers of power and statism. "That was a central flaw in Eastern Europe—the people at the top never asked for approval. They never subjected themselves to any [approval] process." "Power corrupts," concurs lesbian and gay rights activist Michael Goldrosen.

An open system of participatory democracy, which represents all citizens of a society and not a small elite, is the only just way to organize society, argues eco-anarchist Annie Siegel:

> The most important thing about anarchism is that it's anti-authoritarian, and the Left in this country has always been predominantly authoritarian. People have been drawn to Maoism . . . and Castro . . . and they look up to these people. . . . In some sense, what our project is doing *is* a new politics because it's taking this anti-authoritarian Western tradition and also taking on the New Left and the identity politics of the seventies, and we take that all on with a critique of hierarchy, and we are very, very prodemocracy—real participatory democracy. . . .
>
> You've probably talked to folks who have said that [Eastern Europe] wasn't socialism and we can still try this project and anarchists at least have this on their side, with the fall of Eastern Europe it's like, "Look, this didn't work, you can't have these horrible centralized systems where the few run everything for the many. You can't do that. That's a failed project."

For Cheryl Gooding the importance of continual action is an empowering lesson learned through the Eastern European experience.

"The lesson that I took from it," Gooding maintains, is that:

> control is never total, and never totally monolithic. It's porous. In terms of organization and historical changes, it's always like that, those struggles are incredibly important. Even if we feel like we're not getting anywhere, we have to keep articulating that there is another possibility. And organizing people around that is critical. You never know which is the spark that's going to take. I mean I was really astonished [watching the revolution of 1989]—where's this coming from? Like with a lot of grassroots struggle you don't really know what's happening there—it's underground. Like with an earthquake, you think it just happened from nowhere, but it didn't: you just couldn't see what was happening underground.

Many Left activists in the United States learned a lesson of hope in witnessing the revolutions of 1989. These revolutions represented a great victory for human liberation. When people are suffering, they will rebel, and, furthermore, they can succeed.

## No Third Way?

> "Instant diagnosis is a dangerous game, almost as dangerous as instant prophecy."—Eric Hobsbawm

Ralf Dahrendorf and other "death of socialism" theorists insist that there is no third way between capitalism and state socialism, leaving capitalism as the only viable system. Movement participants uniformly rejected this perspective. Warren Blumenfeld said, "There are too many inequities within capitalism and too much disparity between rich and poor. There has to be a system which does not squelch creativity and at the same time has a more equal distribution of the wealth."

The prospect of a world that contained only capitalist societies was extremely worrisome to my respondents. People often spoke of a concern that under capitalism we would soon use up all of the earth's natural resources. "It [capitalism] has no [conception] of right or wrong," explained environmentalist Ron Robinson. "Capitalism fosters the cutting down of the Amazon rain forest. Now, this might alter the climate of the planet and have all sorts of consequences for production forty or fifty years from now, but on my quarterly balance sheet it looks great."

Many of my respondents point out that the victims of U.S. capitalism, particularly those in the Third World, do not see the capitalist system as fair or viable. Cris Costello explains:

> [E]very banana that we eat is at the expense of someone in Honduras (or some other banana-producing country) . . . if we want to live like we live in this country, then I guess it [capitalism] is the only way. But if the rest of the world consumed like we consume . . . we wouldn't have any air or trees left in twenty years. What we have is gotten off the back and off the sweat and off the life of someone else . . . *that* is what capitalism is based on.

But, ultimately, she goes on to illustrate, the system is coming back to haunt those in the United States as well.

> Auto workers or steel workers thought they would work in the plant their whole lives and their sons would work in the plant their whole lives. Now all the plants have run away to Korea, the Philippines, Central America, Mexico . . . so the wool that was pulled over everyone's eyes, *everyone's* eyes, is beginning to thin. People have been ripped off. They thought that the system would take care of them and it's not and it hasn't.

Thus my respondents argue that capitalism is clearly not working. They agree with John Kenneth Galbraith, who pointed out that "people did not flee East Berlin for the South Bronx." Let us then turn to their socialist visions to see how an alternative restructuring of society might work.⁹

## How Activists Define Socialism

If socialism is not dead, what then is the socialist vision of leftist movement participants? In each interview I asked my respondents this question, and it was at this moment that people seemed confused. The issues we were discussing suddenly became much more complex. Where the answers to my questions regarding Eastern Europe had been more or less unified, now there was vast disagreement. Everyone tended to speak of democracy, community, and justice, but beyond that there was little clarity about the concrete character of a socialist society. What would be the role of the state? What of private property? Would there be a market? How would it function?

Many said that certain basic needs like health care, education, and housing should be provided by the state. Others said not, that we must learn from the Eastern European experience and have community-owned institutions with some state regulation. Some argued that we must do away with any type of hierarchical decision making, turning instead to worker-owned factories, collectives, and coops; others said this would never work. Some looked to an Israeli kibbutz-type model; others had no models.

When I pressed my respondents to describe how a socialist society would operate day-to-day, people responded by admitting that they hadn't thought specifically of those issues. "Well, I try not to think of that stuff too much," said one woman. Another respondent confessed, "My flaw is that it's always much easier to point at what is wrong than to envision what the society should look like." When I would press a respondent for a concrete answer, I was often told, "Good question—I don't know!"

I attempted to dig deeper. "If the former Soviet Union was not your vision of socialism," I pressed on, "how would the distribution of goods and services operate?" In return I would hear versions of the following statements: "This would be a society where people are able to maximize their potential. It would be a society where people have full access to fundamental rights—housing, education, medical care. We would have a society that wouldn't abuse the planet and its resources." Another activist suggested there would be "more of a social democracy that allows

## Beyond Socialism and Identity Politics

more control and participation by individuals involved in the process rather than a top-down structure. More collective communities with a looser unifying structure." "Okay," I conceded, "so it would be a form of socialism that is not state run?" "Right," I was told, "but some of the major mechanisms of the state, like health care, like a welfare system, could be organized by the state with collective living situations . . . collective community functioning as more independent units."

In another interview I attempted a different approach. "You get to be the visionary for a minute," I said with a hopeful tone in my voice. But again the answer offered was somewhat vague.

> Well, it's a legitimate question. I always think first of values. What would be the guiding principles? For example, the guiding principle in capitalism is production for profit and everything stems from that. The individual, private property, et cetera. So I would say the guiding principle would be quite different. It would be production for social *need*. And I don't mean to eliminate any possibility for private accumulation of wealth. That's always going to happen. . . . I think there is a lot of balancing that needs to happen. It's like democracy. You can vision it, but then you need to make it pragmatic.

Inevitably, as people became uncomfortable with these questions and my persistence, they would lapse into defenses of socialism as it existed in Eastern Europe. "I don't know what it was like to live in those societies, but I always rooted for them. . . . Whatever existed there isn't worse and may have been better than what we have here." "Well," said another respondent, "at least there was a high degree of social equality in those societies."

Those who had experience in Central America often turned there for models. They maintained that some sort of "third way" between the socialism of Eastern Europe and U.S. capitalism is possible. Debora Gordon's vision, for example, comes from Nicaragua:

> I keep returning to Central America because that's what I'm familiar with. For example, in Nicaragua, when I was there in '87, what was so impressive was the small community organizations that were organized by *barrio* [by neighborhood]. I was there in the year that they were working on the constitution. I was so amazed to hear about how the people participated with drawing up their own constitution. Groups met on the barrio level, then the district, regional, and there was true representation. It was taken from the needs of the people, and that's what I would want . . . coming from the bottom up.

Alexander Lynn argues that the youth leadership movement he is involved with is developing a new model for revolutionary practices.

## On the Death of the Left

> [The organization] believes that the everyday struggles that we as people of the community undertake are part of the larger struggle of all oppressed peoples. By working to create a healthy community, we are involved in a revolution, and each one of us is a revolutionary. In a society that is in its basis self-destructive, the act of taking care of ourselves and our people is by definition revolutionary. Revolution isn't an event, it's the way in which we work for healthy and loving attitudes about ourselves and our people with the goal of creating community based on these healthy attitudes.... Revolution does not equal violence. We understand that the most effective (and sometimes the hardest) method to achieve unity with our people is through gentleness. And it is through the power of our unity that we attain liberation.[10]

By examining Left activists' visions of socialism, one becomes acutely aware of what I have referred to as the Left's "schizophrenic relationship" with socialism. On the one hand, the Left desperately clings to the concept, while on the other hand it displays no credible understanding of socialism or the steps that need to be taken for its achievement.

### Rethinking the Left's Relationship to Socialism

In *Making History* Richard Flacks offers an in-depth analysis of the U.S. Left that begins to clarify the ambiguity and confusion regarding socialism that emerged from my interviews. According to Flacks there are three ideological strands that historically define the Left: socialism, anarchism, and populism—socialism having the most significant impact of these. Among the vast array of social movements that have existed on the left—"abolitionists, feminists, radical democrats, laborists, libertarians, left-liberals, anti-imperialists, progressive reformers, New Dealers, one-worlders, peaceniks, environmentalists"—socialism is only one of several intertwined visions, and it was rarely the exclusive or explicitly unifying theme.[11]

Thus Flacks's phrase the "tradition of the left" becomes critical. Underneath all the clashing perspectives is some inherent unity broader than, and separate from, socialism per se. Once one moves beyond the label "socialism" or other terms used by mainstream culture to define the Left and by leftists as self-definition, one realizes that there is a shared set of values, principles, and sentiments inherent among leftists—and moreover, these values are shared across generations and organizations. Furthermore, this unity, to the great advantage of the Left, comes from a notion that deeply resonates within U.S. culture: democracy. Flacks argues that if one looks at the various Left social movements (labor, feminism, civil rights, gay rights, etc.), the achievement of these movements has been the expansion of democracy.[12]

There are two central components of Flacks's discussion of the Left democratic tradition. The first is the theme of participatory democracy. There is a deep commitment intrinsic within the Left, maintains Flacks, for our society to function as a true democracy with the full participation of all its citizens.

The left vision is "commitment to fundamental restructuring of social institutions and culture so that history making can be a routine feature of everyone's daily life." People have the capability and ought to make their own history, and when we do so we create democracy—"the idea that the people themselves can and should rule."[13] The social movement participants I interviewed, who come from a wide array of social movements, all expressed a commitment to participatory democracy.

Connected to the concept of participatory democracy is the Left's shared vision of community. And community, according to Flacks, is the second concept intrinsic to the U.S. Left's identity. Vibrant and healthy community has always been a core value for leftists. In fact, by understanding this we begin to unravel part of the schizophrenic tension the U.S. Left feels with respect to socialism. For the Left, a socialist vision embodies not only a just economic system but a society in which cooperation leads to healthy interpersonal relationships and to neighborhoods that are able to rely upon one another rather than fear and mistrust one another. One of the reasons the Left has historically embraced socialism, maintains Flacks, is that for many a socialist society represents a vision of "harmonious society." Again Flacks's position is supported by examining my respondents' reasons for their anticapitalist sentiment.[14]

Flacks's analysis and my own interviews suggest that the Left now has an unexpected opportunity for revival and collective mobilization. By setting aside its dubious relationship with socialism and simultaneously promoting participatory democracy and community building, the Left now has the opportunity to recapture its credibility and take a step toward its own healing. That is, mobilizing around these common themes may be a way for the Left in the United States to move beyond the culture of identity politics that has caused it to become so devastatingly fragmented.

As I noted in the beginning, the U.S. Left has experienced two distinct stages and now has the opportunity to move into a third. In the first stage, its identity was predominantly defined by an economic vision in which class politics was at the forefront. The Socialist Party, the Commu-

## On the Death of the Left

nist Party, and organized labor were the primary movements that those who were part of the "tradition of the Left" participated in.[15]

The vision of this first stage of the Left, although tied to differing notions of how economic justice would be achieved, was deeply connected to what Flacks cites as the core values of the Left. This Left was committed to class politics because it believed a true democracy and community could not exist in a society based on inequalities that were intrinsically linked to a capitalist system.

But because this Left focused on class as the only agent of change, it ignored numerous other forms of oppression that were not class-based. Starting with the modern civil rights movement, the Left witnessed the birth of numerous other movements focusing on identity-oriented politics. In this second stage, various collectivities came to the forefront to mobilize around their particular oppression. Identity politics allowed for the establishment of single-issue movements and organizations whose sponsors experienced forms of oppression that had not been addressed by participants in the first stage of the Left.[16]

This second stage of the Left was critical because it allowed for a multiplicity of voices that had been excluded from earlier leftist discourse. Yet it also brought many fundamental problems that the Left is grappling with today. The identity-oriented struggles were predominantly middle-class movements; in the mass struggle of the second stage it was working people and their concerns who were often forced into the background.[17] Many argue that the victories of the women's movement and the Black civil rights movement, for example, primarily benefited middle-class people of color and white middle-class women.[18] Yet perhaps the most serious problem of this second stage is the devastating fragmentation that resulted. Unlike the first stage of the Left, it now seems virtually impossible to sift out a united vision. Nevertheless, within each single-issue movement one still is able to perceive the common values at the core of the Left.

By taking full advantage of its understanding of participatory democracy the Left can potentially see its way through the crisis of the past several decades and with this new strength continue to play the vital role of expanding this country's glaringly narrow vision of democracy. But in order to maximize this opportunity, the Left must move beyond socialism, never forgetting its historical impact (both positive and negative).

The notion of setting socialism aside is stark and alarming, but in fact the more populist leftists that I've spoken with have already done as much in their everyday activism, while clinging to the language of so-

## Beyond Socialism and Identity Politics

cialism out of sentimental loyalty. Although this may be understandable, it is not practical. Left activists should put new energy into a revitalized call for a radical vision of democracy and community rather than rhetorically respond that their dream of socialism, which is vague at best, is still alive.

The advantages to separating the leftist identity from socialism are numerous. As Flacks argues, most people make their personal lives, not history. One of the greatest challenges currently facing the Left is to discover a way to foster a relationship between the average person and the activist. By focusing on concepts that have strong cultural resonance, such as democracy and community, the Left may be able to develop this relationship. In doing so, the Left not only regains credibility, it broadens its base and potentially becomes a force that can bring about radical change.

A third left stage must alleviate the ill effects of the fragmentation that arose out of the second stage. The forms of oppression neglected in both the first and second stage must be addressed, and the themes that have remained at the core of the U.S. Left throughout its history—participatory democracy and community—must be continuously stressed.

The main challenge of this third stage of the Left is for the various submovements that have emerged in recent decades to retain their voices while simultaneously uniting in the common call for radical democracy.[19] A radical and community-oriented vision of democracy is what lesbians, gays and bisexuals, progressive people of color, AIDS activists, and feminists have implicitly been struggling for. Radical democracy and community are also crucial to the labor movement, environmentalists, and peace activists. In the third stage of the Left, the need is for each Left movement explicitly to reframe its own agenda in a shared language of democracy and community.

James A. Vela-McConnell

# 3

## Reflections on the Death of Marxism:

A PARADIGM IN CRISIS

> There are two possibilities: either things will get worse, or there will be a catastrophe.
> —Herbert Marcuse

With the fall of the Soviet empire and the collapse of European communism and socialism, the political world cried out "Marxism is dead!" Echoing this popular sentiment, many conservative and liberal social scientists ask, Who now reads Marx? But they have not bothered to ask that question of Marxist intellectuals themselves. Indeed, nobody has asked the theorists and teachers of Marxism what they are now thinking.

This chapter is an attempt to understand how academics who are familiar with the Marxist tradition and consider themselves part of the Left view Marxism in the wake of these events. Has their thinking changed or been transformed? Where did Marxism go wrong, or did it? What do they think are the implications of these events? Where does the Left go from here?

While my sympathies lie with the Left, I cannot say that my purpose is to defend Marxism. I hope to challenge the Left during a time of crisis, for such a period has the potential for much creative thought. Thus, this chapter is meant to stimulate the Left's creative potential by opening a debate.

I interviewed ten academics in order to understand how they view the collapse of the regimes in Eastern Europe and the Soviet Union. In order to be included in the sample, they had to be familiar with Marxist theory and to identify themselves as leftists or have identified themselves as such in the past. The sample was selected in snowball fashion based on the initial recommendations of several personal contacts.

Taken together these academics represent several fields within the social sciences: sociology, history, and philosophy. While all are educators, some are also involved in the Left as activists. While the majority of the sample is male, two respondents are women. All but one are white. Such a sample may seem narrow in terms of demographic variety, but it reflects a leftist academe that is predominantly white and male. In fact, the domination of the white male in the traditional Left became an issue raised in the interview setting, and it will be discussed further below.

The small size of the sample permits me to give a brief description of each interviewee's character and background. All names have been changed, as has any revealing biographical information:

> Although Kenneth Gates has not finished his dissertation, he is a sociology professor who is much admired by his students. He requires them to become actively involved with social issues, an experience that he believes leads to more learning about society than would be possible from books alone. He notes that it is impossible to be "a Marxist in an ivory tower," and he returns again and again to the importance of praxis.
> Scott Kelley comes from a working-class background and calls himself a "red-diaper baby." His parents were very active in social and political issues when he was growing up. Professor Kelley still feels the pull of the activist lifestyle, although he seems to have found a balance between activism and academe. He claims that his analytical use of the Marxist perspective within the field of sociology actually anticipated the collapse of communism.
> Curtis Parker is a deeply thoughtful man who was very careful in formulating what he had to say during the interview. As a historian, he comments, he would much rather wait a number of years before making any definitive pronouncements on the state of Marxism. However, because of the totalitarian nature of the Soviet regime, he has become more interested in issues involving human rights and the obligations of citizenship.
> Eric Reynolds was trained in the social psychological tradition, although he has consistently related this perspective to social issues of much broader concern. He has thus moved into more macro-sociological topics such as social economy and community within the capitalist world. Despite the acclaimed victory of capitalism, he is still thinking about alternatives. The interview setting challenged his thinking in ways he had not anticipated.
> Christopher Rolston is an intense philosopher who has thought a great deal about the dilemma facing Marxism and the transformations re-

sulting from the collapse of communism. He has written a book about Marx that he has not sent out to publishers because he is "uncomfortable" with it. He jokingly comments that "maybe someone will dig it up sometime and *accuse me* of it!" He is currently interested in the impact of social transformation on legal practice in the former Eastern bloc.

Helmut Schneider is a German emigré and a highly renowned social theorist. He was once a Marxist in the tradition of Trotsky, although he gradually moved away from that tradition. While no longer a Marxist, he is still an advocate of social development from below rather than above and maintains that socialism *"in principle* is a good thing."

Elizabeth Vogel was born in the former Soviet Union, although she and her parents moved to West Germany and then the United States when she was a child. She has an acute grasp of sociological theories, and her intense interest in the Russian transformation is closely linked with her opinion that communism was a "bastardization of Marx's brilliance." In addition to teaching, she is spending much time in the former Soviet Union acting not only as a researcher but also as a consultant. The interview I had with her was informal and went unrecorded. However, her ideas shine through much of this chapter.

During the late 1960s and early 1970s, Gregory Washington was active in the Black Panther movement. Because of this, he has a strong background in the Maoist interpretation of Marxist theory. He has a strong orientation toward activism that is in tension with his academic career in sociology. However, he has a devoted following of African American students.

Sara White is a sociologist and a Marxist to the core, although she avoids using Marxism as a "totalitarian blueprint" with the authority of law. She finds that Marxism is more exonerated than challenged by the events in Eastern Europe and the former Soviet Union, despite all that the media has to say. Her identification with the Left has led Professor White to focus on workplace issues and to make an attempt to apply her work outside of the academy.

John Wilcox is a dynamic historian who approached the interview with much enthusiasm, viewing it as an opportunity to formulate his thoughts regarding the fate of Marxism—something he had not done before, at least not in any thorough fashion. Thus, the interview provided Professor Wilcox with what he called a forum for discussion, one that he found strangely absent in the academic community. While he was once a Marxist and still considers himself a leftist, he feels he has been induced to look elsewhere for his theoretical niche.

From these descriptions, one will note the wide variety of backgrounds and interests of the academics in the sample, a factor that proved to be a great asset in the overall results and presentation of the research.

Three of the interviews were conducted by telephone and the others took place in each respondent's office. They typically lasted from one to two hours. The questions were all open-ended in format and were asked in a conversational style. All of the academics were interested in the topic and found the interview to be engaging. Some mentioned that the interview had brought up important questions that had not occurred to them. In this sense, the interviews were challenging, and one academic even described the process as "therapeutic" in that it stimulated much personal reflection and allowed him to work through the complexity of the issues.

## The Crisis

> The Left is fooling itself; it doesn't exist. Eastern Europe is just a sign of that. It wasn't even really the Left, but was something the Left had a *relation* to. It's more than disillusionment, it's a kind of sudden denuding....
>
> Whether Marxism has a future in its classical forms—whether, as an analytical force, it's going to generate enthusiasm and excitement among new generations of *theorists*—I don't know. My gut feeling is that it doesn't have a future that way. It has essentially a past—a really interesting one....
>
> [A]nd everything [is] getting worse. Marcuse was asked at a conference what are the alternatives before us. He said, "There are two possibilities: either things will get worse, or there will be a catastrophe." I sort of feel like that now. [John Wilcox]

The Left is now experiencing a period of profound disillusionment. Although all would agree that the economic and political systems in Eastern Europe and the Soviet Union were not what Marx meant when he referred to communism or even socialism, these were the only countries in the modern world to claim the Marxist tradition as their origin. They were "something the Left had a relation to."

> These events certainly have caused a weakening of the concept of socialism since any empirical referent or concrete example of what is implied by this term [socialism] is taken away. Not that these societies were examples of socialism in an "ideal type" sort of way, but that these societies were the only ones with even a modest claim to being socialist. [Eric Reynolds]

The Eastern European and Soviet collapse has precipitated a crisis within Marxism; however, academics are only beginning to fathom its depth.

> It is hard to identify how Marxism has been challenged by the events. These events won't reduce its usefulness for understanding capitalism. On the other hand, these events could have a debilitating effect on theory in that they will spark changes in the theory and some rethinking on the part of the Left. It is hard to predict exactly how.... These events should, but won't necessarily, precipitate a lot of soul-searching on the Left. [Eric Reynolds]

## On the Death of the Left

Leftist academics have mixed feelings—bewilderment as to whether one should be glad at the fall of these regimes that misrepresented Marxism or be experiencing a sense of loss. Perhaps this is because these systems were so tied up with what was claimed to be the Marxist ideal. The confusion may also be due to the contagious optimism at the time of these revolutions: tyrannical political systems were collapsing in the face of democracy. Even leftists were caught up in this popular sentiment. Yet they were in a bind because the economic systems—to which the Left was wedded and which placed so much emphasis on state intervention—were also collapsing. Granted, there were some aspects of this economic system that were inadequate; however, with Eastern Europe's embrace of capitalism, even the most positive aspects of state intervention were being abandoned.

> One rational response for the European-American Left—people like myself—might have been, should have been, "good riddance." We're no longer encumbered by the problem of having to explain those regimes, those unwanted cousins, or what have you. That might have been a logical reaction and, I think, to some extent, many of us feel that way—we no longer have to defend regimes that are indefensible. We no longer have to defend a path of socialism which is not going anywhere and which has so many corpses strewn along the way. The problem, though, is that despite a lack of identification with those regimes and the model they employ, I think most people on the intellectual left, and most Marxists and quasi-Marxists in America[1] and in Europe, nevertheless *do* feel a sense of crisis—a sense of loss with the collapse of these regimes. It's not quite clear why. It's not entirely logical and one could have predicted something else; but we all *do* feel a sense of loss and a sense of defensiveness. [Curtis Parker]

The following passage echoes the positive sentiment toward the collapse of "Stalinist" political systems:

> The idea is that, because this Stalinist socialism has collapsed, Marxism is dead.... I don't buy that at all, any more than you could claim that capitalism is finished and you will never see it again on the globe.... In the short term, I think this is a time when Marxists, socialists, leftists... aren't very happy. They're very pessimistic. But I think in the medium-to-long term, there is a possibility that what we're witnessing in the late eighties and early nineties is the fertilizing of the land—an ideological landscape. Out of the wreckage of Stalinism it may be possible to build a democratic socialism. [Kenneth Gates]

Later in the same interview, Professor Gates seeks to separate the economic systems from the political systems by labeling the former "socialism" and the latter "Stalinism":

## Reflections on the Death of Marxism

> People are making all of these assumptions about the death of socialism based on the demise of Stalinism—that doesn't make any sense. The demise of Stalinism had nothing to do with the different types of socialism. This was a reflection on Stalinism and not a reflection on socialist countries. [Kenneth Gates]

At this point one can begin to understand the frustration on the part of the Left. The political and economic systems have become conflated, and while leftists may say "good riddance" to the political system, they are far less willing to give up—at least entirely—the economic system that did bring with it at least some leftist ideals.

In the view of the public, to call oneself a "Marxist," a "socialist," or a "communist" has become passé. The assumption is that one cannot possibly still believe in these ideologies when they so obviously do not work.

> On a pragmatic level, it clearly means that whatever it is that we do, we're doing in the context of a discourse that says "socialism is dead, socialism is irrelevant, the events in Eastern Europe have vindicated capitalism." And so whatever it is that the American Left wants to do, it has to take into account that that is the predominant discourse that it has to struggle with. In some ways, it makes life more difficult because you can't even talk about thinking about socialism anymore because there's such a chorus of voices saying "Why would you want to do that? Why don't you pick your nose instead? This is a dead issue." [Sara White]

Now that the socialist systems of Eastern Europe and the Soviet Union have been discredited, the leftist position—at the political and academic levels—has become one of scorn: "If you called someone a communist now, that wouldn't be a way to make people fear them but a way to make them laugh. It would be a form of ridicule" [Gregory Washington]. Being the object of such derision has become uncomfortable for many leftist academics and intolerable for others.

> I just received a wonderful and very poignant memorandum, sort of "points on my relationship to Marxism," from a humane, deeply intelligent, much admired by me political scientist who I've been in correspondence with for about eight years, which is basically a fond *au revoir* to Marxism. There's no question in my mind, and indeed it's partially explicit in his memorandum, that this stuff in Eastern Europe is the last straw. So I think as a political matter, to call oneself a Marxist is often—depending on the circle that one happens to be in at the moment—a social-psychological experience somewhat akin to saying "I'm a brontosaurus and I love it!" [Scott Kelley]

On the other hand, there are some academics who seem to be unconcerned with the implications of these events and who are able to dismiss them in a flippant manner.

## On the Death of the Left

> I don't know what your interviews are showing, but I experience what I describe as a whistling-in-the-dark mentality in which good social democrats say, "We've been saying these people [in Eastern Europe] are no good for years! Good riddance to them!" The follow-up is that it shouldn't affect us at all. It [such an attitude] may be right morally, but it's not accurate politically. . . . I think that no matter how much you say you're a democratic socialist—emphasis on the democratic—people don't want to hear "socialist"—that's point one. For better or worse, events in Eastern Europe delegitimize the very idea of socialism among a broad range of people. Second, I think ideas that are even vaguely associated with that are similarly delegitimized. The example I like to give is go talk to somebody about the idea of a "right to housing"—that is, the decommodification of housing. I think in the current political atmosphere that's a very difficult conversation to have with all but the most already ideologically committed leftists because most folks would say "What do you mean state solutions? The whole world is moving away from statist solutions!" [Scott Kelley]

Thus, there seems to be a consensus that the Left is in a period of much turmoil. However, the interviewees generally agreed that the current crisis within the Left is much older than public opinion recognizes. It seems that the collapse in Eastern Europe was merely the most visible event in a much larger tide of disillusionment and division that became noticeable especially in the 1960s and gradually built to a peak throughout the 1970s and 1980s.

> My sense is that Marxist theory was already being challenged in major ways *from within* as much as from without. Since the 1950s and 1960s, there has been much critique and revision. In the last ten years—the post-'68 period—there's been an impact on those—at least on *me*—working within and around Marxism. These [revisions] have come from poststructuralist and postmodernist arguments. People like Foucault and some of the deconstructionists were part of a broad-sided challenge to Marxist theory, and *then* came this total disruption in Eastern Europe and the complete fragmentation of the Soviet empire. So it wasn't as if Marxism in general was sailing smoothly. It was an already embattled and tattered ship. [John Wilcox]

And from another academic:

> The American Left, or rather those people in America who think of themselves as the Left or having some interest in Marxism, have been in a state of crisis for a long time. . . . I think during much of the seventies and early eighties there was some hope for a grassroots movement, there were hopes for more links between a Marxist Left and a labor movement. There was disappointment, of course, in the direction of the Democratic Party; but there was a sense that there was a broad constituency interested in reform. I think the victory of Ronald Reagan in 1980 made people more aware of how isolated they were and how few Americans bought into or were open

to a Left vision—or rather how their discontents were easily mobilized by the Right and less easily mobilized by the Left. Therefore, the prospects of the Left convincing more centrist politicians and political coalitions to move in that direction seems more remote. I would say that in most of the 1980s, the Left in America has been in some sort of vague sense of crisis. It's mostly been a matter of reflecting upon the difficulties of bringing about any positive social change in the United States. It's not been a crisis defined by international socialism; it's much more internal and gradual. [Curtis Parker]

Even though this crisis may have been developing since the 1960s, it was not as readily apparent then. It is true that victories became fewer and further between, yet the full extent of the crisis was not known or understood. This may still be the case. However, as the following passage indicates, in the past there may have been enough momentary victories to hide the depth of the crisis while today such a veil has been torn away.

There are lots of achievements of the intellectual Left and the sixties generation in terms of cultural politics and the way we think about the world. So there have been these developments which are encouraging in one sphere or another, momentary victories which have masked the lingering, long-term crisis of Marxist politics. None of us have quite figured out what we're going to do in America to seriously impact the mainstream politics. We have had these crises for a while, and I think it is true that in the last couple of years the crisis has become more critical because that lingering faith in socialist models, particularly of economic change, has been destroyed. [Curtis Parker]

Thus, the Left is enveloped in a state of disillusionment, a spiritual crisis, a "dark night of the soul." This position is characterized by demoralization, uncertainty, hopelessness, and even denial. After gradually building up over the course of several decades, such sentiments are now at a peak. Knowing that there is a crisis, we may now seek to understand what this state of affairs implies for Marxist theory.

## The Debate

The largest single area of disagreement among leftist academics has to do with the relative strengths and weaknesses of Marxist theory within the context of the larger spiritual crisis of a Left bereft of any existing socialist model. Some have cast Marxism aside for theoretical positions that more fully address their concerns. Other cling to the tools Marxism has to offer for the lack of a better alternative. It is over the attractiveness or unattractiveness of Marxist principles in a postcommunist world that the debate among progressive intellectuals comes to bear.

# On the Death of the Left

## *The Continuing Strengths of Marxism*

Marxism continues to present a discriminating critique of power structures within capitalism.

> Marx is extremely relevant for critiquing society, particularly capitalist society. . . . Everything it had to say about how capitalism functioned, who created the wealth versus who benefits, all these basic, fundamental Marxist ideas are very applicable today, or twenty years from now. [Kenneth Gates]

Marxism remains very empowering for the dispossessed within society insofar as it gives them hope for a brighter future.

> [Marxism is] a secular vision of self and world transformation that is incredibly enabling for people who feel themselves to be dispossessed and disenfranchised . . . [I]n secular terms, Marxism survives for many of the reasons that religions survive, and it will have this type of staying power and also be helped by the dilemmas which capitalism keeps confronting people with. [John Wilcox]

Beyond presenting a critique of the power structures within capitalism, Marxism continues to allow one to understand the actual workings of the capitalist economy.

> I think if Marxism led you to anything, it led you to the vision that there was a different way to organize the economy. There were so many ways that Marxism made sense of particular economic problems in American capitalism and European capitalism, and still does make sense of the ups and downs of the economy, the rise and fall of different powers, and so on—all these fronts of critical analysis of the works of capitalism that Marxism seemed to give us still seem to make sense. [Curtis Parker]

Although most academics do believe that Marxism is still very important as a critique, others beg to differ—as the following passage points out:

> What is a critique? And how do we know what the proper critique is? . . . The old Marxists thought they knew. They thought that there was a kind of role that could be played that would grant one a certain kind of knowledge that may not be universally shared with regard to what must be done; and I would be very suspicious . . . I think that people who know what must be done become intolerable and nobody else can stand them. [Christopher Rolston]

Yet even if the value of a critique in isolation is questionable—and this topic will be discussed at greater length below—Marxism provides powerful tools that are indispensable to many.

> Marxism is not a scientific endeavor per se, but a set of tools for looking at social and political phenomena. It remains powerful in that regard. Until there is a more suitable vocabulary or way of talking about those phenomena, I don't have a better set of tools available to me.... The Marxism vocabulary—concepts such as class, exploitation, power, et cetera—are the most powerful tools I have and I can't abandon them totally without some alternative, because that would result in abandoning the problems in social and political phenomena.... Personally, these events won't lead me to shed Marxism for the very fact that there are no alternatives—they are still the best tools. I don't use these tools in an orthodox way, but as a poetic, provocative means of understanding society, polity, and economy. But I'm definitely open to the impact of these events—they definitely have me thinking about the crisis of the Left, alternatives to capitalism, and so on. [Eric Reynolds]

Thus, for some academics, the crisis calls into question the validity of this theoretical framework; and yet the lack of alternative frameworks precludes the abandonment of Marxism.

Others *have* found useful alternatives depending on their interests. Some have moved on to liberal pluralism, or to the postmodern perspective, or to other critical theories such as that embodied in the Frankfurt School. Yet, even those who move away from a strictly Marxist analysis acknowledge that Marxism still has much to offer: "Yes, I guess I would have to say I would sustain some kind of critical perspective. In that sense, I find Marxist historical analysis extremely interesting and delightfully helpful. I think the case that Marx really makes is the case based on historical analysis" [Christopher Rolston]. Thus, the Marxist critique and analytical system still seems, at least for many leftist academics, to be viable and attractive. However, the question is whether these strengths are enough to maintain loyalty to Marxism as a theoretical framework within which to understand the modern world.

### The Failings of Marxism

In the light of the collapse of socialism and communism, academic perceptions of the areas in which Marxist theory falls short are much more varied than the areas considered to be its strengths.[2] Since the topic of the interviews concerned the current crisis in Marxist theory, much more attention was given to its shortcomings than its strengths. It must be noted that all of these concerns are the subject of debate. The ultimate question is whether these failings of Marxism leave enough of the theoretical perspective intact to be worthwhile as a tool for analysis and critique. If the answer is no, there is a follow-up question: If not Marxism, what are the alternative possibilities?

*Basic Assumptions* While basic Marxist assumptions—such as those concerning human nature and the role of production in society—have been the subject of much debate over the years, the events of 1989–91 have brought the attention of Left academics back to these assumptions. At the very deepest level, Marxist assumptions about human nature have been increasingly challenged. One critical approach influencing my respondents is rooted in the postmodern perspective:

> These theorists argue that some of the assumptions Marxism shares with the Enlightenment are really questionable—the way human beings operate in the world, the emphatically rational nature of human beings, and the Marxist view that if only the working class were "sober"—Marx uses that image a lot. He hopes to make workers sober by ripping off all the drugs and narcotics that lay on people through religion, metaphysics, and so forth. Capitalism sort of created this "sobriety." Foucault's view is that Marx hasn't got the faintest idea of what humans are like—they're much more strange, their relationship to power is so bizarre. . . . [Thus,] he focuses on how far out of touch Marx is—that he doesn't comprehend anything. That's why he's so interested in power. And this all comes at a time just when Eastern Europe blows up. [John Wilcox]

Academics argue that Marxism is limited in other ways as well. Marxism, while said to be a theory that is also a form of practice, actually provides little practical guidance for its application beyond calling for a revolution by the proletariat.

> Once you recognize, say, who your enemies are—and that's what Marxism does, it tells you who your enemies are—how does it distinguish the practice of one group from another, or how does it give more detailed practical guidance for how to pursue environmental struggles, union organizing strategies, or anything like that? I don't think it tells you in detail much more. [Curtis Parker]

Some argue that Marxism has obscured any viable political strategy because of its romance with revolution.

> I think that essentially if you feel as I do that most popular mobilizations are very good but limited in that their further development means entering the political system in a serious way, it means you've got to start thinking about what mass-democratic politics is all about—how you influence it. And Marxism isn't a very good guide on that—or at least the kind of Marxism we've had elaborated for us within the academy of socialist parties. [Curtis Parker]

## Reflections on the Death of Marxism

This criticism does not stop with the acknowledgment of the role of political structures, but continues with a more direct critique of the Marxist assumptions concerning the economic base. The following quote is an emphatic denunciation of Marx's elemental focus on production and alludes to the havoc such a focus wreaked on Eastern Europe.

> I agree with Habermas that you have to reconstruct the productive model of Marxism. The emphasis on production is wrong.... There is no way to isolate production from social relations.... There is no transformation without democratization; so the idea that you could have a higher level of freedom by changing an economy independently of dealing with the democratic structures is absurd. In terms of "keeping the faith," I think that element of Marxian analysis is right. In terms of capitalistic monopoly and its distortions, corruptions, et cetera, I think Marx is completely right about that; but one does not change that simply by altering the productive mechanism. This is ineffective from the very issue of productive relations themselves because what happens is you tend to destroy economies. Eastern bloc countries could barely provide for their own needs. These were totally repressive societies.
>
> I think Marx had a pretty simplistic notion of economy—economies require a great deal of direction, and it's not a simple matter of distribution; it's a problem of public wealth and how it's distributed. In the twentieth century, you can't merely take over the means of production; that would never work because whoever takes it over simply controls it—"let's keep it for us." So other mechanisms have to intervene. [Christopher Rolston]

It may even be that such a focus on the means of production ultimately proved to be the downfall of the economic systems of the Eastern bloc countries.

> State-ified central planning apparently is not up to the management of the complexity of a modern technological society. It doesn't seem to be able to generate technical innovation. It did not seem in the Soviet Union and Eastern Europe to properly allocate price mechanisms so that you could evolve successfully from producing goods to consuming goods. It didn't seem to be able to create a set of structures for high-quality production of everyday commodities. I'm not a worshiper of the market, but I think that the socialist end of the Marxist analysis/critique needs substantial thought. [Scott Kelley]

Another perceived weakness is that, as "grand theorists" with a very broad focus, Marxists harbor feelings of grandiosity. Professor Wilcox argued that such hubris has proven to be the undoing of the Marxist experiment.

> That's a Marxist desire: being linked to history. But I feel the lack of the fulfillment of that desire even though I think, "Well, Marxism is dead"

and I'm not a Marxist anymore, so I shouldn't even desire that. Why should I desire being linked to history; that was *always* an illusion. It's *always* what led Marxists down the wrong path and to the worst things that were ever done by them. It's a good thing not to feel bound up to some larger force. [John Wilcox]

On the other hand, there is also the notion that Marxism is too limited in its focus on class. Such a restricted focus on class seems to imply that a single revolution is needed in order to correct the ills of society, a misapprehension borne out by the events in Eastern Europe and the Soviet Union.

[T]here is an assumption that there is *a* revolution which will take place—not forty or fifty revolutions taking place at the same time—and that that revolution will be taking place . . . at the most fundamental point in society. The implication is that changes in all the other points are not fundamental and that focusing on them is a disservice to this fundamental change because once this single change is made, all forms of oppression will be eliminated—including those based on gender, race, and so on . . . that's hard to accept. [John Wilcox]

However, not everyone agrees that the focus on class is a problem with Marxism. Some academics feel that the Left has moved too far away from class issues.

*Stratification Theory* Marx's theory of class stratification, in which he describes the division between the bourgeoisie and the proletariat, is one of the central ideas of Marxism. However, many academics feel that dividing the populace solely on the basis of class blinds Marxists to other divisions within society. The sudden release of ethnic tensions in Eastern Europe and the Soviet Union illustrates the point.

Professor Kelley, who has been a Marxist from his youth, has realized since the time of the events of 1989 to 1991 that his exclusive focus upon class, stemming from his Marxism, was tremendously short-sighted. He now believes that race and ethnicity—and one could also add gender as well as other differences such as sexual orientation—produce equally fundamental divisions and hierarchies within society. He says that this crisis within the Left

is also a challenge to Marxist stratification theory, which is based on the primacy of class over race or ethnicity. You can come up with complicated ways of dealing, say, with the American situation, or even the Western European racial and ethnic tensions; but in the East, these were suppressed. . . . The alleged primacy of class needs to be either defended or reduced, but it certainly cannot stand unexamined by a seeker after truth. [Scott Kelley]

Professor White, a more orthodox interviewee, applies this notion of an inadequate theory of stratification to the more concrete situation in Eastern Europe.

> I think any theory in alerting you to certain things to look out for is also blind to the stuff that's not highlighted. It's clear from the events in the last two years that this theory does not adequately deal with religious and ethnic passions that animate people and a centrist state saying that's "nothing but feudal or early capitalist superstition which we could simply suppress and in the worker state this will wither away." That clearly has not been empirically borne out! So all the attention to class exploitation and class dynamics has really forced the governments in Eastern Europe to conceptualize religious and ethnic difference as being vestiges of a prior system and, if you sweep the system away, believing the ideational accoutrements will wither away by themselves, then that clearly has not been a useful analysis. [Sara White]

However, she is less willing to concede that these problems were with Marxism itself. She argues that such countries—especially the Soviet Union—are tremendously diverse and that it is impossible to unite these areas under one government without some degree of discrimination. Thus, she makes the point that Marxism is not responsible for the ethnic struggles occurring within these systems.

> Yes, there are problems in Eastern Europe which probably do arise out of Marxism specifically; but I think there are certainly problems in Eastern Europe that arose for reasons other than Marxism as well. I'm struck by the author of *Peter the Great* and some of his descriptions of the Russian political system. You can substitute Brezhnev for Peter and it reads very similarly; so there probably is a certain national culture. There's probably a certain degree of repressiveness implicit in any state that is trying to coordinate activities over the land mass that Russia is—over the ethnic and linguistic diversity that Russia is which makes Americans look like incredibly homogeneous first cousins. If you're trying to keep Vladivostok and Kiev in the same political system, it's very hard to imagine how you can do that without a pretty repressive central government. So I think a lot of the difficulties in Eastern Europe are probably not a function of Marxism. [Sara White]

However, this too is a subject of much dispute. Yet another academic argues that the Left is guilty of a striking homogeneity, implying that this reflects upon traditional Marxism itself. John Wilcox presents his argument through a colorful example in which a group of Marxists are criticized for the similarities in their appearance—a symbol of their homogeneity.

> Here's a picture [pointing to the wall behind me: a black and white photo of a large group of white men—dressed in very similar outfits—and two women. There are no people of color]. This is 1923. The leftists I knew in college were men who looked like that—like Marx. I mean, they didn't have earrings, they didn't wear the style that nonintellectuals wore. They didn't model their styles on rock stars or something like that. They all looked the same . . . I look at a picture like this, and it's not innocent. There are some women in it. The men have authoritative uniforms on. They're making a statement about who they are as men in the world and what they do and what their authority is. *One guy* has a sweater, looking informal. That visual image of the leftist intellectual is fragmented—it's now up for grabs. What do you look like? You're a leftist intellectual, but you're interested in style. In fact, they were always interested in style; but they didn't know it, or they didn't want to admit it. [John Wilcox]

The homogeneity of the traditional Marxist Left was "not innocent" in that it forgot people of color, women, sexual minorities, and so on. This has been changing in recent decades, but it still reflects elements of orthodox Marxism that continue today. This lack of attention to the dispossessed other than the working class and the poor has helped cause a fragmentation of the Left into smaller, more focused interest groups.

*The State* Before we can consider the issues surrounding the state, an important caveat is in order. There was wide agreement among the academics that Eastern Europe and the Soviet Union did not represent what Marx implied by his communist vision. As Professor Helmut Schneider said of these political and economic systems, "Marx wouldn't recognize them" as representing the ideal he envisioned. This idea is not new, but it was brought up continually in defense of Marxism. The following passages eloquently describe the feelings of the Left toward these regimes.

> On theoretical and practical grounds, most of us didn't identify with those regimes. We debated what they were. We had a lot of theories about what was wrong with them. None of us regarded them as the embodiment of socialism or practitioners of any kind of Marxism that we would feel comfortable with. It always seemed to us dogmatic. It always seemed to us crude, economistic, heavy-handed, and so I would say that most of the Western Left—by which I mean the American Left and the European Left—had adopted a very critical stance toward the regimes in the East and the kind of socialism and Marxism they seemed to represent. Given that, the events in Eastern Europe and the Soviet Union in 1989, '90, '91

## Reflections on the Death of Marxism

in some ways have simply confirmed our diagnosis that those regimes weren't so great, never represented what we were involved in, and hence their failure, their collapse, ought not to have been a liability for us. . . . Many of us thought that what was wrong in the East was that somehow the political system was undemocratic and the economy had some virtues. What seems quite clear now is that the political system was rotten and the economic system was not working either. Whether that was always the case, whether that was more the case in the last twenty to thirty years, I'm not sure; but I do think that the failure of the economic and the political side of the East European and Russian experiments in socialism was pretty spectacular. . . . [T]hey just seemed to be crude echoes of Marx and Lenin, and they applied Marx and Lenin in dogmatic ways. [Curtis Parker]

There were a lot of socialists—progressive, leftist types—who said that the Soviet Union wasn't socialist or Marxist. The goal of Marxism was all about democracy—political, economic democracy. Many leftists of many different types held that what was going on in the Soviet Union, what was going on in the Eastern bloc, what was going on in China—the various variations—were basically not what socialism was supposed to be about, at least in terms of public ownership and these kinds of things. These places were not democratic at all. They were very authoritarian. It is interesting that when the Soviet Union and communism in Eastern Europe essentially collapsed, socialism was declared dead. It strikes me as odd because socialists did not think it was socialism which existed in these places. It was Stalinism which was going on there and if Stalinism fell, then it would not be a black eye for socialism but a better step toward a democratic socialism. [Kenneth Gates]

[The leaders of these regimes] certainly have no understanding of Marxian theory—but they had power . . . I have complete sympathy with the revolutions which have occurred—their hatred of communism is justified. [Christopher Rolston]

It was a tyrannical state. I think among the things that did it in was that it started out as a "puritan" tyranny and it ended up as a *corrupt* one. . . . A tyrant is one thing; but a corrupt, self-serving, self-seeking tyrant is doubly delegitimized. [Scott Kelley]

While most of the respondents do not believe that the Soviet and East European regimes were what Marx intended, they are reassessing the Left's historic emphasis on state intervention in the economy. As Eric Reynolds notes,

It is apparent that problems arise when concentrating this power in the states. A large part of the Left has put many or most of its eggs in the basket of state, and there is no clear alternative for this. This emphasis on the state needs to be rethought very deeply. The Left needs to come up with alternative systemic formulations. This is a difficult task, and these events may provide more impetus for doing so. [Eric Reynolds]

Earlier in the interview, he said that

> the focus of such rethinking of Marxian theory will be on the state, state planning, organization, et cetera. Overall, there is a deeper disenchantment with the state, and attempts have been made to refine the role of the state within Marxian theory, which have been useful but have not really integrated into classical theory of Marx. [Eric Reynolds]

Professor Rolston went a step further and speculated as to where, exactly, Marx went wrong in his theory of the state:

> Marx may not have understood the consensual aspect of society—civil society. He focused on the economy and set aside legal structures as being dependent on the economy. Marx came to believe that you could organize society on the basis of certain kinds of judgments or demands, and he may have lost the consensual basis within civil society. Because of this, it became too easy for vanguard parties to arise. He was right about Germany: they didn't have any democratic experience and weren't open to pluralism. [But] he didn't understand pluralism, and I think that's one of his serious flaws. [Christopher Rolston]

Marx's neglect of civil society is just one of the many possible reasons that the socialist and communist systems arising out of the Marxist tradition became seduced by totalitarianism. The fact that such a thing occurred indicates that there is something about the state that Marx overlooked.

The following passage serves as an example of the tug of war going on in the minds of intellectuals with regard to the role of the state:

> The model in which the market is completely predominant and the state is weak and reactive is really only true in England and America. In Germany and France, you certainly had a state-managed development of capitalism. Those are certainly successful capitalist models in that certainly there's a high-tech, high level of productivity. I'm not saying that perfect social justice has been achieved in those societies, but those are certainly models of the state being very proactive in economic development.... I think it's kind of a common consensus on some part of the Left that centrally state-planned economies work reasonably well as a transition from preindustrial to industrial economies—that they're good for expropriating the value it takes to get industrialism to a takeoff. But then they become unduly burdensome on the economic process. That certainly is from a market point of view with the assumption that getting a market established is a legitimate objective. Any antidemocratic state is clearly a problem.
>
> I think I would not want to lay the Soviet experiment at the feet of Marxism, basically. If you think of the major totalitarian systems which

> are available to the Eurocentric imagination, there's Russia, where there is some connection to Marxist theory; Nazi Germany, where there is no connection to Marxist theory; and apartheid in South Africa, where there is also no connection to Marxist theory. The Third Reich and apartheid are conducted in the *teeth* of Marxism—against Marxism. So I don't think that there's any real correlation between Marxist theory on the one hand and totalitarian political practice on the other. Unfortunately, there are a number of ways to construct totalitarian experiments. Certain variants of Marxism are clearly one of them, but not one out of three. I don't know that it's coincidental in the Russian experience, but it's not an intrinsic connection so that you can only get from Marxism to totalitarianism or that you can only get to totalitarianism through Marxism. Clearly, there are other ways to get to totalitarianism—racial ideologies being one. Do I think there's a Marxist gap in the theory of the state? Yes. And do I think there are unresolved difficulties with Marxist theory more generally? Yes, of course. There's a sort of strict construction of Marx that says that everything is a relation to production—the determinative power is there and everything else is sort of epiphenomenal, which reduces the state to the errand boy of the bourgeoisie. This is clearly wrong in some ways. . . . Are there problems with Marxist theory? Yes. Is every Marxist guilty of being a proto-totalitarian? No. I don't see any real connection between Marxism and antidemocratic tendencies. [Sara White]

Some would also argue that the problems surrounding a theory of the state are actually greater than those of Marxism in itself. The point is that theories of the state *in general* are inadequate and need much more attention.

*The Lack of Alternatives* One will recall that the Marxist critique and analysis of capitalist systems is regarded as one of its most important assets. However, there is also a point at which this asset becomes a liability in that a critique implies a viable alternative at the risk of losing its credibility. Marxist analysis and critique have been jeopardized. The spiritual crisis facing the Left at this time boils down to the possibilities of finding alternative economic and political structures. Thus, we have arrived at the heart of the predicament in which the Left has become mired.

> The problem is that if there are no alternatives that work, if you can't say "here's a package of policies that national and local governments can adopt which will engineer economic growth, which will stop regional decline, which will allow people to be better off under capitalism"—without those policies, what's the good of critical analysis? Why develop a critique of capitalism if there is no alternative? . . . I don't think there's a crisis internal to Marxism as a theoretical system. The problem is much more what to do with any of the conclusions that would emerge from such a

> theoretical framework. If it produces no conclusions that you can use, or very few practical conclusions you can use—either in the short term or in terms of a long-term vision of change—then the intellectual framework becomes less compelling. Any framework has to produce both intellectual gains—which Marxism can still do—but also has to produce positions, alternatives that you feel have at least a reasonable chance of succeeding; and there's a lot of pessimism in those things.... What I've been trying to suggest ... is that there is some limit to our ability—of those who are intellectual Marxists, or have that as part of our makeup—to find that Marxist analysis, that Marxist style of critique, useful if it never seems to yield practical results. [Curtis Parker]

These sentiments find their echo in this next passage. Here "praxis" is used as the term describing the concrete manifestations of the political and economic systems derived from Marxism:

> Marxism has always been better in its critique—but critique has been closely linked to praxis. Since the praxis side of the coin has been weakened, it may be that the critique has been weakened as well. So these events have implications for critique as well. A critique without a cogent alternative model loses some of its potency in that it is less likely to be taken seriously, because a critique implies a direction for change. It is hard to separate Marxism as an analytical system from Marxism as a normative system. It requires an alternative vision, not just reform, since "the Left" are those who want profound systemic change, not just remedial changes. [Eric Reynolds]

The question that arises is what such a normative system would look like. This is our next topic of concern.

## The Alternatives

If capitalism produces as much injustice as the Left has argued for decades and if the "socialist" and "communist" systems of the East have collapsed under the weight of their own inequities, the question remains, What are the possibilities for an alternative between capitalism and communism that would avoid the shortcomings of each?

### *Capitalism Has Not Won*

Although there is much disillusionment among the Left, there is still a general conviction that capitalism is a system with deep problems of its own. Some even see it on the verge of a collapse: "We can't speak of the collapse of communism/socialism without wondering about the imminent collapse of capitalism, since capitalism is undergoing more strain now than it has in years" [Eric Reynolds].

The observable signs of crisis within the capitalist system are many, although not everyone would agree as to what, exactly, they are. The bottom line seems to be that, as a system, it is just not working for a significant number of people.

> While we're talking of the demise of socialism, capitalism is in dire straits. If you look at this country—the strongest capitalist country in the world—the standard of living is on the decline, wages are stagnant, unemployment is persistent, there's increasing poverty, and so on. And this is the wave of the future? I'd rather not see it. . . . Capitalism is not working for us, and it's getting worse. At the *precise moment* in world history where people are saying that capitalism is the wave of the future, in every capitalist society there is decline. The decline is faster in communist societies . . . but capitalist societies are undergoing these crises too. We spent too much on the military just as they have. We haven't trained our civilian sector, we haven't built up our infrastructure, and we haven't delivered the goods to the people who are demanding and need them. This is happening in a lot of places, so I don't think capitalism in its many forms is the wave of the future. [Kenneth Gates]

Below the surface of concrete indicators, there is the feeling of a global crisis that includes capitalism in its dark embrace. Perhaps there is a more pervasive lack of inspiration which includes capitalist systems since "it's even more bankrupt intellectually; it has no ideas. The Left is a mess, but so is conservatism and liberalism—so is capitalism" [John Wilcox]. Thus, while the Left is caught in an ideological mire of its own and the crisis it is experiencing is much more acute, the malaise in which it finds itself may be an indicator of something much more widespread.

> You look at the collapse of government in Eastern Europe and think that's an isolated incident. But look at the reaction to government in the United States—belief structures, the general collapse of the Bush administration, the need to fight wars to keep the thing going, the great disaffection that people have. I wonder if there's not some kind of worldwide movement abroad or at least some paralysis that's occurring in Western societies. [Christopher Rolston]

### The Third Way

Economic alternatives lying between capitalism and communism have oftentimes been grouped under the term the "third way." Usually this term has implied some sort of social democratic system in which a "capitalist" economy is closely regulated by a strong, quasisocialist state. However, some social scientists, such as Ralf Dahrendorf, argue that even social democracy has lost its viability and that an economic "third way" is no longer credible.

My respondents generally disagree, continuing to believe in the possibility of a wide range of alternatives to capitalism. At one end, you have those who are convinced that socialism or communism, not social democracy, are the only alternatives that will ever be able to work in an equitable fashion.

> I think what will happen is you'll see Marxism, with major retreading, coming back to address questions that capitalism doesn't feel like it has to solve any more. Unopposed, it can go back to assaults on the lives of workers—to accumulate capital internally in terms of developing a more voracious appetite than it used to have, judging from the salary of people like Iacocca.... You can say that anybody is dead, but then you go back to Mark Twain who said "Have you heard that the reports of my death have been greatly exaggerated!" Show me something—what third way? Has somebody happened onto it already? You can say social democracy is dead. Socialism isn't dead—it's just going to have to look at what it can do and can't do again. It'll be around again in a very healthy form in another twenty-five to fifty years with another hundred different variations on how to apply it. [Gregory Washington]

Then there are those who are open to the possibility of a third way but do not have any notion of what it would be. In the following passage, Sara White is critical of some of the "third ways" that have been proffered and gives only a vague affirmation to the idea of an alternative.

> Clearly—I haven't read Dahrendorf—but it sounds to me like another work about the end of history and the end of ideology. Those works almost always, thirty years later, end up looking just plain stupid; so I find it very hard to get invested in an end of history argument of any sort.... They're playing with the idea of a third way and, I must say, I don't find them that intellectually very persuasive because I think they are way too Eurocentric and not really dealing with a global economic context. So the answer to your question about the third way is I have no idea; but I don't think history is going to end, and I don't think we're going to live in a market economy forever. [Sara White]

At the next point on the continuum is the position that capitalism, while continuing for the short term, will be succeeded by some sort of social democratic vision.

> [N]othing in the events in Eastern Europe disproves the viability of the extension of a social democratic capitalism. The Swedes ... cruise along with a very different structure of equity and a very different sense of

> security and, arguably, a different sense of empowerment amongst the classes. . . . I think that that is both technically viable and morally preferable to what is going on in the Anglo-American world. [Scott Kelley]

However, the third way would probably involve some sort of variation on the social democratic model because, as this next excerpt informs us, that model has problems of its own.

> Socialism is a position which is now difficult to defend. At the same time, social democracy is experiencing problems. It seems to me that we need many of the things they have done. [However,] they have done too much from above—there is not enough concern with civil society, i.e., what do people at the bottom think about what is being done? But if we are to go forward, it must be forward from the Swedish model. Generally they have done very well—there isn't much poverty, but taxes are extremely high—and not just for the rich, but everybody. But it is still an effort to strive for the common good. [Helmut Schneider]

Professor Gates was willing to outline a more radical alternative he envisions. His alternative involves decentralization and a focus on distribution and rights.

> Yes, social democracies are under attack and the Labor Party is retreating in Britain, Social Democrats have lost in Denmark and Sweden, and the Socialist and Communist parties are moving to the right; but—what it's going to look like, I don't know—there's going to be a society which has the rights of the working people at the forefront. I think the oppressed class is extremely large around the world, and it always has been. What the oppressed class needs is the open market; but it also needs labor protection, it needs guaranteed health care, and various kinds of guarantees like that. I think that's the kind of world we're going to live in. It may be very decentralized—probably not anarchist, but one can imagine a more decentralized system which may be worker-owned and where health care is delivered on a community basis. Again the problems of bureaucracies in capitalism, socialism, and communism point to a future of decentralization; but I think there's going to be societies that have a fairly heavy basis in socialist principles—from each according to ability, to each according to need, or whatever. There will be a more equal distribution of resources, that people have enough to survive, a guaranteed job, all these kinds of things. . . . I see a third way which is guided by socialist principles of equality, social justice, more decentralization than we have imagined it in the past, and so on. [Kenneth Gates]

At the other end of the continuum, one academic takes up the torch of human rights and raises it within the context of agreement with the position Dahrendorf has taken.

> I think he's [Dahrendorf's] right, basically. I'm not quite sure about writing off social democracy, but I think that any realistic political-social

thinker today has to grant that, in any vision of the future, markets will have to play an enormously important role. State economic policies will have to be subordinate to market considerations. It will have to fit in with the dictate of the international markets; there's no getting away from that. Within that, I think states can do a lot. States can be much more humane—can force many more rights—and so I think there is a lot that states can do that is good. However, I think one has to grant that, overall, markets have a big role to play in the future. With regard to those grander visions of state planning or systems that transcend the marketplace, I think that the intellectual argument has been won by the Right. I think that that's over. I think what can happen is that people who have commitments on the left and who have critiques of the market economy and its workings can make arguments about the framework within which the market is operating, both nationally and internationally. Those frameworks can involve a set of definitions of rights that individuals and groups have. Therefore, the future of the Left and the center has to be the elaboration of a politics of rights—citizen rights.... I think you'll find that many of us on the left are developing our political thinking along the lines of rights, arguments about social rights and human rights and the rights of groups and activities and so on. The point of which is to suggest that, yes, capitalism and a market may be fundamental, but that whatever kind of social economic system we have, there are certain rights that groups and individuals have—anything from the right to a trial by jury, to a decent standard of living, to the expression of their sexual identity—which have to be safeguarded. [Curtis Parker]

This position would involve a focus on democratic participation. Socialism and communism have failed in this regard, but so has capitalism. Thus, it is very difficult to avoid consideration of a "third way."

Although there are no concrete theories of alternative political and economic systems other than that of social democracy, academics do seem to have some sense of what such an alternative would include. The argument is that the long-term agenda of the Left should include a focus on human rights and moral autonomy, both of which were denied in the regimes of Eastern Europe and the Soviet Union as well as arguably constrained within capitalist systems. Thus, the alternative is basically conceived of as a building up of civil society within a democratic system. Ironically, as some argue, Marxism has always fit within the tradition of democracy: "The goal of Marxism was all about democracy—political, economic democracy" [Kenneth Gates]. Christopher Rolston feels that the revolutions in Eastern Europe and the Soviet Union may actually be a return to a purer form of Marxist ideology than was in place there for the past seventy years, at least in terms of civil society.

One could make an argument that there has been a move from "vulgar Marxism" to what Marx is really about—to an internal, democratic revolution. This may be a wild argument, but there is some indication that this is what happened—at least in Poland. But of course, that's not the whole story. This has less to do with Marxian theory than it does with power structures and disillusionment with a system which gave all the wealth to those in power—and it became very corrupt. [Christopher Rolston]

Professor Schneider argues that a civil society is built up from below, in stark contrast with the regimes in the Eastern bloc.

> Essentially, Marx was a democrat, which comes out of the eighteenth-century Enlightenment. The difference is in civil society. In a good socialist society, as much as possible, everything is built on what is going on down below, in the community. Emphasis is on the democratic, the low, civil institution and what Lenin called the slow death of the state—and Marx said something very similar. [Helmut Schneider]

Since these societies were lacking a civil society in any real sense, they must take a step back in order to develop one. In this next passage, moral autonomy is identified as the missing factor at the root of the civil society.

> I think they have to go back. They don't have a sense of moral autonomy. This concept was essentially lost and this is what's coming back. If people are morally responsible in this public sense, in having a sense of moral obligation for the whole society—without this, nothing will happen. The sort of thing that makes a political democracy wasn't there. In modern society, we need a post-conventional morality—a morality that's not based on nationalism but on modalities of autonomy. You cannot have a good social system unless that happens. [Christopher Rolston]

Thus, it can be argued that the revolutions are an attempt on the part of the masses to build up a civil society and that this would be more in keeping with the spirit of Marxism than the actual systems that claimed to be Marxist in origin.

### A Danger

At the same time that there is so much optimism in the West about democratic systems in regions of the world that until recently were dominated by totalitarianism, there is also the specter of other potential forms of tyranny, such as fascism. Kenneth Gates makes an analogy to the David Duke campaign in Louisiana, an example arising frequently in my interviews. The argument is that fascism is likely to develop out of the frustration of the masses depending upon who taps into that frustration and provides the answers for which the public is looking. If a David Duke, representing fascist tendencies, can arise in response to the frustrations of people in Louisiana, who are relatively well off compared to those in

Eastern Europe, then there is all the more reason to fear the possibility of fascism in those areas.

> There has to be a democratic socialist alternative. In the absence of that, there is a danger—if I can turn this toward a domestic problem—such as a David Duke who taps into the working class's frustrations, the same kind of frustrations that socialists could have been tapping. Working-class people have been working a life that's shitty. They can't buy their own homes; they can barely stay in their own apartment. So there is a lot of frustration there, and Duke was able to tap into that in the absence of any kind of Left alternative. I think the danger, just as we've seen fascist parties in the East, [is that] there could be the rise of fascist parties in the West, in Western Europe. Extreme right-wing parties in such countries as Belgium, Germany, France, and Italy may be small, but they are *growing*—we can't write them off. In the absence of any socialist, progressive, working-class alternative, fascism is going to march in. This is also true here and in Eastern Europe. [Kenneth Gates]

Whatever the outcome may be, it will have an impact on the future of the Left in many parts of the world. While nothing is definite or predetermined, at this time it is possible to make projections about where the Left will go from here. It is to this topic which we now turn.

## The Vision

How will the collapse of communism influence leftist activists around the world? How have they been affected by the general demoralization both during its development and now, in terms of the more immediate crisis? Where will they go from here? Where *should* they go? Before these questions can be addressed, we must first examine who falls within the category called "the Left."

### *What Is the Left?*

As was mentioned briefly before, it is more difficult to define who belongs on the left than it was thirty years ago: "It used to be that when people described themselves as socialist, it was perfectly clear what that meant. Now we have a confusion of tongues, and it's not as obvious what socialism means" [Helmut Schneider]. Professor Scott Kelley lends a humorous tone to the same notion when he says that "for a whole generation, we have been in what I like to think of as the 'Heinz 57' varieties of Marxism and the political practice of nominal Marxism."

However, there is also a contrast between a sense of something having been lost in the process and a positive regard for the increased inclusivity of the Left.

> In the past, when something horrible happened, I knew many people who were going to react to this news just as I am—there's going to be *this* rally, *this* demonstration, *this* article. Now there are the usual horrible things happening, and I feel totally alone. I know that many other people are reading these things and feeling alone in the sense of not feeling part of something coming from within the system aiming at transforming it. There is no sense of being linked to some historical possibility.... I don't know what it means to be a leftist. The Left is part of the problem here: who's the Left? where's the Left? It's problematic. Who the hell *knows* what it is? [I knew what the Left was] when I was a child—a red-diaper baby in the fifties—the Left meant the communist and fellow-traveling Left, the Left of the thirties, of the forties. But I didn't know there was a socialist left—Trotskyist—that was critical of the communists. Another Left that was coherent to me was the New Left of the 1960s and early 1970s. There were some differences; but, broadly speaking, when you entered into discussion, you knew what the terms would be. But, in retrospect, that was a coherence that was ready to explode because there were women who wondered "Why aren't we ever invited to the microphone?" and others raising all sorts of issues, "Why do *we* have to keep silent?" [John Wilcox]

For John Wilcox, the transition to greater variety within the Left is a move toward a much more democratic leftist movement. He sees the lack of such variety as oppressive.

> I think that so often the social movements that I've had the strongest feelings about are even *themselves* social movements which, in retrospect, were powerfully engaged in isolating people, in pressing people psychologically, and often very indirectly, to not speak what they actually felt or thought, to not present themselves as they would like to, but as they thought they had to because this was the way the movement for liberation was going. There is probably no such movement which can resolve that mass of problems; but when I say a *democratic* movement, I mean a movement where there is open and democratic discussion of the nature of the movement, where it's going, and so forth.... You're not going to have a Marxist movement which can be antifeminist or homophobic, when Marxist movements have *always* been homophobic. It's never taken a decent position on the issue of sexuality with the exception of various radicals who end up getting pushed aside. [John Wilcox]

Thus, this breakdown or explosion in what it means to be "left" is seen by some as a positive development. However, that is not to say that variety itself is something new: it only happens to be more pronounced now than it was in the past. While the Left was quite homogeneous in the past, it still had factions dividing it. The notion of a seamless garment—a unified front—was an illusion.

> It's a myth that revolutions and social movements are unified. The only one that came close to that was Nazism, and even that was fragmented. Bolshevism was totally divided. Communist parties are always splitting off, hating and killing each other. There's this widespread notion that there has been a unified movement—this is nonsense, there have never been unified movements. [John Wilcox]

These strong sentiments find their echo in the following passage in which variety is seen as something necessary and a lesson to be learned on the part of the Left as it proceeds into the future.

> There's always variety in confronting advanced industrial society. I expect there will continue to be variety. I don't expect there to be one path in the future. I think you have to encourage a variety of political developments—that's one thing that's learned. That may be one of the ways to keep yourself on your toes as a Marxist—to be able to not have a safe haven by saying "now we've achieved power and can sit back like fat cats—*we* can become the bureaucrats." [Gregory Washington]

### *The Future of the Left*

Where does the Left go from this point of spiritual crisis and turmoil? I was surprised that the majority of the interviewees had a generally united outlook—one of pessimism. This is especially true of those who consciously think of themselves as within the tradition of Marxism, as is suggested in the following passage.

> I think the extent of disillusionment on the American left in the 1980s was probably greater than the disillusionment of European leftists. Hence, the recent turn of events had a less dramatic impact because we were already moving in what people might regard as a pessimistic path or direction—pessimistic and moving toward passivity. At least that applies to the leftists who think of themselves as Marxist or socialist. [Curtis Parker]

The idea is that the U.S. Left has been in a decline from which it will be difficult to extricate itself.

Overall, the future of the Left depends on many things—from the unfolding of history outside of its control to the decisions it makes in terms of the directions it will take. Again, the expectations of the academics are mixed. While showing some uncertainty in his position, Professor Wilcox feels that, even as social movements of the Left continue, Marxism—at least in a purer or even normative sense—will not continue to be the basis of inspiration and vision. This will be the case even if it continues to be used as a source of critique and analysis, although he does not seem to expect that either.

> My sense is that, to the extent that there are practical movements of opposition, nobody is going to care about Marxism. The oppositions are going to take very different forms, and it's a strange period where everything has broken down. My feeling is—and this is one of those things where one wants to be proven wrong—is that Marxism doesn't have a future, really—at least as a basis for opposition in Western industrialized society. On the other hand, there is a profound Marxist critique of the socialist systems we have encountered in the real world—a critique of the whole experiment. You can't create socialism in a place like Russia. Michael Harrington would have argued that "Marxism is now *more* relevant to the situation in the United States than it's ever been. Marx was so wrong and so right at the same time. He was so wrong in his timing—in his sense of time elapse—but he was so right in his analysis of what's really happening. Marxism's future and whole meaning is around the corner." This idea sort of haunts me. But it seems Marx, in certain ways, may become relevant now because there can be the possibility of a democratic, proletarian movement for social transformation in the industrial societies. But, even if that's possible, the intellectual self-expressions of that—of Marxism as the self-critique of reality—will prove inadequate, ultimately. [John Wilcox]

The Left has been changing for some time now, moving away from its Marxist heritage. Another academic feels that, as these changes continue, a point will be reached in which Marxism as a theoretical system and a source of direction will be left behind.

> I think our intellectual orientations are changing—those of us on the intellectual left—and have changed a lot in the past twenty years anyway and the last two or three years have changed us even more, although they've only pushed us in the same direction. If you keep getting pushed in the same direction, at a certain point there's a kind of qualitative transformation. I think that's what we're approaching. [Curtis Parker]

Even one of the most dedicated of leftist academic activists has a sobering view of the near future of the Left.

> I think the lesson they ought to be learning—and that they're not learning at all—is that capitalism is the wave of the future. Socialist parties for a long time have been turning conservative. Leftist parties have been making a move to the right. It's amazing that many parties are changing their names away from "communist" when they never really bought into Soviet communism all that much. I think what we have to do—what leftists have to do—is use this as an opportunity. I know there is a problem in the decline of these states, but it also seems to present an opportunity for a more democratic socialism. [Kenneth Gates]

## On the Death of the Left

However, several academics agree that only time will tell, for in time everything can change. Those taking this perspective are optimistic about the future of the Left but concede that much will have to happen before such a positive outcome is reached.

> I can envision what the empirical and logical requirements are for the kinds of ideas that made up the socialist project . . . to once again have viability. . . . That would be when the global industrialization is much further along than it is now; when national, racial, and ethnic divisions between laborers recede in importance and their common interests as wage laborers increase in importance across national lines. That is to say, when capitalist development really works out its logic on a global basis, then I think once again people will say there must be some other way to do this. I think that's a long moment away; but I'm also guessing that's a logical requirement for a recrudescence of an alternative vision. Of course, so much will happen in the course of that environmentally and technologically—world culture will have changed dramatically. So it is very hard to determine what the outline of those alternative ideas will be; but I think they will have some resemblance to a transcendence of the market and private appropriation of the product of human labor. [Scott Kelley]

The conviction is that, "in the next twenty years or so, things will be gradually sorting themselves out" [Helmut Schneider]. The current crisis presents an opportunity such that

> Out of the wreckage of Stalinism, it may be possible to build a democratic socialism. In the medium-to-long term, it is easier to be optimistic. For a long time, it was difficult for socialists to make any kind of headway because for many, socialism meant Stalinism. Now we have the opportunity to let people know that socialism and Marxism are *not* Stalinist oppression. [Kenneth Gates]

This positive outlook is summed up in the following passage in which a premium is placed on long-term imagination.

> After this stuff is over and after a couple of fascist regimes have committed their own atrocities, the people are going to start looking back and saying "those good old bad days weren't so bad after all. What can we salvage from that experience?" Right now, people are running away from that experience as fast as they can, but they're about to hit a stone wall. Once they hit the stone wall, they'll think "I thought we were running away from that thing"—then they'll have to process it. . . .
> I think first of all, they [the Left] need to take a long, historical view. . . . My view is that, if you take enough of it into account, then you'll probably become a Marxist. Even if you don't, you have to understand what works and what doesn't and understand the "why" of the functioning of the system. You have to have an understanding of history to deal with it. History informs your ability to see the future. If you can't see the future in

broad strokes, you're not going to be a Marxist. You easily become demoralized. But I'm one for great leaps of imagination. [Gregory Washington]

However, the long term is also problematic, and the dilemma has to do with a concrete vision more than with imagination.

> Popular movements have always been a source of leftist activity, and this isn't likely to change. They have the same problems to deal with. But they [movements] have been handicapped by a long-term alternative vision—and now that vision may be more muddied and confused than before. This leaves an intellectual and spiritual vacuum in terms of knowing its longer-term identity while, at same time, it still concentrates on the more immediate, pressing issues it seeks to address. This is where these movements get their energy. [Eric Reynolds]

It is the conviction of this academic that, without a viable, long-term vision, the Left loses direction and is easily demoralized. Yet, on the other hand, short-term, immediate issues and concerns provide the needed impetus to keep the Left moving, even during this time of crisis. Thus, there is one more area of concern relevant to a consideration of the future of the Left: the relative values of short-term visions of reform versus a long-term vision of systemic change.

### *Visions of Reform and Systemic Change*

It is the leftist—especially the socialist—vision that has been called into doubt within the spiritual crisis of the Left. The old vision of a state-run economy has largely been discredited and has tainted the Marxist theoretical framework as well. While Curtis Parker believes that a vision of long-term change is still theoretically important, it is no longer viable or compelling in a practical sense.

> I think theories, such as Marxism, that are systemic and talk about long-term capitalist development and propose theories of long-term, systemic change remain useful theoretically. You do better to try to grasp capitalism systemically. . . . [B]ut it's not at all clear to me that any social democratic thinkers, parties—any socialist thinkers, parties—in Europe have a particularly compelling vision of long-term social transformation. They refer to such visions, but I don't think anybody believes them. . . . There would clearly be a benefit to having a long-term vision of change if you could believe in that vision—if that vision genuinely provided guidance. However, I don't know that many people on the left today in America or Western Europe really have a vision that's compelling. They may have aspirations and utopian feelings or sentiments, but I don't know that they have much of a vision of how it will happen or where they're going. [Curtis Parker]

## On the Death of the Left

Helmut Schneider says that, in the absence of a viable, long-term vision, it is best to remain committed to short-term issues and concerns.

> In a way, we have again become utopian—even though Marx didn't like the idea—insofar as we imagine a society that's better than what we have now. We must keep a long-term vision, but also get involved in the little things.... Trotsky said this when he reflected on what must be done if a revolution didn't occur: then we must do the elementary things that must be done to help workers, immigrants, women, and so on. One goes down below to the people—while giving up more grandiose things—and does some work; and I think that is a sensible idea.... I think it's valuable to build up a vision for those who are dissatisfied with society the way it is. [Helmut Schneider]

However, a long-term vision gives guidance and a means—a set of criteria—for judging short-term activism. Without such a vision, reformist activism becomes directionless and of questionable value.

> Even if you're doing a variety of practical, reform-type things, if you have an alternative vision, you have criteria by which to judge your everyday action. If you don't have an alternative vision, you are, I think, intrinsically more inclined to act in a less integrated fashion and also less able to inspire yourself or others with another vision.... [I]n general, I think that the loss of an alternative mode of civilization as a vision has negative implications—at least I experience it that way. [Scott Kelley]

On the other hand, while a long-term vision has definite advantages, it also has its problems when carried to excess. Such a vision can become dogmatic and inflexible—"monolithic" is the term used in the following passage. The idea of a vision toward which we "march in long step" is suggestive of where the Soviet Union and Eastern Europe went wrong. The goal became something to be achieved at all costs, even to the point that ordinary people with everyday concerns had to suffer for this "greater good." It is possible that such a dogmatic vision led to totalitarianism (although, as the respondents have observed, this is only one of many roads leading to totalitarianism). Thus, the argument in the following excerpt is that a balance must be struck between visions of long-term systemic change and short-term visions of reform such that they temper one another.

> I think the long-term reform—it's very hard to imagine how you're going to get there except step by step from the present. It does clearly help to have some idea of where "forward" is and in what direction you would like to move things; that would certainly be helpful as a point of reference.... I do think that a long-term vision is helpful ... in terms of picking your shots; there are a vast array of social improvement efforts out there. Between, on the one hand, having this monolithic vision of the

perfect future to which we all have to march in long step and, on the other hand, this completely "do whatever feels good, light any candle, thousand points of light" kind of strategy, there's some middle ground of having a vision either toward which we are moving or at least having priorities set for the issues which are important to address. [Sara White]

The balance between visions of reform and systemic change is delicate but necessary.

## The Academy

### *Implications for Academics*

Who will be more concerned about the collapse of the Soviet experiment and its implications for the Left, academics or activists? The general agreement among academics is that this spiritual crisis is much more of a concern for academics than activists. These events are very distant from activists' everyday concerns in the United States, especially when weighed against the more pressing issues they face. Although academics acknowledge that they are more likely to be worried than the activists about the implications of these changes, some are not so sure that this position is a luxury. Scott Kelley says that academics will be more concerned about these events

> because that's what they're paid to do! We pay each other to think about things that aren't on the agenda of the state senate next week. You can call it a luxury, but I don't particularly see it that way—some people do. I think, more broadly, the intelligentsia will be more concerned with this than grassroots organizers. By the way, my impression is that not too many [intellectuals] are all that concerned.... [The activists'] much more immediate problem is how to find a language that is persuasive to Americans, that advances equity and equality, transforms some of the things that are now commodities to matters of right and decency. I don't know that reflection on the collapse of the Soviet or communist system is very helpful in that. [Scott Kelley]

Academics, if they are concerned at all, are experiencing the spiritual crisis "for" the Left, but surprisingly their teaching of Marxism—if they still teach it—has not changed in a dramatic or obvious way as a result of their concerns. However, they do raise discussions in class about these events and their implications.

> I don't think it really affected the way I taught the material. I defended Marxism. We took the line that Marxism got entwined with political movements in areas that Marx was not intending it to be entwined

> with. . . . I tell the students that I used to teach it as a living thing and now it's not. . . . But in the course, a critique of capitalism is part of it. We say that capitalism isn't so victorious, we shouldn't feel so triumphant. But we were doing that already. [John Wilcox]

> I tell my students that, as far as I'm concerned, this stuff could go on for a thousand years, easily, before these questions can be resolved. It seems a lot more viable than any other sociology that was created up through 1925. [Gregory Washington]

> [My teaching of Marxist theory has not yet changed] because my use of Marxism in my primary research area, and which I teach, actually anticipated some of these events. I actively talk about events in Eastern Europe. I'm trying to talk with my students about how the Eastern European countries will fit into the global capitalist system. [Scott Kelley]

> [T]he part of Marx that I teach is the analyses of capital. So, no, I don't think it has changed tremendously. [Sara White]

The dissenting opinion comes from one who has not changed his teaching of Marxism because he no longer teaches it at all, although this switch predated the current crisis.

> I used to teach a regular course on Marxism during its heyday. But I don't do that anymore—for the last four to five years. I still do critical theory; but I wouldn't say that was only the result of recent events. . . . I even wrote a book on Marx which I didn't publish because I was uncomfortable with it; maybe someone will dig it up sometime and *accuse me* of it! [Christopher Rolston]

Even though academics have not consciously changed their approach to teaching Marxist theory, their scholarly work has responded to the crisis in a variety of ways depending on the individual's personal interests.

> I'm sure that over the long term, my scholarly interests and research agenda will be impacted by recent events. . . . I'm sure that whatever I write five years from now will be influenced by what's happening now. . . . The impact that it has had is that I'm beginning to do some research, reading about and thinking about questions of citizenship and social rights. I'm thinking in the direction that the reforming, social democratic Left, or the Marxist Left is going in, or has to reenter in a serious way the political discourse of the world we live in. That's something that I have been doing for a while. [Curtis Parker]

> I just wrote a book that isn't scholarly in the sense that I'm not a specialist in the sense of the issues I raised. It came from the inside: I just had these perceptions and thoughts and feelings. It never would have occurred to me before to make my own thoughts about something a subject of analysis. I raised issues that I would not have raised when I understood myself

primarily to be a leftist. I still felt on the left, but I couldn't address these issues as a leftist. [John Wilcox]

I've been trying to figure out what to do when you change the legal structure—when you're changing to a democratic society but you have no legal structure. Do they [the former Soviet and Eastern bloc nations] buy into the legal structure? do they recreate it? do they generate it? what do they do? I'm interested in how legal practice is associated with social transformation. [Christopher Rolston]

I'm much more actively trying to think through the question of which kind of social cleavages are primary. I resisted political correctness in the eighties and the first part of the nineties. That is, I continued to think and to argue that class was primary over gender and race. On a world scale, ethnic tensions are now at a height. I think it is incumbent on me as a person who wants to have an accurate view of the world to think about that carefully. [Scott Kelley]

These events have passed on a new set of problems and in that sense have affected my thinking. For instance, although I have had doubts about social economy—which is a way of thinking of economic alternatives to capitalism that are democratic and community-based and don't involve a reliance on central state systems—I am now looking at social economy in a new light as an approach which is removed from statist thinking—even though social economy has its own problems. [Eric Reynolds]

In some ways, I think the events in Eastern Europe are cause for great optimism, and all the things that theorists [such as Weber] said could not possibly be done nevertheless were done. I certainly think the strengths of a disorganized resistance are of interest to me and how resistance can be effectively mounted really very much at a local level. I think there's a tremendous undertone in sociology to think strategically, to think structurally, and to try to capture the major citadels of the state, the labor movement, and so forth. Yet one of the things that happened in Eastern Europe is that you had a state that was clearly not constrained by civil libertarian sentiment. It clearly was willing to ruthlessly crush every form of organized opposition, as was also the case, for example, in South Africa. So the resistance *could* not be organized because to be organized was to be suppressed—to martyr yourself. So there is this kind of bizarre and very hopeful strength of weak resistance or power of disorganized opposition that I think the Left in America—which is very much in the position of being localized, fragmented, pretty disorganized, not having any central organizational power or strategy—needs to look at how you managed; where that opposition came from when everybody was organized and active and identifiably oppositional; how you maintain resistance in church groups, theater groups, carpenter's groups, etc. I think that is absolutely fascinating, and I think that's something that maybe we could learn from. . . . And that's where I think my Marxism—intellectually—doesn't serve me well, and sociology as well. I always think myself into this corner

# On the Death of the Left

where the structural forces raised for maintaining the status quo are so much more powerful than the little, voluntaristic, fragmented, ad hoc forces that can be brought to bear against it; and yet, in fact, in Eastern Europe, forces very much like that prevailed in the long run . . . and I think that's grounds for tremendous optimism! [Sara White]

## A Paradigm in Transition

> Progress is impossible without change; and those who can't change their minds cannot change anything.—George Bernard Shaw

In interviewing these academics, I was struck by their willingness to examine the crisis faced by Marxism. Although there was little consensus about the extent or depth of this crisis, there was general agreement that theoretical Marxism is struggling through one. In addition, while it was noted that this crisis had been building gradually since the late 1960s, the collapse of the Eastern European and Soviet systems in which Marxism was actually implemented is seen by many as the proverbial straw that broke the back of Marxist thought, immersing Marxists in a state of confusion and demoralization.

Anselm Strauss notes that crises of this sort will provoke at least two different reactions.[3] Representations of the "old guard" hold that the crisis has not really changed the standing of theoretical Marxism, while others argue that it is of such a severe degree that basic changes are required. The academics who made the latter argument have generally abandoned much of the Marxist paradigm and have opted for other perspectives, such as postmodernism or some form of liberalism. Between these two positions are a majority who are still wrestling with the issues, although to varying degrees. Their thinking has gone in many different and sometimes conflicting directions. It is here that the observer is able to detect the confusion and demoralization present within the Marxist tradition.

What is one to make of this state of confusion? Thomas Kuhn's theory of scientific revolutions may be helpful in making sense of the intellectual crisis within the Marxist world. Kuhn begins with a description of "paradigms" and "normal science." A paradigm is a commonly held perspective for understanding nature or, in this case, society. As such, a paradigm presents scientists with the relevant problems for investigation and the approach for solving those problems. Defining the relevant questions for understanding nature not only opens scientists' eyes to areas of research but also blinds them to alternative questions not raised by that

## Reflections on the Death of Marxism

particular paradigm—that is, the object is to find evidence that *supports* the dominant paradigm. This is the state of "normal science," a state in which the paradigm is universally supported by scientific evidence.[4]

However, in the course of the development of normal science, anomalies to the paradigm are unwittingly found. These anomalies, since they present evidence that fails to support the dominant paradigm, are at first ignored or suppressed. However, as anomalies begin to accrue, they are explored in an attempt to reconcile them with the paradigm. In this way the paradigm is gradually altered in order to account for the anomalies. This is the process of discovery, which strengthens the paradigm by giving it a broader descriptive and explanatory power.[5]

At the same time, these discoveries and the consequent altering of the paradigm imply a gradual move away from the original perspective offered by that paradigm. A variety of versions of the paradigm may develop, and this, as Kuhn points out, is an indicator of a coming crisis. At some point the stability or balance of a paradigm is tipped—whether through the accrual of many anomalies or through an anomaly that challenges some of the most basic assumptions of a paradigm. In either case, a paradigmatic crisis is characterized by "a growing sense . . . that an existing paradigm has ceased to function adequately in the exploration of an aspect of nature to which that paradigm itself had previously led the way." A transition away from the dominant paradigm has begun.[6]

Such a transition involves not only moving away from a beginning point but also moving toward something new.[7] Thus, the scientific revolution or paradigm shift presumes, and indeed requires, the existence of an alternative: "The decision to reject one paradigm is always simultaneously the decision to accept another." Without an alternative, a paradigm may continue to exist in the face of glaring anomalies. Even when there is an available alternative, a transition will not take place unless two conditions are met: the new paradigm must adequately solve the problems presented by the anomalies to the old paradigm, and the new paradigm must also be able to solve the problems that the old paradigm had successfully solved itself. Even so, the transition is accompanied by much resistance, especially from those scientists—the "old guard" mentioned above—with the most personal investment in the old paradigm. Because of this, Kuhn notes that younger scientists, who generally have much less commitment to the old paradigm, are more likely to be at the forefront of a paradigm shift. In other words, a crisis and the existence of an alternative, while necessary, are not sufficient to create a paradigm shift. "There must also be a basis . . . for *faith in* the particular candidate [alternative paradigm] chosen." Because of these requirements for a paradigm shift, it is possible for much time to pass between the beginning anomalies and discoveries and the final transition to an entirely new paradigm.[8]

Kuhn notes that although the world has not changed with the shift in paradigms, the new paradigm highlights new aspects of that world. A paradigm shift "is a reconstruction of the field from new fundamentals, a reconstruction that changes some of the field's most elementary theoretical generalizations as well as many of its paradigm methods and applications." The alternative becomes the new dominant paradigm, and the cycle of scientific revolution is able to begin anew.[9]

As a paradigm, Marxism in its original form gave progressive social scientists a perspective through which to view the world, a means of social analysis, and an approach for solving the problems posed by the paradigm. However, as in the development of the natural sciences, anomalies that could not be solved by the existing conceptual framework began to appear. As the anomalies multiplied, subsequent theorists expanded upon the original Marxist perspective in order to reconcile these anomalies with the paradigm. A significant difference between the natural and the social worlds is that the social world changes quite dramatically over the course of time. This only serves to encourage the development of anomalies to a social paradigm as "grand" (to use the term of C. Wright Mills) as theoretical Marxism. The result was a rapid proliferation of variations on the Marxist framework—the development of the various forms of neo-Marxism.

Another significant difference between Marxism and paradigms within the natural sciences—and even with other social science paradigms—is that Marxism has a direct application beyond the realm of theory: it inspires activists to mobilize. Thus, the roles of the theorist and the activist, although they are conceptually distinct, are closely intertwined in relation to the whole of the Marxist framework. Because of this, the uses to which Marxism is put are quite relevant to the more theoretical aspects of the paradigm and vice versa. While the theory provides the ideal vision that inspires the activists, in order to apply the theory to a real, ever-changing situation, certain adjustments, or distortions, must be made. Insofar as these distortions reflect back upon the original theory, they also constitute the development of anomalies. Again, adjustments are made to the theory in order to account for the anomalies—that is, in order to reflect the political realities of the times.

A crisis does not develop until some anomaly tips the balance and destabilizes the paradigm. Generally, but not necessarily, this is an anomaly that strikes at the heart of the paradigm's most basic assumptions. In the case of Marxism, the collapse of the Soviet empire and the Eastern bloc was what tipped the balance and plunged the Marxist paradigm into crisis.

As several interviewees have noted, the greatest strength of Marxism was in its critique of capitalism. Insofar as the critique of a social system implies an alternative system, the value of the critique is indicated by the practical alternatives it presents. Since the Soviet and Eastern bloc systems represented the most powerful and widely known alternatives to the Western capitalist systems that Marxism criticized, the value of the Marxist critique suffered a tremendous blow when these systems collapsed. The collapse of communism precipitated a paradigm crisis, leading to demoralization, confusion, and inconsistent responses on the part of Marxist thinkers.

These academics, at least those most open to considering the implications of the events in Eastern Europe and the former Soviet Union, are in an interesting state of limbo: they are still *within* the Marxist tradition but not necessarily *of* that tradition. They have begun to distance themselves from the old Marxist paradigm and have begun looking for alternatives. Herein lies the crux of the situation: without a viable alternative paradigm, the transition cannot be completed—a full paradigm shift cannot occur. As discussed earlier, there currently appear to be no appealing alternatives to which these Marxist or formerly Marxist academics can turn. The transition has stalled at the point of crisis. It is this condition of being "stuck" that explains much of the current state of confusion: academics from the Marxist tradition are caught in a directionless state of limbo.

In the introduction to this chapter, I mentioned the creative potential that arises in the wake of this kind of crisis. Periods of doubt, struggle, and debate have an immense potential to bear fruits of which one could not possibly have dreamt when caught in the mire of inner turmoil. As Anselm Strauss points out, "innovation . . . rests upon ambiguous, confused, not wholly defined situations. Out of ambiguity arises challenge and the discovery of new values."[10] A crisis such as this has the potential to light the spark of creative thought and action.

However, as of yet, the disillusionment and confusion among leftist thinkers has prevented them from formulating a coherent response. Without any alternative, the state of crisis is perpetuating itself. Thus far, it seems as if these thinkers are forfeiting the creative opportunity it has presented. That is not to say that on an individual level the academics are not responding to the challenge. Quite the opposite. As I have discussed, they are in a productive mood and are looking in many new directions. Yet, the multiplicity of directions only serves to further fragment the Left; and this is occurring just when the Left's influence is at a low ebb.

There is too little organized discussion of the current state of Marxism or of "what is to be done." Leftist academics do not seem to be talking with one another beyond a superficial level. This may be because their disillusionment is still fresh and each is embroiled in his or her own attempt to deal with the crisis. Such individualistic responses go against the very leftist tradition of collective organizing that gave the Left its spirit.

Evidence of this problem emerged in the course of the interviews. Invariably, the academics would say something like "I'll be very interested in seeing what others have to say." Only later did I wonder why they had not asked others themselves. One academic even pointed out that the interview itself had sort of a therapeutic function, forcing him to think about issues to which he had not paid much attention. He acknowledged that similar topics would come up in conversations, but they were never pursued so relentlessly as in the interview. Thus, the interview setting opened a type of "private forum"—an oxymoron indeed!—within which important issues concerning Marxism and the Left could be considered in a systematic manner.

Such discussions need to move out from behind closed doors. A "public forum"—a redundant but necessary phrase—is needed in which these same issues can be formulated and discussed. Perhaps that is a part of the function of this chapter: to stimulate thought, objections, agreement, questioning, and debate. Only through engaging in such discussion will it be possible for leftists to assess the options faced by the Marxist tradition.

Given our analysis of the current crisis, the goal of such discussion is clear: to formulate an alternative paradigm. Some may object, believing that no alternative could possibly be as "left" or as radical as Marxism. However, a reminder is in order. Before an alternative can emerge as the new paradigm, it must fulfill three conditions. It must adequately address the problems posed by the anomalies to the old paradigm. At the same time, it must be able to solve all of the problems solved by the old paradigm. Finally, the alternative must be appealing enough to warrant the faith of leftist social scientists. The result might not resemble Marxism at all, yet it remains true that Marxism as a theoretical framework will have an impact on all succeeding frameworks, informing the course they take whether or not they are labeled "Marxist." The Left will remain, but what defines it as the Left will have changed.

In order to tap into the creative potential of a moment of crisis one must be willing to change. Most of the academics I interviewed are beginning such a process—a change of outlook in which directions and conclusions are as yet undetermined. The possibilities are limited only by the imagination and, as some academics stated, there is much cause for optimism. Progress toward a brighter future for the Left requires dropping its dogmatism and rigid adherence to outmoded principles, allowing change to become legitimized within a tradition that has prided itself on the notions of dialectical change and historical progression.

Karen Marie Ferroggiaro

# 4

## Reframing Revolution:

### THE REBIRTH OF THE LATIN AMERICAN LEFT

> In our time, the bureaucrats have stigmatized
> hope and befouled the most beautiful of
> human adventures; but I also believe that
> socialism is not Stalinism. Now, we must begin
> all over again. Step by step, with no shields but
> those born of our own bodies.
> —Eduardo Galeano

In Latin America, a surprising phenomenon is emerging in the dawn of the post–Cold War era: many of Latin America's armed revolutionary movements are putting down their guns and attempting, once again, to work for change within a pluralist political system. The strategy of revolution through violence is giving way to the strategy of revolution through reform. In the process the very concept of revolution is being reframed and redefined. Though often not explicitly stated, there appears to be a correlation between recent world events that have made the "communist threat" disappear and the attempt by leftist groups to utilize a nonviolent interinstitutional strategy for change.

While leftist groups are changing to work within a pluralist political system, the programs that they intend to implement in the economic and social realms are still quite revolutionary. In other words, their vision remains transformative; they are still searching for alternatives to the existing social structure. The programs proposed by such groups demonstrate a level of economic pluralism and a conscious effort to strengthen and maintain civil society heretofore unknown in Latin America. It is an attempt to create a uniquely Latin American version of social and economic democracy, by which I mean a qualitatively different way of structuring the economic, social, and political realities of these countries. At the forefront of this movement are El Salvador's Farabundo Martí National Liberation Front (FMLN), the Frente Sandinista (FSLN) in Nicaragua, the April 19 Movement, or M-19, in Colombia, and Brazil's Worker's Party.

The extent to which any form of social democracy will take hold and flourish in Latin America is largely dependent upon its acceptance by these countries' powerful right wings and by the United States. It must not be forgotten that in the not too distant past, attempts by leftist parties to effect change within the political system were met with violence and terror. While most Latin American countries have been capitalist, they have not been democratic but rather "closed" authoritarian capitalist societies. When attempts were made to open these societies through democratic reform, repressive national and international capitalist forces have closed them once again. This was most evident in the coups that deposed Guatemala's Jacobo Arbenz and Chile's Salvador Allende. Consequently, challenges to the closed authoritarian capitalist system took the form of armed revolution.

The end of the Cold War has created the possibility for an end to that violent strategy. The end of the "communist threat" means that leftist parties may be able to integrate themselves into a less overtly repressive system and work for change through electoral politics without fearing for their lives. Traditionally, cries of a "communist threat" have been used as a justification for suppressing movements working toward effective social change. Thus the United States readily backed the coups that overthrew Arbenz and Allende declaring communist threat, even though neither of these freely elected presidents was officially communist.

Theorists of the "death of the Left," however, argue that the failure of communism has universally marginalized the Left, that electoral politics cannot rehabilitate the Left, and all one need do is look at the worldwide swing to the right for the proof. Yet it must be remembered that Latin America is not like much of the world. In fact, there is little in common between, say, Guatemala and Germany, or even Guatemala and Poland for that matter. The face of capitalism in Europe or the United States is not the face of capitalism in Latin America. As Uruguayan writer Eduardo Galeano has succinctly stated, "for us, capitalism is not a dream to be made a reality, but a nightmare come true . . . we must begin all over again."[1]

## On the Death of the Left

Many "death of the Left" arguments have explicitly excluded the so-called Third World. Their arguments are inherently Eurocentric, failing to take into account the different reality of capitalism in poor nations. As stated above, in Latin America, capitalism has never been synonymous with democracy, and the Right in many of these countries has never advocated democratic forms of capitalism. Yet the Left appears poised to do so and may be the champion and beneficiary of a new democratic ideology emerging in the post–Cold War era. Thus while the industrial capitalist First and Second Worlds may be moving right, the Latin American capitalist Third World may be moving left.

A further problem with many "death of the Left" arguments is that they tend to collapse struggles for economic justice and civil society into the struggle for political freedom. As we point out elsewhere in this volume, the end of the Cold War does not close the debates over economic justice and community. This is particularly the case for the Left in some Latin American countries where we can see programs developing that vigorously attack systemic problems of economic justice and civil society within a pluralist, or open, political framework. In this process, an active reframing and redefining of the concept of revolution is occurring.

In this chapter, I argue that the end of the Cold War has opened the opportunity for a peaceful revolution in Latin America to create a new form of social and economic democracy, and this opportunity is being embraced by the Left. Contrary to popular opinion, the post–Cold War period has not marginalized the Left in Latin America but rather reinvigorated leftist political parties. In many countries, these parties are enjoying a significant degree of success working within the political system, while at the same time advancing a political platform that, if implemented, would amount to nothing less than social revolution by reform. This revolution, however, is not "communist" but rather a revolution to create precisely what Latin America has never before enjoyed: a truly democratic form of social organization characterized by political and economic pluralism, self-determination, and self-sustaining development. Though this change is visible throughout Latin America, it is occurring most notably in El Salvador, Nicaragua, and Colombia. I will, however, focus my attention primarily on the experiences of El Salvador since its potential for social reform is perhaps the most significant and far-reaching.

I am not predicting the imminent success of a "New Left" in Latin America. Rather, I believe the Left in Latin America has the possibility to embrace political opportunities and adapt to international conditions while maintaining its historical commitment to a transformational social and economic project. Essentially, what I am arguing is that rather than disappearing into the margins of political life the Left in Latin America is claiming its rightful place in the foreground. By adapting to international political changes and learning from the economic failures of state socialism, the Latin American Left is demonstrating to the world that it is developing, advancing, and adapting. As Carlos Gabetta writes: "The left [is] slowly emerging from the guerrilla debacle. What we are witnessing reflects a mature coming together of Guevarists, communists, Trotskyists, socialists, Christians and nationalists in a democratic transformational project."[2]

## The FMLN and the Hope of El Salvador

In order to understand current events in the tiny country of El Salvador, it is important first to understand that attempts to open Salvadoran society go back a long, long time. The country has been ruled since 1821 by a small and very powerful oligarchy. Approximately 80 percent of the population has been marginalized throughout the last 170 years, and attempts to change the balance of forces through interinstitutional means have never succeeded. In 1972, three leftist organizations, the Salvadoran Communist Party (PCS), the Christian Democratic Party (PDC), and the National Resistance Movement (MNR), formed a coalition and won the presidential elections with José Napoleón Duarte and Guillermo Ungo as their candidates. Perhaps encouraged by the recent Allende victory in Chile, this coalition campaigned with a progressive socialist platform aimed at improving the living conditions of the country's marginalized majority. Though freely carried out, the electors were deemed null and void by the Salvadoran military; the victors were imprisoned, tortured, and forced into exile. A military junta took their place.

Soon thereafter, right-wing paramilitary groups began killing and "disappearing" the civilian members of left-wing organizations with increasing ferocity. By 1980, this activity would result in more than eight hundred deaths per month. Worldwide attention was attracted with the assassination of Archbishop Oscar Romero on March 24 of the same year.

The FMLN was officially formed by five political-military organizations on October 11, 1980. On January 10, 1981, the FMLN launched what was anticipated to be its final offensive, a large-scale urban campaign that is credited with having wiped out approximately 80 percent of the Salvadoran military's air power. However, the "final" offensive actually became the first initiating a brutal civil war. The United States, under the leadership of Ronald Reagan, who vowed to stop the spread of communism in Central America, responded to the January offensive by sending military aid, advice, and training to the Salvadoran military. By the end of the war, this country, which is roughly the size of Massachusetts, had received approximately $4.5 billion in aid from the U.S. government.

The war lasted some twelve years, cost the lives of more than seventy-five thousand Salvadorans, most of whom were civilians, and displaced nearly one-quarter of the country's population of approximately five million. During these twelve years, the FMLN gained and retained a large following of active members and sympathetic communities. It was instrumental in organizing rural areas located in its zones of control and providing them with a minimum of community health services, schools, cooperative production structures, and autonomous local governmental systems. In this way, the FMLN helped improve, even if only minimally, the quality of life for the peasants in these zones and gained their sympathy.

On December 31, 1991, a negotiated settlement was reached between the FMLN and the Salvadoran government after more than two years of painful negotiations. The agreement was signed on January 16, 1992, and a cease-fire went into effect on February 1. This settlement is not simply a cease-fire agreement but rather an attempt to open Salvadoran society. Among other things, the FMLN has won the right to exist as a legal political party able to participate in any and all elections. If the agreements are put into place as outlined in the settlement, the FMLN will have gone far in attaining its original goals of social justice. In short, the peace accords "open up space in the political arena for the left to press for reform by peaceful means for the first time in Salvadoran history."[3]

Now that the Cold War is over, a political opportunity has been created that may allow the FMLN to continue its struggle by utilizing nonviolent, pluralist strategies. The negotiated settlement is an attempt to restructure Salvadoran society. For the FMLN, the peace accords amount to nothing less than a negotiated revolution.

## A Negotiated Revolution?

In a ninety-five-page cease-fire agreement, the FMLN and the Salvadoran government agreed to certain important ground rules for a negotiated end to the armed conflict. The peace accords address five general topics:

a reduction in and restructuring of the armed forces, the creation of a national civil police, judicial system reforms, electoral system reforms, and economic and social questions, including the issue of agrarian reform. Though the agrarian question is dealt with rather vaguely and has already proved to be a point of contention between the FMLN and the government, it is both important and a remarkable accomplishment for Salvadoran society that the issue, one of the conflicts that initiated the war, will be formally addressed by the government. The concerted efforts at demilitarization are similarly significant. Yet perhaps the most important gain by the FMLN in this agreement is its institutionalized legality. Chapter 6 of the agreement guarantees the "legalization of the FMLN as a political party through the adoption of a legislative decree to that end."[4] According to the timetable provided for in the accords, the legislative decree announcing the legalization of the FMLN as a political party was to have occurred no later than the first week of May 1992. In actuality, the legalization of the FMLN as a political party was not accomplished until October 1992. This final accomplishment allows the FMLN to continue its struggle utilizing an institutionalized, internationally accepted strategy: elections.

The FMLN has characterized the settlement as a "negotiated revolution." FMLN commander Joaquín Villalobos, in an interview conducted shortly following the signing of the peace accords, state that "in my opinion, what is happening in El Salvador is a revolution. That's why it is not easy. We are touching sacred cows." Another FMLN commander, Fermán Cienfuegos, has asserted that "this is the first negotiated revolution in Latin America." Yet the revolution is not over; rather it has just begun. What has changed is the battleground: "The revolution that erupted in the final arid years of the cold war is moving from the jungles and mountains of El Salvador to the National Assembly and the streets of the capital."[5]

Having won the right to exist as a political party, the FMLN has plans to forge ahead with the social reforms necessary to bring about true economic and social justice for Salvadoran society. Top FMLN official Shafik Handal asserts that he is "still a socialist who has learned a fundamental lesson from the collapse of Communism: Socialism can be created only by free citizens." Handal adds that the FMLN will "be politically successful only if they are able to offer 'a national project' that a majority of Salvadorans will support." This is precisely their goal for, as Salvador Samayoa states, "it is absurd to talk to the end of history. Current forms of capitalism haven't begun to satisfy the material needs of the third world, much less its moral needs." FMLN field commander "Ulises" states that "we are going to have to continue the fight on other terrain" while his *compañero* "Chano" asserts that the FMLN will now "continue the political struggle."[6]

## Reframing Revolution

Thus we see that the concept of revolution is taking on a new meaning. Revolution, in FMLN terms, need not be accomplished using a total-war of zero-sum strategy. The revolution can be democratic, and it can be fought in the halls of the National Assembly; the revolution is a process and not an event. This reframing, however, is not the result of the negotiated settlement; rather the negotiated settlement is a result of this reframing. We can trace this change in strategy back to 1984, when the FMLN participated in three meetings at La Palma, El Salvador, with then-president José Napoleón Duarte. These meetings, however, proved unfruitful as the right wing, tightly allied with the United States, proved too large an obstacle to overcome. Yet the FMLN continued to consider the possibility of a negotiated revolution, and by 1989 Joaquín Villalobos wrote an article for *Foreign Affairs* entitled "A Democratic Revolution for El Salvador."

The article essentially outlines the FMLN's thinking on revolution by reform. The concept of revolution began to take on a different meaning. Specifically addressing the need to move beyond the traditional Western understanding of revolution as closed and authoritarian, Villalobos stated that in the current world "it is absurd and antihistorical to adopt a closed model of revolution. Such an approach blocks the development of revolution and leads to its isolation." The FMLN, according to Villalobos, is capable of learning from the experiences of others and is thereby able to avert their errors as well. As with everything else that is dynamic, revolutions too must evolve. Part of this strategy is deepening the essential democratic nature of revolution. "We [the FMLN] do not view this evolution as a concession but rather as a purer expression of the democratic nature of revolutionary change. For revolutions are essentially dynamic. . . . The aim is to create a real democracy for the entire people in the economic and political arenas." The document goes on to assert the primary importance of participatory democracy at all levels of society, noting that "democracy must be forged from above and below. . . . Democracy must be based on the popular will."[7]

Following from the above, an essential part of the democratic revolution will be elections and political parties. Yet these concepts must be popularized in order for the revolutionary transformation to true democracy to occur. Elections and political parties must not be separate from, or superior to, institutions of civil society. "The purpose of political parties is not only to compete in elections, but to help lead and educate the people in the daily exercise of power," Villalobos observes. The inclusion of elections and political parties into the FMLN platform began at this time to command a central importance. Revolution and elections were no longer diametrically opposed. "Elections are part of the FMLN's program," writes Villalobos. "The FMLN does not fear elections. Under fair conditions the majority of Salvadorans would opt for revolutionary change." Villalobos explicitly acknowledges the FMLN's reframing of the concept of revolution when he writes: "Are all of these positions just tactical maneuvers by the FMLN? Conversely, do they indicate that the FMLN is ready to abandon revolutionary aims? The answer is that, whatever the process might be called, El Salvador needs profound change; and what the FMLN proposes, others would call a revolution [but] the FMLN does not advance a dogmatic view of what it means by revolution or socialism."[8]

Thus we see the FMLN, as early as 1989, responding to a real-world context and formally advocating a reframing of the concept of revolution. This reframing would ultimately prove essential for ending the war through negotiation. Through it the FMLN demonstrated its ability to be critical and self-reflexive, to adapt to a changing world, and to mature and evolve as a leftist organization. Now that a settlement has been reached through much patience, compromise, and determination, the FMLN may be able to continue its struggle for revolution utilizing an open society. That the FMLN intends to continue the struggle for economic justice and civil society is evident in its postwar plan for reconstruction.

## The Postwar Plan for Reconstruction

Chapter 5 ("Economic and Social Questions") of the United Nations peace agreement states that "within 30 days from the signing of the agreement ... the Government of El Salvador shall submit to FMLN the National Reconstruction Plan ... so that the recommendations of the FMLN ... may be taken into account." In February 1992, the FMLN submitted to the people of El Salvador its preliminary plan for reconstruction. Titled "Reconstruction Plan for the Development of the New Salvadoran Society," the document outlines the FMLN's position on the social and economic changes that will be needed for the creation of a better El Salvador. The document is in many ways a manifesto of the political position taken by the FMLN. It states as its main objectives: "A. To attack the causes that originated the war . . . in order to encourage social and economic development that is equitable, participatory, and self-sustaining; B. To contribute to the consolidation and display of democracy . . . ; C. To strengthen the organizations and institutions of civil society, articulating and consolidating the foundations for the development of the popular sectors."[9]

These three objectives coincide directly with the social, economic, and political sectors of society. Hence it appears that the FMLN is continuing its struggle to transform Salvadoran society within a system of democratic political pluralism rather than armed guerrilla warfare.

The central organizing concept of the plan is sustainable economic development. It must be remembered that as a result of twelve years of devastating warfare, including mass bombing campaigns, El Salvador is the most environmentally stressed country in Central America, and it faces serious problems of deforestation, soil erosion, and water pollution. The FMLN acknowledges the great importance of this problem and has called for measures that will ensure a speedy recovery of the rich ecological balance in the country.

The principal beneficiaries of the plan are intended to be "the majorities who have been historically marginalized,"[10] and specifically those most directly affected by the war, including former FMLN combatants, peasants from war zones, cooperative communities, small landholders, and urban and suburban marginal communities—in short, those in Salvadoran society who have traditionally been neglected. Furthermore, the plan addresses not only questions of political freedom but questions of economic justice and civil society as well.

### *The Economic Realm, or Justice*

The FMLN acknowledges that profound and persisting economic disparities gave rise to the war, one that, in the postwar period, call for a concerted attack on poverty that will lead to long-lasting solutions. "The enormous social and economic problems that have accumulated throughout the history of the country must be confronted with a plan that addresses the basic problems, rather than one that is of an emergency and compensatory nature. In our understanding this necessitates adapting the general political economy to be in agreement with the consensus of the diverse sectors of the society." In keeping with its stated objectives the FMLN has called for multiple types of ownership, favoring "cooperative, union, communal, micro, small, and medium-sized businesses," the forms of which may be "state-cooperative, state-union, state-private, and/or state-communal."[11] Furthermore, the FMLN acknowledges the need to participate in the world market but calls for a change in the traditional relationship El Salvador has had with it. In the past El Salvador has been an exporter of raw materials, principally coffee, sugar, cotton, and indigo. The land upon which these products have been cultivated has been owned by a very small percentage of the population who benefit from their sale on the international market, yet the labor used to produce them comes from a large and very poor peasant class. Despite the wealth brought in by the sale of these materials, the poor have remained poor.

Rather than for El Salvador to continue to participate in the international economy exclusively as an exporter of raw materials, the FMLN has called for the creation of a Central American production bloc that will strengthen the productive capabilities of the region as a whole. Furthermore, production is to be expanded to include products and services that will benefit the large majority of poor Salvadorans as well as create a vertical rather than horizontal industrial infrastructure. Production priorities for El Salvador include a system of agricultural foodstuffs; industrial production of medium- and high-value agricultural products and other goods to be used for internal consumption or export; and the production of goods and services with a social character as a core of economic development.[12] The social nature of the FMLN plan is evident in its classification of people as a resource that needs developing as part of strengthening the objectified "economy."

The FMLN also calls for an agrarian reordering that will be more redistributive, new forms of land transfer, development of the productive capacities of the cooperatives, and solutions to the credit problem. Here the FMLN is explicit in asserting that the "democratization of credit will only be possible [with] the democratization of the ownership of the means of production and of the financial system."[13] As stated above, ownership can take many forms, but all ownership must be democratic. Hence the FMLN is calling for a democracy that encompasses not only the political, or questions of "freedom," but also the economic; the idea is to create a sort of economic justice.

## On the Death of the Left

### Democracy or Political Freedom

The FMLN acknowledges the great importance of creating a Salvadoran society that is truly democratic. The development and nurturing of a truly democratic state is, in many ways, the only thing that will keep peace in El Salvador. Democracy for the FMLN includes all Salvadorans, and not, as was the case previously, the privileged few.

> The construction of a new society must rely upon the participation of all Salvadorans. All political actors and social forces, as well as the [government] and the FMLN must participate in the elaboration and practical application of the Reconstruction Plan . . . [which] will contribute to the consolidation of a new culture and institutionalized democracy.

The plan goes on to call for a truly participatory democracy wherein the popular sectors will be allowed a say in the policies that will directly affect their destiny:

> The participatory philosophy that animates the FMLN proposal is expressed concretely in that the [executors] are fundamentally those same subjects of the Plan. . . . The philosophy is established in the fact that it is not the plan of a government or a party; it is the plan of a nation in which only the road of consensus can assure the political stability that this or any other plan requires.[14]

The plan outlines processes for decision making at the national, regional, and local levels and proposes the creation of an interagency advising committee whose task would be to assure consensus in the distribution of funds for reconstruction. The use of consensus at all levels of society demonstrates an active effort to popularize decision making, thereby expanding the definition of democracy to incorporate diverse social agents and not just a small elected elite. Furthermore, the central importance of democracy is explicitly addressed in the definition of the Salvadoran revolution as a democratic one (see above).

### Civil Society or Community

A general objective of the FMLN development plan is "to strengthen the organizations and institutions of civil society." The FMLN maintains that the sustainable development of El Salvador will only be possible if it includes the development of its people. The plan acknowledges the importance of social development; social forces are understood by the FMLN as an important "factor for the development of the country." Therefore it proposes to "[p]romote the institutional participation and self-sustaining economic growth of new socioeconomic agents [and] to contribute to the amplification and diversification of a national system of social security: employment, health, education, and housing."[15]

Noting the extreme importance of bringing up the lower two-thirds of Salvadoran society, the main beneficiaries of the plan are intended to be those who make up this vast majority, including landless peasants, workers, and former FMLN combatants.

Because large numbers of FMLN members are indigent, the plan stresses the need to promote their reintegration into the civil, political, and institutional life of the country. It also acknowledges the need to "legitimize and institutionalize the harmonious participation of diverse organizations and institutions of civil society."[16] Similarly, the plan calls for the social distribution of resources and the strengthening of forms of local power that emanate from civil society.

The above are only a few specific examples of the FMLN's advocacy of policies aimed at strengthening civil society and incorporating aspects of civil society into the political system. By calling for decision making by consensus, the FMLN is explicitly acknowledging the role of civil society in the political arena. Civil society is noted as an important and active aspect in the development and execution of all political and economic policies ranging from environmental recuperation to the distribution of credit. It is in this way that the revolution proposed by the FMLN is democratic in the most essential manner.

In sum, the FMLN's plan for reconstruction calls for the complete restructuring of Salvadoran society in order to strengthen its economy, promote self-sustaining development, eradicate poverty, and preserve the environment. Guiding principles for attaining these goals are the importance of civil society and institutionalization of participatory democracy. These are revolutionary changes by any standards, and they will be worked for through the institutions of an open society within a pluralist political system.[17]

## The New Initiative for Popular Self-Development

The FMLN does not exist in a vacuum and does not act alone. On the contrary, there is a large organized social movement that, although very sympathetic to the FMLN, is composed of autonomous organizations. As Salvador Samayoa has stated: "The FMLN has not been isolated from the re-emergence of the popular movement, and it wields enormous political influence in the movement. Most people in the popular movement believe that the political line of the FMLN works to their benefit. But it is not true that the popular organizations are an organic part of the FMLN, that they are subordinated to the FMLN. This is not true now, and has never been true." In the wake of a negotiated settlement, seven nongovernmental economic and social development organizations in El Salvador formed the Inter-Institutional Coordination (CII). In a document titled "The New Initiative for Popular Self-Development in El Salvador," CII has identified its postwar challenge to be "to discover and construct an alternative model of development, a unified, coherent effort... with a strong component of democracy and self-development." The document argues that the implementation of austere IMF-style neoliberal economic policies, which began with the installation of the right-wing Alianza Republicana Nacional Party (ARENA) in July of 1989, has increased misery and poverty throughout El Salvador. CII asserts that structural adjustment has had only limited success while increasing poverty for the majority. CII is calling for radical change, saying that the "search for an alternative social-economic model is literally a matter of life and death" for El Salvador's poor majority.[18] Admitting that there is currently no social force powerful enough to introduce an entirely new model to substitute for the neoliberal one now in force, they insist that an alternative economic pole is nevertheless possible. Therefore, CII is working toward the creation of an alternative economic sector that will focus on long-term development and self-sufficiency, a project that admittedly will depend greatly upon the success of the popular democratic movement.

The idea is to create an internal market as a second pole of the Salvadoran economy and as an arena for generating capital to be reinvested in participating communities. Based on ideas of popular self-development, the initiative is an attempt to coordinate the efforts of community organizations and unions to generate long-term community development. The model rests upon the assumption that cooperation and cooperative ownership can provide optimal economic results. CII will provide technical support and help raise capital. Projects will be both economic and social in nature and will work toward upgrading and strengthening already existing projects of which there are many since El Salvador's rural areas were organizing and developing along these lines throughout the twelve years of civil war. Funding will be provided on a case-to-case basis. Most important, CII states that it will not impose any economic models on anyone but only insists that certain criteria be met. To qualify projects should:

—assist in guaranteeing community survival;
—organize the communities they serve and have clear objectives;
—help communities defend their rights;
—develop people as well as the economy because "human development is a central aspect of economic development";
—be connected regionally and nationally to create economic linkages that will bring mutual benefit;
—be designed to conserve resources and minimize harm to the environment.[19]

Ownership may take a variety of forms including, among others, cooperative ownership, union ownership, and community ownership. Here we see a strong similarity between CII priorities and what has been proposed by the FMLN. Coordination and organization will be keys to success. And apart from this, these efforts must be accepted and respected by the Salvadoran right wing and the international community. This is true not only for the CII projects but for the FMLN's plan for reconstruction and all other proposed reforms. Herein remains perhaps the biggest obstacle for the Salvadoran Left and for Salvadoran society in general.

## Resistance from the Right

Though the FMLN may be framing revolution in a new and innovative way, thereby maintaining its strong popular support, it may be further alienating itself from El Salvador's powerful right wing. In many ways, the war may be over, but the battle has not yet been won. The Salvadoran right wing has never been receptive to changes that threaten its all-encompassing economic and political power.

Unfortunately, armed conflict was unavoidable if El Salvador was ever to become an open society. Many analysts agree that it was precisely the very violent, repressive, and closed nature of the state in El Salvador that forced a military response by the FMLN. Noted Salvadoran leftist scholar Mario Lungo asserts that "what unequivocally could not be avoided was the militarism." Sara Gordon, scholar with the National Autonomous University of Mexico's Institute for Social Research, has analyzed the situation that led up to the armed conflict. Gordon asserts that "expressions of popular discontent and collective actions . . . sporadic until 1977, became ever more frequent as a result of official repression and private violence of ultra-right para-military organizations." Top FMLN member Salvador Samayoa has asserted that "we were forced to take up arms to change the balance of forces in El Salvador." Even in the *New York Times*, this reality is acknowledged:

## On the Death of the Left

In a direct challenge to the received political wisdom of our time, El Salvador was a place where neither elections nor capitalism were by themselves capable of bringing fundamental change to a nakedly unfair and brutal society. The sad truth is that only war could budge the clique of army officers and oligarchs who dominated the country in a militarized, colonial form of capitalism. And the only ones willing to wage that war were Marxists, radicalized priests, organized peasants, trade unionists, and angry students who formed the five groups making up the guerrilla Farabundo Martí National Liberation Front.[20]

There is no reason to think that the clique will acquiesce easily this time. Although international pressures may ultimately work to the advantage of the FMLN, this must not be taken for granted. Already right-wing and military figures have given the FMLN cause to worry. Citing his skepticism of the FMLN, Salvadoran military spokesperson Lieutenant Colonel Hernández López said in an interview "The FMLN is going to cause chaos. They will use elections to take power and impose a totalitarian system." As U.S. State Department official Bernard W. Aronson has observed, "The great fear of the right is that the rebels will use this peace accord as a Trojan horse to infiltrate and take over."[21]

Unfortunately, the Right did not delay in imposing a new reign of terror. An April 9, 1992, news item in El Salvador's *Salpress* stated that "since February 1, when the cease-fire went into effect, 38 persons have been murdered, seven of these with their throats cut, a trademark of the death squads." Other reports indicate that the government failed to uphold the accords by refusing to incorporate the National Guard and Treasury police into the army by the agreed-upon deadline. The government also delayed the formation of the National Civil Police and the dissolution of the National Intelligence Authority. These actions prompted a FMLN delegation to travel to New York in April 1992 to address the United Nations directly with their concerns. As the United Nations Commission to El Salvador, (ONUSAL) has stated, "There are serious problems in El Salvador's pacification . . . enormous difficulties that could derail the process."[22] And these problems continue even today.

Rubén Zamora, vice-president of the National Assembly and presidential candidate of the Democratic Convergence/FMLN coalition at the time of this writing, has stated that "if the government intends to go back on its agreements, we're prepared to be the strongest and hardest opposition to this government we can possibly be." An August 1992 report by the American solidarity group CISPES indicates that in El Salvador "structural violations of human rights persist, including summary executions, violent deaths, and death threats" and that well-known death-squad tactics such as throat-slitting and decapitations continue in an attempt to "leave a message of fear." One UN official admitted the difficulties in transforming the attitude of confrontation into one of cooperation, "from hate to reconciliation."[23]

As I write, this has not yet occurred. Currently, there are serious threats to free and fair elections. Voter registration has been an ongoing problem. The legal process for obtaining a voting card is extremely complex and places a heavy burden on average citizens, especially peasants and those who are illiterate. Human rights groups and nongovernmental organizations have accused the government of unduly complicating the process. Politically motivated killings continue on an alarming scale. In 1993 alone more than thirty-five death squad–type killings took place. In January 1994 Oxfam America noted that twenty-five activists and candidates had been killed before the March 1994 elections. A 1993 Amnesty International report notes that "several FMLN leaders were wounded in separate attacks by unidentified gunmen." A recent report from Hemisphere Initiatives (a Cambridge, Mass.,–based research group monitoring the peace process in El Salvador) asserts that "a democratic society cannot be built upon a foundation of political killings. Failure to stop the killings by identifying those responsible will undermine the credibility of the elections."[24] To date there appears to be no reconciliation in sight.

Yet this is what must occur if El Salvador is to ever experience true democracy and justice. The right wing must be willing to open Salvadoran society to participation by all sectors, and international pressure must assure that it does. It is in this respect that the role of countries such as the United States, and organizations such as the UN and the Organization of American States, may be most helpful. As Bernard Aronson has stated, "Our (U.S.) mistake was to ignore democracy in the past in El Salvador. If we had vigorously defended the democratic election there in 1972, perhaps we could have avoided the polarization that drove some [people] to become guerrillas."[25] Though I do not think that Aronson is correct in assigning the United States such a decisive role in the history of El Salvador, we can only hope that the United States does not repeat the same error. Unfortunately, the current administration does not appear inclined to actively promote democracy in El Salvador. Where the Reagan and Bush administrations were aggressive interventionists, the Clinton administration is complaisantly silent. Furthermore, the United Nations' ONUSAL, COPAZ (a bilateral commission on peace accords implementation), and organizations such as CISPES and Amnesty International agree that international pressure will be important in assuring the effective implementation of the peace accords as well as fair, democratic elections.

Unfortunately, the March 1994 elections have demonstrated that truly free and fair elections have yet to come to El Salvador. The elections, though deemed acceptable to the United Nations, were marred by a number of "technical irregularities" which resulted in the disfranchisement of numerous Salvadorans. Nevertheless, the FMLN was able to obtain some twenty-one seats in the National Assembly and force the presidential elections into a run-off, attesting to their popular support. Sadly, however, death threats to now-elected candidates continue and a true reconciliation is nowhere in sight.

The implications of all this are clear: though the guns may have been silenced, the peace is fragile, and if not treated with utmost care it may be violently broken at any time. History has adequately demonstrated that the largest obstacle to justice and democracy in El Salvador has traditionally been the Right and not the Left. Perhaps, then, it is time to give the Left a chance to demonstrate whether it can bring true democracy to El Salvador.

## Moving beyond El Salvador

What has occurred in El Salvador is not unique. There is now a historic opportunity for the Left in all of Latin America to take its place in the forefront of Latin American politics with a transformational program that will explicitly address the structural social and economic problems the region faces. We turn briefly now to developments in Colombia, Nicaragua, and Brazil.

Perhaps it is not coincidental that Colombia is a member of the "Group of Friends," a coalition of officials from four countries who have assisted the FMLN in its negotiations with the Salvadoran government. Colombia too has had its share of guerrilla activity and in 1990 came to a negotiated cease-fire agreement involving the Movimiento 19 de Abril, or M-19.

M-19, like the FMLN, was formed in the tumultuous years of the early 1970s as an armed guerrilla organization whose goal was social revolution. Led by Carlos Pizarro León-Gómez and Antonio Navarro Wolff, the group is perhaps best known for its 1980 occupation of the Dominican embassy in Bogotá and the November 1985 occupation of Colombia's Palace of Justice. Because of the army's severely aggressive response, this event led to the deaths of over one hundred people, including eleven of Colombia's twenty-three Supreme Court justices (none of whom was killed by the M-19). Prior to this incident the M-19 had attempted a negotiated settlement with the Colombian government, and in August of 1984 an agreement was reached but failed due to repeated violations by the Colombian army and the right wing. Thus there is a parallel with the case of the FMLN in El Salvador: both organizations had proposed peaceful settlements to the armed conflicts and both propositions were rejected by the countries' right wings.[26]

Following the Palace of Justice event, talks ensued. In February 1990, Navarro and Pizarro were formally pardoned for their roles in the taking of the Palace of Justice, and in March of 1990 the M-19's entire force laid down its arms. They, like the FMLN who would follow them, gained the right to exist as a legal political party and continue the struggle for change within the political arena.

The party ran Pizarro as their presidential candidate in the upcoming May election, but he was assassinated before it took place. Navarro ran in his place and captured some 800,000 votes. On August 7, the day after presidential victor César Gaviria took office, Navarro was named Minister of Health. In congressional elections that took place the following December, a short nine months after laying down their guns, the M-19 scored a major victory by capturing some 26 percent of the popular vote and nineteen of seventy congressional seats.

It has been asserted that the M-19 runs on an anti-establishment platform and that it is composed of "nationalists who advocate . . . a Colombia of property owners." Furthermore, Navarro who recently served as copresident of the Constitutional Assembly, has called for "anti-trust legislation to break up Colombia's industrial monopolies, privatizing state enterprises by selling shares to employees, and promoting free-trade with Venezuela." For the M-19, any form of capitalism must work to the benefit of all Colombians and be truly democratic. Selling state businesses to their employees is an innovative method of promoting social ownership. In a recent interview with NACLA, Navarro is quoted as asserting that "we are fighting for democracy, for political democracy, for democratization of the economy. We are fighting for social justice . . . a different notion of development for Colombian society."[27] The policies promoted by the M-19 are popular, and Navarro is seen as a potential successor to president César Gaviria in the 1994 presidential election.

Though the M-19 may be the most successful thus far, it is not Colombia's only guerrilla group to disarm and become a political force. Colombia's People's Liberation Army (EPL), a Maoist organization formed in 1967, reached a truce with the government in June of 1990 and officially disarmed in October 1991. EPL commander Bernardo Gutiérrez has now traded his uniform for a business suit and hopes to follow in the footsteps of Navarro. Gutiérrez asserts that he now believes in a "pluralist, democratic state" and claims to have learned this directly from the experience of Eastern Europe. "Our conclusion from the recent events [in Eastern Europe] is the need for democratic socialism." Gutiérrez states that he now "dreams of a nation 'where you can conduct politics without bodyguards.'"[28]

In February of 1990 the Left worldwide was shocked by the electoral defeat of Daniel Ortega and the Sandinista revolution. Although all signs had appeared to point to an FSLN victory in Nicaragua's presidential election, the National Opposition Union (UNO) candidate, Violeta Chamorro, was a clear winner, receiving 900,000 votes to Ortega's 680,000.

Internationally, the Left was quick to respond that the elections did not reflect the social advances made by the FSLN. Rather, Nicaraguans were voting with their stomachs. The Sandinistas had suffered years of United States–sponsored counterinsurgency as well as a paralyzing economic embargo. The country was war torn, inflation ridden, and, above all, tired: "what liberty in voting could exist among a people harassed, anguished and insecure after eight years of war, disaster, tension, and pain? . . . Nicaraguans did not vote against the Sandinista front; they voted against the war."[29] And they voted for Violeta Chamorro. Chamorro, unlike the FSLN, was able to guarantee an end to the economic embargo and $2 billion in U.S. aid should she win. Furthermore, the UNO party received substantial monetary contributions from the United States for Chamorro's campaign. In this way, it has been argued, the United States essentially bought the Nicaraguan election.

Yet what is most significant about this historic event is the heroic way the FSLN peacefully handed over power to the UNO victors. In fact, the FSLN was able to do what no other governing party in the history of Nicaragua had done: peacefully admit its defeat. Thus though the FSLN may have lost the elections, in a sense it did win the war for a democratic Nicaragua.

Though Daniel Ortega is no longer president of Nicaragua, by no means has the FSLN "lost." Winning some 41 percent of the popular vote, the Sandinistas still maintain thirty-eight of ninety-one seats in the National Assembly. And since a 60 percent majority vote is required for constitutional changes, none can occur unless the Sandinistas are in agreement. Daniel Ortega has asserted that the "Sandinistas will resist attempts to change the labor code, to restrict the right to strike, or to form trade unions," all of which are constitutionally guaranteed.[30]

Interestingly, the right-wing UNO government is bound to accept and work within a constitution written by the Sandinistas. As Rafael Solís, a Sandinista deputy in the National Assembly, has succinctly stated, "If you accept the results of elections, you have to accept the constitution. That is democracy."[31] Thus though Violeta Chamorro has won the right to govern, she must do so within a Sandinista-designed framework.

The Sandinistas have set a precedent for the Latin American Left. They utilized a democratic pluralist strategy and abided by its results, yet continue the struggle to implement transformative policies aimed at creating a true democracy and improving the quality of life of the impoverished majority. Thus the Sandinistas have demonstrated to the world that a revolution can be and must be democratic. When election time rolls around again in 1996, the people of Nicaragua are likely to recall Sandinista policies that attempted, against innumerable odds, to improve the quality of life for the country's marginalized majority—especially given that the Chamorro administration has thus far proven itself unable to improve Nicaragua's economic crisis.

Though these three cases provide examples of formerly armed revolutionary organizations that transformed themselves to play a vital role as institutionalized political parties, this is by no means the only path to effective leftist politics in Latin America. Throughout the region new parties of the Left are springing up in an attempt to work toward social and economic transformation through the political system. Brazil provides an excellent example.

Brazil's Worker's Party, or PT, was founded in 1979 by a coalition of parties and organizations that included the Brazilian Communist Party, various worker's unions, and leftist intellectuals. Their objective was to develop a political party that would effectively address the needs of Brazil's poor. In 1988 party candidates won mayoral elections in São Paulo and other large Brazilian cities. In a further display of popular support, the PT's 1989 presidential candidate, Luis Ignácio da Silva (Lula), "came within six percentage points of winning the first direct presidential elections in Brazil in almost 30 years."[32]

It has been asserted that the success of the PT lies in its "unusually rich reinterpretation of the importance of socialism to democracy and vice versa." Furthermore, the PT consciously chose to utilize an interinstitutional strategy and work for change within a pluralist political system rather than to opt for a violent revolutionary strategy. Organizers and founding members of the party maintain that this will ultimately prove to be the most effective strategy. "Party organizers believed that by remaining rooted in civil society the PT would eventually win elections, because those it sought to represent were a majority."[33] Other examples of the resurgence of Left political parties in Latin America that have consciously chosen a nonviolent, interinstitutional strategy are Peru's United Left and Chile's Humanist Party, both of which have had members elected to public office.

## Conclusion

Far from being marginalized, the Left in Latin America appears to be experiencing a strong renewal. Left parties from El Salvador to Chile are coming away from elections as the victors, demonstrating significant popular support. Their visions remain essentially transformative. Struggles for social justice and economic equality continue, indicating that those who equate the fall of communism with a necessary marginalization of the Left are in error.

"Death of the Left" arguments are inherently Eurocentric, and they fail to address the specific political, cultural, and historical realities of Latin American countries. Disregarding them, or evaluating them according to European or U.S. standards, diminishes the sovereignty, individuality, and integrity of these countries and constitutes a serious form of intellectual imperialism. This is a historical and intellectual error that it would behoove us to correct.

The Latin American Left's creative responses to the current political opportunity indicate that they are a social and political force that can adapt to changes in the international climate while maintaining their historic commitment to real social transformation. Yet with all this said, I do not wish to paint a utopian picture of the current political situation in Latin America nor predict the future of its Left. History gives us no reason to believe that this new Left will be more successful than the old one. At any moment this opportunity may be eliminated and the forces of the Left once again violently repressed. Nor do I wish to imply that the role of armed struggle has been made irrevocably obsolete. In fact, the recent appearance of the armed Zapatista Movement in Mexico exemplifies the still quite volatile existence of inequality and oppression and the dangers of bureaucratic authoritarian rule. The point, however, is that if democracy fails in Latin America, it will be, as is historically the case, the responsibility not of the Left but of an unchanging, militarized, and oligarchic Right.

# Part II

## A Postcommunist Left Agenda

# 5

## Four Futures of the Left:

DEFINING THE NEXT STAGE

What is to be done? That famous question has never been more important for the Left than it is today. In this second part of the book, we review the possibilities and offer one road forward.

Four different visions now compete for the Left's attention. One, advanced mainly by Marxists, proposes that the Left unify around the struggle for an authentic, democratic socialism. The fall of Eastern Europe liberates us from the burden of a false socialism. Now is the time to find the true one.

The famous Marxist historian Eric Hobsbawm makes one of the most compelling cases for a new socialist Left. He argues that market systems are incapable of solving three of the largest crises threatening the twenty-first century: looming ecological disaster, the growing division between rich and poor countries, and the unraveling of the moral and social fabric in both East and West. Eventually, all of these problems "will require systematic and planned action by states.... They will require not just a better society than in the past, but as socialists always held, a different kind of society."[1]

Hobsbawm is no doubt correct, and in the long run socialism may emerge back on the agenda. But there are several reasons for believing that it is not the task of the coming stage. First, the collapse of Eastern European socialism, rightly or wrongly, has destroyed the political viability of the socialist idea in the near future. It will take time, and considerable further political disillusionment with the enchantments of Western capitalism, before citizens in most of the world will be predisposed to consider a socialist alternative. In the meantime, any move-

## A Postcommunist Left Agenda

ment wrapping itself in the socialist banner is committing itself to electoral irrelevance.

Second, the fall of Eastern Europe robs the socialist idea of any empirical referent whatsoever. No Third World socialist experiments have proved themselves, and European social democracy is suffering its own reverses, symbolized by the Swedish voters throwing out their labor government in 1991. Without any practicing socialist models, a socialist movement appears hopelessly utopian.

This is not a call to abandon the idea of socialism entirely. "Socialism" is still a term that connotes perhaps better than any other the core values of the Left, including the idea of an alternative economic order that puts people ahead of money and profit. Hobsbawm points out that the term "socialism" originated as "an opposite to individualism," not capitalism. In this cultural sense as well, it is still vitally relevant to the Left's mission in a world increasingly dominated by hyperindividualistic values.

In the coming stage, those on the left still attracted to the socialist vision must work hard to give it a new meaning. We have seen in the first part of this book that the Left is now largely bereft of any coherent, credible, and consensual vision of socialism. Socialism stands mainly as an emotional symbol for those who hate capitalism, and until a well-developed vision and program is attached to that symbol, it cannot be the core of the Left's identity. If there is a socialist content to the next stage, it is the formative task of conceiving and elaborating a new socialist vision. Only then will we know, in the stage to follow, whether the Left should once again embrace the struggle for socialism.

A second vision calls for the Left to embrace "identity politics." The rallying point for many feminists, African American activists, multiculturalists, and postmodernist theorists, this is less a call for change than a recognition of what the Left has already become. In the 1970s and 1980s, the Left threw off the straitjacket of unity imposed by white males, emerging as a coalition of groups organized around gender, race and ethnicity, sexual preference, age, and other "identity formations." This unleashed an explosive new "politics of diversity" to combat the multiple forms of domination ignored by the traditional socialist Left.

Identity politics helped save a Left that had not been honest about its own internal stratification. Intellectually, identity politics spawned feminist, multiculturalist, and other new theories that revealed the limits of an economistic Marxism. Identity politics also made politics more textured and personal, an avenue of hope for millions of women, African

Americans, gays, and others who had not before connected their "personal troubles" to public issues. It spoke powerfully to people's need for self-esteem and belonging and proved such an electric mobilizing force that social scientists who studied social movements in the 1970s and 1980s described identity politics as *the* emerging form of dissent in "postindustrial" societies.

Identity politics is hardly spent, but it is unlikely to be the same defining force in the coming stage. As Cassie Schwerner has written in this volume, identity politics has created a devastating crisis of fragmentation on the left. The possibilities of common cause between men and women, whites and blacks, heterosexuals and gays, old and young have eroded; the many "identity" movements do not see themselves as part of a common struggle. Ironically, as the Left embraced identity politics, it lost its own identity.

This breakdown in solidarity, while a life-threatening problem for the Left, is viewed by many as a necessary stage. "Where silence and taboo reign in the name of unity," Sharon Kurtz writes, there is no real unity. "Recognition of diversity," Kurtz continues, "has the potential to yield a more frank, a more true connection." The socialist Left faltered on a contrived unity based on denial of difference, and identity politics offers the potential to build a more enduring solidarity.[2]

Perhaps, but time is of the utmost importance. In the current era, the burning task is rediscovering a politics of inclusion and an idea of community that can unite people of every race, gender, and sexual orientation. A Left that cannot find its own common ground can hardly speak credibly to the national crisis.

The Left has to urgently rededicate itself to the problem of its own solidarity. The solution is not likely to come out of the same identity politics that helped give rise to the problem. Identity politics arose to affirm the differences of race, gender, and sexual preference that had earlier been submerged and to right the wrongs associated with them. This remains a task of great urgency, but it will take a new politics to discover the common ground.

This is not a call for the end of identity politics. It is hard to imagine a struggle against racism, sexism, or heterosexism without the movements created by identity politics. Moreover, since the national crisis of civil society is so intimately linked to racism, sexism, and heterosexism, it is impossible to see a solution that does not build on these movements. As practitioners of identity politics struggle to build a broader coalition crossing race, gender, and other lines of difference, they have the potential to help invent the bridging politics that can heal the wounds of civil society.

A third vision calls for a Left wedded neither to socialism nor to identity politics but to "radical democracy." This idea has been advanced by influential Left writers such as Richard Flacks and Stanley Aronowitz, and it reflects the sensibilities of many of the activists we interviewed. In a spirit reminiscent of the New Left's 1960s call for participatory democracy, the "radical democrats" argue that the struggle to deepen democracy in every social sphere reflects the core of the Left's tradition and speaks to the most urgent crises of the coming stage.

Flacks argues that the Left historically can be defined as "that body of thought and action that favors the democratization of history making, that seeks to expand the capacity of the people themselves to make the decisions that affect the conditions and terms of everyday life." In his book *Making History,* he elaborates the view of the Left as the political tradition devoted to empowering people. "The tradition of the Left," he argues, is "to change social structures so that, ultimately, historical decisions will be made by those affected by them" and "to encourage and enable individuals to participate in history before—as well as after—democratic social restructuring has been achieved."[3]

Democracy, unlike socialism, is an idea whose time has come. The "postcommunist" era is one in which virtually all political traditions accept the legitimacy of the democratic ideal and where publics are hungry to gain more control over their lives. The revolution in Eastern Europe itself was a struggle for democracy, and it has rekindled the energy of the democratic idea around the world. Meanwhile, leaders in Western capitalist democracies, who offer mainly lip service to the democratic ideal, are increasingly vulnerable to movements that raise the banner of authentic and deep democracy.

Democracy is part and parcel of the solution to all our most pressing problems. Democracy in the workplace is overwhelmingly important, essential to revitalizing the American economy, empowering workers, and nourishing community in and out of the workplace. Economic democracy can also rejuvenate political democracy, which is the only way to get a government promoting equality, peace, and ecological sanity. And more democracy in family life, churches, and voluntary associations has a big role to play in restoring civil society.

What, then, is wrong with the vision of the radical democrats? Nothing, except that it is dangerously incomplete. Radical democracy is very much what the Left in its next stage should be about. But no amount of democracy, as we show below, can fully solve the problems of values and community that lie close to the core of our current malady. And democracy itself cannot be created or deepened without a revitalization of the moral and social fabric.

The agonies of Eastern Europe today illuminate the interconnection of democracy and civil society and simultaneously the limits of the "radical democracy" perspective. Poland, Czechoslovakia, Hungary, Bosnia and other countries in the region first and foremost need democracy. But all democratization strategies in Eastern Europe are foundering not only on disastrous economic problems but on crises of civil society. As Eastern Europeans watch their democratic dreams go up in the toxic flames of "ethnic cleansing" and protofascist nationalism, they are discovering that political democracy cannot simply be legislated. Democracy presupposes a certain development of the moral and social fabric, including a culture of trust, tolerance, and inclusion or solidarity, as well as a flowering of voluntary association. Eastern Europeans themselves now recognize that to win democracy, they first have to rebuild civil society and that it is impossible to separate a politics of democracy from one of community.

In the West, the unraveling of the social fabric also puts all democratization strategies at risk. The breakdown of community—whether in the neighborhood, the workplace, the family, or the nation as a whole—will profoundly frustrate initiatives for radical democracy. In an atomized and hyperindividualistic society, it is not only difficult to mobilize democratic participation but possible that democratic initiatives will yield only a more fractious and divisive politics. In a broken civil society, democratic politics can easily degenerate into the sociopathic populism of Christian fundamentalists such as Pat Robertson or the electronic politics of Ross Perot, whose proposed national computer referenda can only produce a pseudoconsensus for a pseudocommunity.

The two overarching, intertwined political crises of Western society now involve power and community. Radical democrats address the first by proposing to democratize the economic and political hierarchies that are permitting wholesale looting of Western societies by the governing elites. But they neglect the second, which can only be addressed by an explicit concern with the moral order and the social fabric.

This then leads to a fourth vision, the one that we expand on in the rest of this book as the most compelling for the United States and that we call the politics of democratic community. It embraces the view of radical democrats that exploitative hierarchies in the economy, state, and cultural life remain the central structural problem, for which democracy is the only antidote. But it also starts with the premise that the disintegration of the social fabric overshadows all other problems in the current era, and that any viable political agenda must offer new values and a positive vision of community to guide social reconstruction. Calling for democratic community, it also recognizes that community cannot be built on democracy alone.

The Left approach should not be confused with the politics of civil society that many conservatives propose to save the family or community in the United States or that some liberals propose to save Eastern Europe. Unlike conservatives such as Ronald Reagan and Dan Quayle, whose trumpeting of traditional "family values" celebrates a mythical civil society of premodern capitalism, the Left approach has no nostalgia for traditional communities, which stifled freedom and were authoritarian, patriarchal, and racist. A Left politics of community, then, is not a rush to civil society on any terms. The Left's challenge in the coming era is to offer a fresh idea of community whose "glue" is neither repressive nor authoritarian.

In contrast to liberalism, the Left approach does not regard activist government—the liberal panacea—as an adequate prescription for reconstructing civil society. One of the great lessons of Eastern Europe as well as of the Scandinavian welfare states is the limits of states as tools of social morality and community building. Solidarity cannot be legislated and ultimately arises in social domains outside of the state.

A Left politics of community departs most clearly from both conservatism and liberalism in its democratic vision. Conservatives see community being subverted by the "excesses" of democracy, leading to runaway demands for rights without any corresponding sense of civic obligation. They propose that civil society can be restored only by traditional authority that reins in democracy. Liberals espouse greater democracy but also want to put the brakes on at a certain point, fearing that too much democracy in the economy or state will undermine the authority, property, or efficiency that make modern civil society possible. Liberal Paul Starr writes that the problem with radical democracy is, among other things, that it "takes too many evenings," espousing his own view of excess democracy and, indeed, excess community. In contrast, a Left politics of civil society weds the politics of radical democracy and community, seeing them as core principles that are mutually reinforcing rather than in conflict, and calls for democratic community in every sector of social life.[4]

Democracy, however, is only one part of the scaffolding of community, which ultimately lives or dies on the oxygen of social solidarity. Solidarity, a fragile and problematic gift in Western individualistic societies like the United States, makes possible collective commitments and the transcending of the very human preoccupation with self. The building of solidarity, the great challenge of the coming stage, requires the nurturing of moral responsibility as well as social entitlements. The Left, we shall argue, can help inspire a new politics of obligation by drawing on its historical vision of solidarity and a moral tradition that has always recognized the limits of the Western individualistic tradition.

Two different ideas of solidarity need to be reconciled in the Left's new agenda. Historically, the Left has favored what might be called "universalistic solidarity," uniting all peoples—regardless of race, gender, religion, ethnicity, or nationality—in shared commitment to justice, equality, and democratic human rights. Universalistic solidarity is, necessarily, a rational, abstract, and demanding vision, insisting that people embrace high moral ideals and care for those radically different and remote from themselves. Such solidarity ultimately points to a world community in which the sense of mutual obligation diffuses outward and yields mutual cooperation among vastly heterogeneous and dissimilar peoples.

A profoundly different form, one more associated with the Right in the United States than with the Left, is "particularistic solidarity," the "blood ties" associated with family, neighborhood, race, ethnicity, religion, and nationalism. This is the solidarity of tribalism and gemeinschaft, the face-to-face communities that have dominated the human experience for most of its history. Such solidarity grows out of the primal glue of kinship: it is the bonding of birth, locality, likeness, and necessity. In contrast with universalistic solidarity, particularistic solidarity is organic, rooted, concrete, and emotive.

The Left needs to meld these two apparently contradictory ideas of solidarity in its new communitarian politics. Universalistic solidarity is too abstract, impersonal, and bloodless on its own to be viable, while particularistic solidarity tends, unmodified, to yield racialism, parochialism, and, in extremis, the "ethnic cleansing" we have seen in Bosnia. Reacting against the terrible oppressiveness of traditional society, the Left has typically advanced universalistic solidarity as the only viable alternative to capitalist individualism. But the failure of the Left, especially the Marxist tradition, is deeply connected with its repudiation of particularistic identity as parochial and reactionary.

Marx rejected his own Jewishness as a shameful and reactionary tribalism and passionately embraced the side of capitalism that swept away the communal legacy of feudalism. Successive generations of Marxists largely treated religion as the "opium of the masses" and the particularistic solidarities of ethnic and racial communities as little more than obstacles to the achievement of class consciousness.

As Sara Evans and Harry Boyte have written, Marxist socialists have assumed that "a sundering of people from their historical and organic connections—from their 'roots'—is the indispensable preliminary to freedom." Marxism suggested that the crumbling of traditionalism would yield a more cosmopolitan worker who would replace his or her parochial identities with a universalistic class consciousness. But workers were never completely "liberated" from particularism, nor could the abstract form of solidarity connected with class position ever fully replace the old "parochial" identities as a source of connection and meaning. Ironically, a close reading of labor history suggests that workers' movements only succeed when they build on the dense connections and personal loyalties of ethnic and religious communities, both in and outside of the workplace.[5]

Making a mistake opposite to that of the socialists, identity politics is being fatally seduced by the "particularistic solidarities" of race and gender. As noted earlier, racism, sexism, and homophobia have been so devastating in the American experience that minorities, women, and gays have had to bond tightly in their own communities for self-defense and collective empowerment. But identity politics subverts its own purposes when it becomes the ethnocentric particularism that socialists have rightly feared. Stripped of any vision of universalistic solidarity, identity politics degrades into balkanized and antagonistic communal movements or into a new form of individualism modified to permit minorities, women, and gays to join the mainstream ratrace on equal terms. To contribute to the next stage of the Left, racial and gender movements must reinvent themselves around common themes of justice, democracy, and community, building a deep solidarity across as well as within the lines of difference.

In contrast to socialism and identity politics, radical democracy seems to have a better chance of joining an enlightened universalism with a robust particularism. The political model here is the New England town meeting, which in theory joined all citizens—whatever their race, ethnicity, gender, class, or religion—in a face-to-face community of passionate dialogue devoted to the common good. The particularistic solidarity of radical democracy is built through the sweat of grassroots civic participation. As neighbors work together on local issues, they talk, argue, empathize, and negotiate toward agreement, building a civic bond promoting trust, loyalty, and responsibility to the group. This is not the thick solidarity of blood or tribe, but for that very reason, as political theorist Benjamin Barber argues, it is a particularism that nurtures cross-community respect and a larger civic universalism.[6]

In this abstract formulation, radical democracy seems to merge with Left communitarianism. But, as implied earlier, civic participation offers too thin a concept of solidarity. Engaged citizens may share a sense of community, as Barber argues, but even in what he calls "strong democracy" it is not sociologically robust enough to meet our needs for connection and meaning. When democratic participation is extended from the town meeting to the workplace, its potential to strengthen the communal fabric is greatly enhanced, making workplace democracy central to any communitarian Left project. But to build civic and workplace democracy, Left politics needs also to help build and reshape in progressive forms the particularistic solidarities of family, occupation, ethnicity, race, and religion.

Radical democrats tend to share the Marxist aversion to the "blood ties" of traditionalism. Barber argues that "the blood brothers of the organic community" are likely to create a tyrannical politics of exclusion and fear, like that of the Muslim fundamentalist Ayatollah Khomeini in Iran. This danger is real and helps explain why the Left should not romanticize or emulate traditional communities. But the Left needs to commit to its own "roots" project that nourishes the communal habits of the heart at every level of society.[7]

Radical democracy detached from a larger communitarian politics can easily follow the larger experience of American democracy into a radical individualism. Sara Evans and Harry Boyte observe that the American republican tradition itself, "though prizing service to the community, became fused with an eighteenth century individual rights philosophy that emphasized the liberation of the individual from constricting traditions and communal ties. Indeed, in many ways the hallmark of American democracy became the stress upon individualism." Evans and Boyte cite Ralph Waldo Emerson, a leading theorist of American democracy, as illustrative: "Take away from me the feeling that I must depend upon myself, give me the least hint that I have good friends and backers there in reserve who will gladly help me, and instantly I relax my diligence ... and a certain slackness will creep over my conduct of affairs."[8]

In a capitalist, individualistic culture, as noted above, democratic participation tends to degenerate into the politics of self-interest, mirroring the habits of the market. Political participation becomes just another means of getting "mine," manifested in such current phenomena as the politics of NIMBY ("not in my back yard"). Radical democracy is a powerful vehicle for building both particularistic and universalistic communities, but it cannot, by itself, complete the communitarian project we need.

Despite the overriding importance of saving civil society, many leftists will have healthy skepticism about any form of communitarian politics. Communitarian movements, such as the counter-cultural politics of the 1960s, often degrade into purely cultural politics. Most have lacked a structural analysis, an economic agenda, or a coherent political program. Many, like the nineteenth-century Owenites or Fourierists, become an exercise in utopianism, seeking a communal paradise for the converted at the expense of the problems of the larger society.

Such communitarianism, however, has little to do with the politics we propose. The commitment to rebuilding community is not a revival of the dream of living in communes nor an effort to dictate people's lifestyles. Indeed, it is not any stripe of "culturalist" politics. A Left politics of community, while deeply concerned with the quality of everyday life, is focused on changing the dominant economic, political, and ideological arrangements that are shredding the social fabric. There can be no community as long as we have an economy that systematically creates profit by destroying jobs and neighborhoods, nor as long as government remains the servant of a ruling elite that, in an orgy of excess of recent decades far more spectacular than that of the nineteenth-century robber barons, has abandoned even the enlightened class self-interest that might sustain it in the long run. A communitarian Left must thus commit to economic transformation through movements for economic democracy and what we shall call the social market.

A Left politics of community will not be driven by an abstract form of cultural alienation—by privileged, disaffected youth seeking paradise, as many characterized the politics of the 1960s. Its agents and constituencies, broad enough to sustain a majority Left, must include those who have fallen—or been pushed—through the gaping holes in the tattered social fabric. This not only includes inner-city dwellers, the black and white poor, and other abandoned groups, but huge categories of the labor force including displaced blue collars, underemployed white collars, "contingent" workers shorn of job security and benefits, as well as racial and ethnic minorities, gays, and other identity groups who have been read out of the larger moral community. A politics of community starts with the pain of those already impaled on the sharp edges of a splintering civil society.

But it hardly stops there. As the social fabric unravels, the vast majority of the population feels at risk. The sense of instability, fragmentation, and disconnection from community and public life—and concrete fears of crime, reduced wages or job loss, divorce, and isolation—stretch deep into the suburbs and well into middle management. As social breakdown accelerates, these fears become the driving concerns of a large majority of the population seeking to survive in the wreckage. The Left, like all other political traditions, will have no choice but to address these problems; politically, they will increasingly constitute the only game in town. Fortunately, as we show in the next chapter, Left history offers glimmerings of the communitarian vision and the remedies it might offer.

# 6

# Beloved Comrades:

A HISTORY OF THE LEFT AS COMMUNITY

The idea of community has always had a home on the left. The history of that idea—both its strength and weakness—needs to be rediscovered if the Left is to revive itself and the nation as a whole is to heal the crisis of community that now haunts it.

This chapter takes up three pivotal communitarian movements in Left history. We have passed over many others: the agrarian Populists of the late nineteenth century who preached the "gospel of cooperation"; the revolutionary "Wobblies" of the early twentieth century who sang of their brave community of lumberjacks, hoboes, and gypsy workers as "a power greater than [the capitalists'] hoarded gold"; the civil rights movement of the 1950s and 1960s, which rekindled the conscience of the nation with its dream of "beloved community"; and the women's movement of the 1970s and 1980s, which proved "sisterhood is powerful" and demonstrated that politics is inescapably about love, caring, and community.

Communitarian politics offers community in two senses. One is the "micro-community," bonding members of the movement itself. The other is the "macro-community" and the effort to remake the larger society and economy in the image of community. The Left, we shall see, has practiced both, although the one is not necessarily found with the other, and nowhere do we find the robust melding of the two that a rich communitarian politics requires.

Neither the Left nor the larger society can find in this history the magic formula for repairing our tattered social fabric. Instead we find a rich but ambiguous legacy that can help point us toward the politics of democratic community that we desperately need.

## An Injury to One Is the Concern of All: The Knights of Labor and the Idea of Solidarity

The Knights of Labor was arguably the first national organization of the Left in the United States. Formed in 1869 in Philadelphia, it became for a brief period in the 1870s and 1880s the most important labor movement in the country. Its great legacy is the communitarian idea of solidarity, which defined the Left in the nineteenth century and can help guide it in the coming millennium.

The Knights captured the imagination of workers everywhere with its slogan, "An Injury to One Is the Concern of All." These words helped the Knights, as labor historian Philip Foner writes, to establish "a magnificent record of labor solidarity, of a workers' unity strong enough to surmount differences of race, creed, sex, national origin and skill." This remarkable practical achievement, largely unequaled by the American Left before and since, testifies to the power of the Knights' idea of solidarity and its potential importance to an America that is losing its common ground.[1]

The Knights' idea went well beyond the class solidarity that Marx was writing about in Europe when the Knights were organizing. The Knights drew on the socialist tradition but believed in a true universal community encompassing all but the most outrageous parasites on society (among whom they included lawyers, bankers, and labor scabs). They sought to appeal to farmers, artisans, and small shopkeepers as well as workers, a practice that earned scorn from both more conservative and more Marxist-oriented rivals in the labor movement.

The Knights' idea of solidarity was rooted in spirituality and deep moral conviction. The founder of the Knights, Uriah Stephens, spoke of a "universal brotherhood" in which "the babel of tongues is hushed ... the discords of party strife are stilled, the war of creeds gives place to the white-robed angel of charity. Creed, party, and nationality are but outward garments, and present no obstacle to the fusion of the hearts of the worshippers of God ... and the workers for man, the universal brother."[2]

With this idea of universal solidarity, the Knights infused the American Left with a charismatic communitarianism. The Left of the Knights would most of all stand for community itself—a community of "all the

## A Postcommunist Left Agenda

world's workers." "Cultivate friendship among the great brotherhood of toil," Stephens thundered, "beget concert of action by conciliation; confidence by just and upright conduct towards each other; mutual respect by dignified deportment and wise counsel by what of wisdom and ability God . . . may have endowed us with."[3]

The purpose of the Left was to bring this community into full self-realization and to give it expression, as the Knights saw it, in "one Big Union." But this was hardly a narrow trade union community seeking higher wages and shorter hours (nor only a male one, as Stephens's language implies). The Knights envisioned a struggle for the economic and spiritual "uplifting of humanity," one seeking not only "complete emancipation of wealth-producers from the thraldom and loss of wage-slavery" but moral elevation of the human race as a whole "to a higher plane of existence, a truer, nobler development of its capabilities and powers."[4]

The Knights' idea of community was always closely linked to a passionate concern with the moral development of the individual. Education, temperance, and other forms of "moral uplift" championed by the Knights required both individual growth and community support. The Knights' "communitarianism" joined features of American individualism (notably the concern with individual rights and personal development) with the recognition that humans are social beings who cannot fulfill their natures in isolation.

The Knights' ideas of solidarity and community were closely associated with the idea of democracy. The full version of the Knights' famous slogan was, "That is the most perfect government in which an injury to one is the concern of all." Taken from Solon, the famous Grecian sage, the motto evoked the image of a civic community rooted like classical Athens in political democracy. The Knights saw democratic participation as the key to the moral community they sought, recalling the memory not only of the Greeks but American democrats like Jefferson and Madison.

The Knights championed democracy in the economy as well as in government. They became known—and were often disparaged—as cooperativists because of their early and passionate advocacy of worker-owned business. Going against the grain of both trade union thinking and the Marxist orthodoxy of their day, the Knights pioneered a Left communitarianism that put worker cooperatives on the national agenda.

Solidarity, the Knights argued, could only be the product of voluntary association, neither commanded by the state nor dictated by the boss.

Workers and citizens had to come together themselves, in their families, churches, neighborhoods, and unions or worker assemblies, to build their collective strength and sense of community. Stephens proclaimed: "This we must do for ourselves. If we neglect or refuse to do it, let things remain as they are; we shall justly be the prey of monopolists, the serfs of lords of land; slaves of lords of labor, and victims of lords of law."[5]

Their communitarianism led the Knights to recognize the vital importance not only of the workplace but of all the institutions of civil society. As social historian Leon Fink observes, the Knights "looked to self-organized society, not to the individual and not to the state—as the redeemer of their American dream." The Knights worked closely with religious, ethnic, and neighborhood associations, and their worker assemblies built on and deepened the social networks in the community. One Knights leader could thus honestly proclaim, "We stand as the conservators of society."[6]

The Knights' critique of capitalism was rooted in their stance as Left "conservators." They saw their members' dignity and community life threatened by a ruthless marketplace. Terence Powderly, the national head of the Knights at their peak, conceived economic competition as the curse of modern society, inspiring a war of each against all. Powderly approvingly cites French socialist Louis Blanc: "And of how many tears is composed the good fortune of those we call happy? Is it, then, a good state of society which is so constituted that the prosperity of one fatally corresponds with the sufferings of others?"[7] Powderly charged that "the results of the last thirty years have demonstrated that the present competitive system is rotten to the core, that it is crumbling of its own weight; it is unhealthy, it is baneful and through its operations a few men have rushed on to a point which other men could not reach. A few have grasped all."[8]

Unlike their Marxist rivals, the Knights did not seek a complete dismantling of capitalism but a shift toward a cooperativist market system compatible with the preservation of community and moral virtue. Powderly proclaimed that "the basic principle of the order of Knights of Labor is cooperation," and in their constitution the Knights pledged to "endeavor to associate our own labors; to establish co-operative institutions, such as will tend to supersede the wage system by the introduction of a cooperative industrial system."[9]

The cooperativism of the Knights was emphatically neither state collectivism nor a denial of individual rights. The rise of the robber baron monopolists and their takeover of the state had disenchanted much

## A Postcommunist Left Agenda

of the working population from any faith in government redress. The Knights shared this distrust of government, believing that workers and communities would have to act on their own behalf. Regarding the rights of the individual, Powderly never saw cooperation as antagonistic to individual empowerment, arguing that cooperation "will make every man his own master—every man his own employer."[10]

The Knights viewed worker cooperatives as a vehicle for moral as well as economic transformation. Cooperatives would require and help create a new kind of human development. The Knights observed "That in establishing our cooperative institutions we must not forget that men reared under the conditions of wage service can not jump at once to the much higher level of cooperation. The man who has acted for a lifetime under outside pressure, when that pressure is suddenly removed becomes listless, apathetic, incapable of exertion." Creating worker cooperatives was a long-term project, closely associated with building a new culture and moral order.[11]

The Knights established a cooperative fund to ensure that all its members would personally share in a form of ownership. The Knights' constitution mandated that every member "of the order shall ... pay to the Financial Secretary of his local, a sum equal to ten cents per month as a cooperative fund of the order. ... Every member shall receive from the Financial Secretary a certificate of stock in the Cooperative Association."[12]

Along with many small cooperative grocery stores, often housed in the union halls themselves, the Knights helped establish scores of cooperatively owned manufacturing enterprises, bakeries and other worker-owned enterprises across the country, including one large, cooperatively owned coal mine. Many failed, in large measure because "[i]n every case, the capitalist class fought the cooperatives tooth-and-nail and the labor projects faced interference by wholesalers who withheld supplies, and rank discrimination by railroads in rates and facilities, and by banks in the matter of credit."[13]

What most famously distinguished the Knights beyond their vision of cooperativism was their solidaristic strategy, which offers important lessons for a Left today that cannot find its common ground. Uniting all workers regardless of background was an open challenge to employers, who consciously mixed nationalities of workers to heighten friction in the workplace and hinder worker solidarity. It was also an affront to the trade unionism of the day, especially craft unionism, which created hierarchies based on skill, race, and gender.

Their vision of solidarity led the Knights, as noted earlier, to achieve "what no other American labor organization before the 1880s had succeeded in doing—the organization and unification of the American working class."[14] Frederick Engels was among the first to acknowledge this accomplishment: "The Knights of Labor are the first national organization created by the American working class as a whole; whatever be their origin and history . . . here they are, the work of practically the whole class of American wage-earners . . . to an outsider it appears evident that here is the raw material out of which the future of the American working class movement, and along with it, the future of American society at large has to be shaped."[15]

The Knights tackled the divisive "nationalities problem" by organizing Poles, Hungarians, Irish, and others together into "mixed assemblies." The Knights translated their pamphlets and manuals into numerous languages, insisting that their organizers become, in effect, linguists capable of reaching each group in its own tongue. While thus respecting the national traditions of each group, the Knights forged them together with the idea of universal brotherhood and sisterhood. In their anthem, "Storm the Fort, ye Knights of Labor," they highlighted the refrain, "Equal rights for every neighbor."[16]

The Knights understood that solidarity meant bringing women and men together in the labor movement and were among the first to do so. Of the thirty national trade unions existing between 1860 and 1880, only two—the cigar makers and printers—accepted some women. While the Knights originally also excluded women, they passed one of the first provisions for equal pay for women in 1878 and admitted women members in 1882. Ultimately, more than fifty thousand women joined the Knights, including mill operatives, shoe workers, housekeepers, farmers, chambermaids, hatters, weavers, and laundresses.[17]

The Knights remained male dominated, but they elected some women officers, established a Woman's Department, and appointed national committees to investigate the conditions of and collect statistics on women's work. Leonora M. Barry, originally a hosiery mill worker, became a full-time organizer of women for the Knights. She lectured all over the country, telling groups like the suffragists that a feminism based on winning the right to vote was not enough; women and men would have to unite to challenge the "root of all evil, the industrial and social system."[18]

Solidarity in action, such as the 1885 New York strike joining women cloak and skirt workers with male compatriots, led to important victories, boosting the confidence both of women and of the larger labor movement. Militant strikes among female textile workers in Fall River, Massachusetts, and carpet weavers in Yonkers, New York, contributed to a growing national assertiveness of women workers. One member of a woman's assembly in Chicago described in 1882 how "timid young girls—girls that have been overworked from their cradles—stand up bravely and in steady tones, swayed by conviction and the wrongs heaped upon their comrades, talk nobly and beautifully of the hope of redress to be found in organization."[19]

The most important division threatening the solidarity of American labor was race. The Knights were slow to recognize the problem and never fully committed themselves to the struggle for racial equality. But while they did not succeed in eliminating racial discrimination even within their own ranks, they established an unprecedented solidarity across the races. As Philip Foner writes: "For the first time in the history of the American labor movement, widespread Negro-white unity flourished as Negro and white members of the Order acted together for common purposes," prefiguring the "rainbow coalition" needed today to unite a racially fragmented Left.[20]

At their heyday, in 1886, the Knights had brought between sixty and ninety thousand blacks into their ranks, perhaps a tenth of total membership. The majority of these blacks had never been part of the labor movement before, reflecting the fierce antagonism of employers and the crafts to bringing black and white workers together. Many black Knights were in the South, a notable accomplishment given the dangers involved both for organizers and for black workers, including the threat of lynching.[21]

Even in the South, where separate black worker assemblies were usually organized, the Knights made progress in overcoming prejudice and building racial solidarity. One labor newspaper in Charleston, South Carolina, reported in 1886 that, "The white and colored mechanics and laborers are working in great harmony as K. of L. This is a grand stride. The organization of the K. of L. has done this much for the South, uniting the white and black worker out of the bond of poverty."[22]

In parades, rallies, and festivities, the Knights encouraged public displays of racial solidarity that shocked many onlookers and were often illegal. In Louisville, Kentucky, the Knights-sponsored parade of six thousand black and white workers entered National Park, although all Louisville parks were officially closed to blacks. In Dallas, Texas, black and white workers marched together in a Knights Fourth of July parade and held a rally in which a black speaker joined a white on the podium. A local newspaper reported, "This is the first time such a thing happened in Texas."[23]

Racial solidarity paid off in strikes, such as that of shipyard workers in Baltimore starting in August 1885. White and black workers struck for almost a year, maintaining solidarity despite rabid attempts by the press and employers to fuel racial divisions. They joined together to drive out strike breakers and maintained close working relations after succeeding in preventing massive wage cuts or increases in hours.

In Richmond, Virginia, the former capital of the Confederacy, the Knights achieved one of their most publicized triumphs of racial solidarity. White and black workers in Richmond after the Civil War were deeply divided racially, working in racially segregated occupations, living in separate parts of town, and joining segregated churches and fraternal associations. Richmond elites closed down the few places—such as gambling and prostitution houses and prize fights—where the races mixed. When the Knights began to organize in earnest in 1885, they had to organize separate white and black worker assemblies.[24]

Their dramatic success with black assemblies in Richmond reflected their communitarian approach. Richmond blacks were already knit closely together by a remarkable network of over four hundred secret societies that provided health benefits, pensions, and aid to orphans, widows, and the sick. Rich with ornate rituals and arcane ceremonies, the secret societies held public parades and rallies that drew the black community together in public displays of internal solidarity.

The Knights' strategy, which always sought to build its worker assemblies from the social networks already established in the community, proved auspicious in Richmond. Black workers flocked to the Knights' assemblies—so rapidly that they filled twelve new assemblies in a two-week period in 1885 alone. The cooperative philosophy and communal rituals of the Knights attracted a proud and assertive black community accustomed to the bonding and ceremonies of fraternal societies.

In May 1886, the Richmond Knights built support for a boycott leading to unprecedented solidarity between their white and black assemblies. The boycott was directed at the use of mostly black convict labor by a local flour mill, a practice that threatened the wages and livelihoods of both black and white workers. The Knights saw the flour mill's action as "an injustice done honest labor" and, as was their wont, used both patriotic and Christian references (the Boston Tea Party, the "divine right to boycott accorded us by the Holy Bible") to justify acting against it. Reconceiving the boycott as not a right but a "Christian duty" helped bring together blacks and whites as never before and led to a sweet victory.

This organizing success was converted a few months later into a political win by a biracial Knights reform slate in local Richmond elections. The Knights had challenged business elites in political contests in such cities as Rutland, Vermont, Rochester, New Hampshire, and Milwaukee, Wisconsin, almost always as a workers' reform movement bridging ethnic, racial, and religious differences. In Richmond, the reform slate dramatically challenged the traditional Southern caste system aligning white workers and employers against blacks; it successfully united white and black workers to clean up the patronage system of Richmond's ruling business elite and provide more jobs and benefits for workers. The biracial working-class coalition did not survive long. It was unable to sustain a candidacy for Congress the following year by the local Knights leader, but it afforded a brief glimpse of the momentous political realignments and new multiracial communities offered by the Knights' vision of solidarity.

The Knights collapsed by 1890, supplanted by less visionary trade unions oriented toward bread-and-butter issues. Part of the problem was that the abstractness of their prophetic thinking about cooperativism made them vulnerable to a utopianism removed from the immediate struggles and needs of their members. The Knights lacked the capital, technical skills, political organization, and intellectual understanding to create a sustainable worker cooperative sector of the economy. They could thus never deliver on the cooperative "city of refuge" for their members that their rhetoric promised.

If Left communitarianism always has to guard against utopianism, it also has to repudiate a common-ground philosophy, prevalent in mainstream communitarian thinking today, that blurs the real conflicts of interest between workers and employers. The Knights' leadership, particularly Terence Powderly, thought they could appeal to all sectors of society and sought an image of moderation and respectability that might attract the Catholic church hierarchy and even large employers. Powderly personally opposed political action, arguing that the "Knights of Labor is higher and grander than party," and took a position against strikes in favor of arbitration and conciliation, often undercutting his own members to curry favor with the likes of railroad tycoon Jay Gould.

Growing differences between the Powderly leadership and the rank and file revealed the failure of the Knights to live up to their own standards of democratic community. Powderly accumulated autocratic powers over local assemblies and leaders and stacked the national committees of the organization with his own loyalists. Many, like Powderly, were middle-class intellectuals or small business proprietors with fine oratory but little feel for working-class life. Had members been able to overthrow the Powderly machine and exercise real democracy in the Knights, they might have created a more enduring legacy of left cooperativism and community.

## Communist Habits of the Heart: Community in the Old Left

The Communist Party (CP) in its heyday created as intensely communitarian a movement as ever practiced on the American left. In wonderfully moving interviews with elderly former communists active in the 1930s, journalist Vivian Gornick found it was the spirit of community that they carried in their memories—and that defined what the practice of communist politics was all about. Selma, a Brooklyn-born activist, spoke for almost all the old communists when she told Gornick that being a union organizer for the party "was the best ten years of my life. . . . Deep inside me I was a wounded, homeless person. The party healed me, gave me the kind of home I could never have made. . . . It gave me a home inside myself."

Selma explained that the party healed her loneliness, which was "entirely absent from my life while I was Communist. . . . Whatever else we were as Communists we were not lonely. This disease that's slowly killing off everybody today, that's killing me, this disease was unknown to us as Communists." Selma left the Party, but she says there still lingers in her soul, "the vision of thousands of people, strong and united, made whole, marching beneath the Communist banner, toward a better world, toward their lives." This vision of community, binding her passionately both to her party comrades and to the whole human race, is what made her a communist.[25]

For Jim, a party organizer for twenty years who originally came from a Nebraska tenant farm family, the party was also a community where "the drifting stopped. I'd come to rest. I had a home again. And for the next twenty years, no matter where I was, I had that home. And in that home, I discovered I could think, act, learn, be." Jim says that it was "the pull of connectedness," his own "longing for connectedness," to which the party really spoke, and from the moment he joined the party, he "felt connected up to the world." The party gave him a spiritual as well as social home: a community of meaning. It helped him "make sense of it all," making the world "larger, richer, something to place yourself in."[26]

Gornick, herself a "red-diaper baby" raised in the bosom of a passionate communist family, concludes that the party brought "to astonishing life the kind of comradeship that makes swell in men and women the deepest sense of their own humanness, allowing them to love themselves through the act of loving each other." While aware of the party's tragic limitations, she says one could aptly claim, as did the famous author Richard Wright, "There was no agency in the world so capable of making men feel the earth and the people upon it as the Communist Party."[27]

The communitarianism of communism lay partly in its universalistic vision of solidarity, a secular faith that connected every believer with all of suffering humanity. To join the party was to share the noblest struggles of others, especially the wounded and dispossessed, for dignity and equality. Almost by definition, a communist could not be lonely because he or she was doctrinally bound to the soul of the whole human community.

In the early thirties, communists led hundreds of thousands of the unemployed on the streets of New York to demand food, an end to foreclosures, and the creation of jobs and new unemployment benefits. By the late thirties they became front-line soldiers in John L. Lewis's fight for a new Congress of Industrial Organizations (CIO) uniting workers of all crafts and backgrounds. The communists were thus practitioners as well as theorists of a great new human community reflecting the spirit of workplace solidarity.

The party's official language of Marxism, and its vision of macrosocietal transformation, however, were less communitarian than those of many of its Left competitors, such as the anarcho-socialists and the cooperativists, who spoke in a more personalized language of caring, connection, and sharing. The communists used the dry discourse of economics and "scientific socialism," which carried an intellectualized idea of solidarity removed from the immediacy of daily life. The dreary economism for which the communists are famous helps to explain why it is so surprising to learn of their rich communitarianism; their politics of community was obscured by their own political rhetoric.

To build community among their own cadres, the CP helped create a dense network of institutions that would wrap members in a secure social cocoon almost from cradle to grave. Richard Flacks writes that if you were a New York party member in the 1930s, you could "read the Party's daily newspaper, go to work in a shop represented by a Party-affiliated union, eat lunch or dinner at a restaurant run by Party sympathizers or frequented by comrades, participate in a Party organized softball or volley-ball league, sing in a Party-organized chorus or theater group, attend two or three meetings a week, send your children to a Party-allied summer camp or after-school program, get medical care through the Party-sponsored medical society, go to lectures or concerts or rallies put on by Party-related organizations, read books by writers celebrated by the Party cultural magazine or published by the Party publishing house, vacation at a Party-owned resort, spend retirement recreating at old people's activity centers sponsored by the Party, be buried by the Party-sponsored burial society." Flacks concludes that "virtually every aspect of one's everyday life could be lived in relation to the Party's institutional framework."[28]

The party did not create this remarkable infrastructure of community life on its own; it had to build a relationship to the neighborhood associations, religious and ethnic organizations, and cultural groups in which the party's members were already embedded. The party's housing coops, medical and social insurance associations, newspapers, and summer camps typically were operated through the auspices of Jewish, Finnish, German, or other ethnic and religious organizations affiliated with the party, which had long histories preceding their communist affiliation. Against the grain of the party's official Marxist doctrine, which tended to dismiss such "blood ties" or traditional communal roots as destructive of class solidarity, the party began to recognize that they were essential ingredients.

This insight transformed the party's understanding of how to build the labor movement. The party's abstract doctrines of class consciousness could not inspire the same loyalties and cooperation that the churches, ethnic associations, and fraternal groups in the community had long commanded. Communists leading CIO organizing drives in the auto plants of Michigan or the steel factories of Ohio and Pennsylvania "soon realized the necessity of building broad community support in company towns by working through ethnic associations, churches and black associations."[29] Ethnic, religious, and racial identifications helped divide the working class, but they also created habits of caring and associations of mutual aid nourishing "the type of cooperation that would be necessary for the eventual triumph of the CIO."[30]

This understanding crystallized officially during the Popular Front era of the late 1930s, when the Party pronounced that "it is necessary that our comrades be not only good Communists, but . . . good Jews, good Irishmen." The idea paid quick dividends. Historians Harvey Klehr and John Earl Haynes write that party-controlled fraternal organizations "structured to provide low-cost life insurance and organized by ethnic units (Hungarian, Jewish, Slovak, Serbo-Croat, Italian, and so on), boomed during the Popular Front, reaching 150,000 dues payers by 1939 and spreading Communist influence throughout foreign-born communities." The communists were discovering that traditional communities could be mobilized and linked to fight for a universal vision of liberation and community.[31]

The new practice—instructive for a Left today that no longer knows how to mobilize racial, gender, or ethnic communities for shared universal goals—was best exemplified by the Jewish communists, who constituted the largest subcommunity in the party and created a universalistic labor movement melding Yiddish culture and socialism. Its roots were in the Bund, a famous Jewish socialist labor movement originating in Russia and Poland during the 1890s. Lev Martov, one of the Bund's founders, believed that the achievement of socialism required the awakening of suffering ethnic or national communities, such as Jews who were being massacred, to their own distinctive forms of economic and cultural oppression: "A working class which passively accepts its own national status, such a working class will hardly be able to revolt against its inferior class status. Because the national passivity of the Jewish masses prevents the development of class consciousness, the tasks of awakening both the national and the class consciousness must proceed on parallel lines." The Bund's founders believed that "a Jewish socialist organization did not imply the surrender of or even a deviation from the major long-term goal of all socialists—an international classless society." Jewish socialists would fight for the liberation of all humanity.[32]

Bundists joined hundreds of thousands of other Jewish immigrants to America after the bloody pogroms at the turn of the century. Their impact on the American Communist Party, the unions, and the Jewish community itself would be dramatic. Out of the many mutual aid associations that honeycombed the Jewish immigrant community in New York and other large cities, the new movement helped build housing coops, newspapers, summer camps, choirs, and overarching fraternal and sororal labor organizations advancing the cause of Jewish socialism. These included the Workmen's Circle (WC), formed in 1900 and linked to the Socialist Party, and later, the International Workers Order (IWO), a descendant and rival of the Workmen's Circle formed in the 1930s and linked to the Communist Party. Both associations knit Jewish workers together socially, provided them mutual benefit plans for housing, medicine, and pensions, offered schools and adult educational programs, and ran summer camps for children.

The central mission of the schools, as expressed by one leading Jewish communist educator and publisher, was to help educate a Jew who "will know how to link the progressive forces of the Jewish people to the progressive forces of all other peoples . . . and who will, at the same time, remain a Jew, a son of his people, a fighter for the future of his people." Likewise, the summer camps, such as Camp Kinderland, "wished to educate and socialize its charges so that they would acquire both a Jewish and a Left identity. . . . Thus the daily life of the campers was . . . filled with songs, poems, lectures, and games designed to make the children aware of their Jewish-Progressive heritage and the struggle for social justice that united Jews with other people."[33]

The camps taught Yiddish songs and poetry dealing with the political struggles of Jewish and non-Jewish immigrants, and invited non-Jewish black and other Left activists and musicians to speak and entertain. As Camp Kinderland administrator Elsie Suller, who viewed Jewish socialism as a movement for the liberation of all people, said, "We must be committed and every day in these two precious summer months, 24 hours a day, we try to invest our children with this kind of conscience, with the understanding that there cannot be a commitment as a Jew unless there is a commitment as well to [universal] brotherhood."[34]

The Jewish Left press, especially newspapers such as the *Jewish Daily Forward* and the *Freiheit*, played a central role in creating the ideology of the new movement and winning Jewish workers to the socialist cause. As one scholar put it, "Socialism was the message and Yiddish the medium." Editors such as Abraham Cahan of the *Forward* and Moissaye Olgin of the *Freiheit* were critical intellectual figures, helping redefine Jewishness in terms of socialist principles. Thus, Cahan would write that "The Law of Moses was invoked on behalf of striking workers. Thou shalt not withhold anything from thy neighbor, nor rob him; there shall not abide with thee the wages of him that is hired until morning. So it stands in Leviticus. So you see that our bosses who rob us and don't pay commit a sin, and that the cause of our unions is a just one."[35]

Efforts to organize Jewish and other immigrant workers in the needle trades and other industries had begun in the 1870s and 1880s, long before the Bundists arrived with their vision of Jewish socialism. But after the turn of the century, as the Bundist influence took root, socialist and communist labor organizers found themselves working with rather than against the grain of the community. Simply using Yiddish in meetings and rallies had an electrifying effect on the receptivity of Jewish workers. The Jewish press gave the labor movement an almost miraculous new means of winning Jewish workers' hearts and minds. The Jewish schools taught the struggles of the labor movement to students, while the summer camps invited union activists to come and tell stories and sing songs with their young charges.

The Workmen's Circle and International Workers Order cajoled, instructed, and pushed Jews into the embrace of the labor movement. They were essentially the community arm of the unions, weaving the concerns of the Jewish community together with labor's economic agenda in a seamless web. The unions helped finance and organize the community-based institutions, which in turn recruited and campaigned for the unions. To be eligible for WC and IWO membership and benefits, Jews had to join the union and vote for the socialists or communists. Most important, these organizations socialized the whole community to feel that being Jewish meant joining the struggle to liberate all of humanity.

The Jewish communist experience was replicated in lesser degrees by the Irish, Finns, Germans, blacks, and other communities. Each of these groups formed its own fraternal labor organizations and presses, which worked diligently in the service of the Communist Party and the larger struggle for human liberation. But if the communist experience shows that movements for universal solidarity cannot divorce themselves from traditional communal roots—and in fact can succeed only by helping reshape them in the service of universal ideals—it also demonstrates the dangers inherent in this kind of Left communitarianism.

Arthur Liebman, a leading scholar of the Jewish socialists and communists, writes, "the very same components of the Jewish labor movement that fostered and consolidated a positive relation between Jews and the Left also undermined it." Liebman observes that the historical conditions that helped catalyze a magical connection between the Jewish community and the labor movement reversed themselves. "The Jewish labor unions," he writes, "came into existence with two souls—one Jewish, the other socialist. In the early decades of the twentieth century, each reinforced the other as the Jewish community in this period was largely working class and disproportionately prosocialist. However, with the passage of time and the accompanying improvements in the socioeconomic circumstances of the Jewish community, the Jewish and socialist souls no longer complemented one another."[36]

The Jewish socialist presses and fraternal organizations slowly became more Jewish than socialist. Financial, bureaucratic, and ideological forces—related not only to Jewish economic mobility but to such external events as the Stalinist purges, the rise of Hitler, and the advent of the Cold War—all conspired to make the national theme more powerful than the class one. The Yiddish newspapers and schools began cultivating Zionist and religious themes unrelated or even hostile to the Left and class consciousness. In the aftermath of the Second World War, the culture and institutions that had animated Jewish communism were joining the Jewish mainstream, becoming politically liberal but increasingly bourgeois in sensibility and more concerned with Jewish prospects than social revolution.

Powerful tensions inevitably exist between particularistic and universalistic communities and ideals. Even the Jewish community, historically defining itself as a beacon lighting the path of all nations, is pulled by strong insular identities. While the task of the Left is to help nourish the universalistic aspirations of all particularistic communities with which it must align itself, there is no sure formula for insuring that it will prevail over the forces of parochialism within them. Historically, the Left has often lost the battle, unable to sustain common ground and universal commitments among ethnic, racial, or religious groups succumbing to chauvinism or nationalism. American communism thus offers hints but no conclusive answers for communitarian leftists today seeking to reshape and unite the Left's fragmented communities and movements in a new common ground.

There were other serious limitations of communism as a model of the democratic communitarian project. The party was stiflingly authoritarian, and it slavishly toed the Soviet line. It was run on Leninist principles of "democratic centralism," not democracy. This drove many out of the party and destroyed its credibility as a symbol of freedom and community.

Moreover, as noted earlier, the party, despite its communitarian practice, was economistic in its official vision and rhetoric. The party needed a language more humanly expressive than Marxism of the spiritual and cultural sensibilities it sought to promote. If the party had been more democratic, it might have found that language in the voices of the workers themselves, whose stories of suffering and struggle conveyed a richer understanding of the Depression than the party's arcane economic theories of surplus value. Had it found this more organic, rooted voice, it would have expanded the circle of beloved comrades far beyond the limited numbers who rallied to its cause.

## Communities of Privilege: The Tension between Individualism and Community in the New Left

In fund-raising meetings in the mid-1960s of the New Left's leading organization, Students for a Democratic Society (SDS), students sometimes enacted an odd ritual. They reported their parents' occupations or incomes before announcing their contribution. "My father's a vice-president at General Electric; here's a hundred dollars. . . My father's a downtown corporate lawyer; here is one hundred twenty-five. . . My mother's a surgeon; I'm giving a hundred fifty."

The students were playing on guilt as a way of raising money for the movement. They were paying (only partly humorously) for the sin of being born privileged. The New Left was a self-conscious new class of revolutionaries drawn from the elite of the most powerful society in the world.

Their privileged status is the secret to understanding the complex history of the New Left as a communitarian movement. Freed from material need, these student radicals had the luxury to focus on the questions of values and human connection that animate communitarian politics. These "post-materialist" concerns gave the New Left its unique flavor, liberating it from the official economism of the Old Left.

Within its post-materialist politics, however, two partially conflicting themes developed. A communitarian hunger for connection and loving relations—with each other and with the oppressed of the world—propelled New Leftists into communal lifestyles and intensely participatory collective action for social justice. An equally deep individualistic thirst for uninhibited self-expression and personal authenticity also inspired them, spawning not only the existential "personal politics" of the New Left but the countercultural ethos of "doing your own thing." While radical students saw community as a vehicle for helping their own and others' individuality flower, they never fully understood nor resolved the tensions between their communitarian and individualistic sides.

The quest for both community and individuality grew from the same source: the impoverished quality of life that America's bureaucratic capitalism had to offer even to these, its most privileged youth. In 1964, students at the University of California campus at Berkeley wore signs saying, "Do not Fold, Spindle, Staple or Mutilate." Huge, impersonal classes, professors they never got to know, and a sprawling administration that saw them only as a computer number all helped fuel the famous Free Speech Movement (FSM), which launched the New Left on campuses across the country.

The University of California's president, Clark Kerr, had himself called the campus a "knowledge factory," implicitly acknowledging the coldness of the enterprise and the fact that professors were paid to do research, not teach. The FSM linked the disregard for the student with the larger institutional callousness expressed in bulldozing poor neighborhoods and building weapons for Vietnam-style wars. America and its universities, as Mario Savio, the fiery leader of the Free Speech Movement, put it, were becoming a vast unfeeling machine: "There's a time when the operation of the machine becomes so odious, makes you so sick at heart, that you can't take part. And you've got to put your bodies upon the gears and upon the wheels, upon the levels, upon all the apparatus, and you've got to make it stop."

The communitarian side of the New Left was its vision of remaking society in the image of a caring, moral community. In the 1962 Port Huron statement, the founding philosophical document of SDS and the New Left, principal author Tom Hayden denounced the bureaucratic "depersonalization that reduces human beings to the status of things" and produces modern society's "loneliness, estrangement, isolation." Bureaucratic capitalism, Hayden wrote, turns our relationships into "partial and fragmentary bonds of functions that bind men only as worker to worker, employer to employee, teacher to student. Hayden concludes that this dehumanization 'cannot be overcome by better personnel management, nor by improved gadgets, but only when a love of man overcomes the idolatrous worship of things by man."[37]

Hayden acknowledged his debt to the civil rights movement and particularly to the Freedom Riders and the Student Non-Violent coordinating Committee (SNCC). Drawing on the nonviolent philosophy of Martin Luther King, Jr., SNCC, like Hayden, had spoken about politics in the language of love and community. Its founding statement spoke of "a social order of justice permeated by love" and a "redemptive community" or a "beloved community" that would bond all those struggling for freedom.[38]

According to sociologist Wini Breines, the New Left was an essentially communitarian impulse that sought to create "a network of relationships more direct, more total and more personal than the formal, abstract and instrumental relationships characterizing state and society." The New Left, she suggests, saw that "the struggle to defend community, both the 'sense' of community and actual community institutions, becomes political in the context of the changes that capitalism has brought in the everyday life of the individual," changes involving loss of control at work and "impersonality and competition in all areas of life." For the New Left, the "desire for connectedness, meaningful personal relationships and direct participation and control" over institutions moved to the center of political life, defining a Left communitarianism never before seen in America.[39]

Breines's view obscures the deep tensions between the communitarian and individualistic souls of the New Left, but it captures the most innovative side of the movement. On the one hand, the New Left advanced a "micro"-communitarianism, seeking to create more egalitarian and loving relations in their own movement. These would prefigure, as Breines writes, the "non-capitalist and communitarian institutions" of the new society they wanted to create. Mario Savio was frank about the personal needs that this micro-communitarianism addressed, asserting that students "are all cut off from one another and what they need is a spark, just one spark to show them that all these people around them, likewise, are quite as lonely as they are, quite as cut off as they, quite as hungry for some kind of community as they are." "Free speech," Savio asserted, "was in some ways a pretext. . . . Around that issue the people could gain the community they formerly lacked."[40]

While some activists in SDS feared that the concern with personal relations and transforming the self would derail the movement, many leading SDS figures believed that it was the cutting edge of their new politics. Student activists Pat Hansen and Ken McEldowney wrote that it was not civil rights or Vietnam that ultimately built SDS but "a sense of community and opportunity to affect at least a portion of our lives." Students recognized that something was deeply amiss in the "way that people relate to each other," and they flocked to the New Left because it offered a political analysis of what was wrong and a communal refuge.[41]

Greg Calvert, an SDS national secretary, agreed that the quest for more loving and meaningful relations helped define New Left politics: "Cynicism easily dismisses such sentiments as naive. And yet, no sentiments seem to be more revolutionary in the society in which we live—because there is no clearer denial of human freedom on the most immediate level than the destruction of the kind of community which makes human relatedness and love possible."[42]

The New Left always viewed its own quest for community in the context of a larger moral mission involving all of society. Its concern with personal relations could easily become navel-gazing, but this tendency was tempered by its intense sense of connection to the world and a hunger for moral authenticity as deep as that for loving comradeship. The New Left's communitarian impulse joined issues of love to those of moral responsibility, seeking not the privatized community of the suburban family or the shopping mall but the civil rights movement's "beloved community" united in its commitment to freedom and social justice.

Sociologist Richard Flacks describes the New Left as a "laboratory for moral vocation," underscoring the importance of values and moral authenticity in radical student culture. Flacks's own research, based on interviews with student activists and their parents, revealed predominantly liberal parents who had established themselves in business and the professions and "were strongly impelled to encourage their children to seize opportunities to do more with their lives than make money and win status." Radical students, Flacks found, put moral authenticity at the top of their own list of values. They were acutely sensitive to hypocrisy both because of the strength of their parents' moral commitments and the parents' failure to commit to an activist life embodying those commitments.[43]

New Left students, believing too fervently in American values of freedom and democracy, were unprepared for the gap between reality and rhetoric they discovered in America's racial problems or the Vietnam war. Thus, SDS National Secretary Carl Oglesby in 1965 would remark about his reaction to learning that the United States supported dictatorships in the Third World: "Others will make of it that I sound mighty anti-American. To these I say: Don't blame me for that. Blame those who mouthed liberal values and broke my American heart."[44]

Thus was born a personal crisis of authenticity that colored the New Left's communitarianism. Students needed a community that supported them in a life of moral commitment to the larger world. The movement's impetus was thus radically different from that of the inward-looking utopian communities of the nineteenth century. Founded on a solidarity of moral obligations to others, especially the dispossessed of the world, the New Left was relatively invulnerable to the retreat from larger social commitments often associated with communal lifestyles and movements.

## A Postcommunist Left Agenda

Their "prefigurative" politics—in which activists sought to create in their own movement the democratic and cooperative community that would guide their struggle for a just society—put a charismatic stamp on the idea of Left communitarianism. SDS leader Greg Calvert made the idea explicit: "While struggling to liberate the world, we would create the liberated world in our midst. While fighting to destroy the power which had created the loveless anti-community, we would ourselves create the community of love—the Beloved Community."[45]

As early as the Port Huron statement, the New Left had discovered its political formula for creating community both in the movement and throughout the country. Its roots were authentically American, drawing on the country's deepest ideals and traditions of democracy. The guiding idea of the Port Huron statement was "participatory democracy," which meant that "the individual [should] share in those social decisions determining the quality and direction of his life," that "decision-making of basic social consequence [should] be carried on by public groupings," and that "politics [should] have the function of bringing people out of isolation and into the community." When participatory democracy is extended from government into the workplace, the family, and all other institutions, it can become the basis of the "radical democracy" that many New Left theorists, such as Richard Flacks and Stanley Aronowitz, now argue must animate the Left in the postcommunist world.[46]

The Port Huron statement conceived participatory democracy as the means to both individual freedom and community. Opposing the "dominant conceptions of man in the twentieth century," the assumption that he is "incapable of directing his own affairs," Hayden wrote that people have "unrealized potential for self-evaluation, self-direction, self-understanding and creativity. . . . The goals of man and society should be human independence," which would be fulfilled through participatory democracy by ensuring that each would have his or her own say.[47]

But Hayden hastened to say that "this kind of independence does not mean egotistic individualism. . . . Human interdependence," he insisted,"is contemporary fact" and needed to be transformed into a "human brotherhood" that is "the condition of human survival." Participatory democracy would help create such a community by bringing everyone into a shared forum for deciding the great questions of their common life, as in the old New England town meetings.[48]

Democratic participation would then resolve the great tension between individualism and community, eliciting the full expression and development of each person's right and views, while bringing everyone together in a consensus built around the common good. In long meetings—especially during dramatic protest actions such as sit-ins against the military draft in university administration buildings—student activists had gotten a personal taste of the exhilarating potential of participatory democracy: the heady sense of self-expression and personal growth combined with the oceanic feeling of being emotionally bonded with others in a common cause of historic and noble purpose. It was thus understandable that SDS leader Carl Davidson could write, "Participatory democracy is often like a chronic and contagious disease. Once caught, it permeates one's whole life and the lives of those around. Its effect is disruptive in a total sense. And within a manipulative, bureaucratic system, its articulation and expression amounts to sabotage."[49]

The participatory democracy idea was attractive because it seemed a way not only to gain community without sacrificing individuality or freedom but also to unite community with justice. A community of participatory democracy would, by definition, be empowering, guaranteeing a voice for all the poor and dispossessed who in the capitalist system didn't even have a place at the table. As SDS leader Richard Rothstein said, this made the vision of participatory democracy something like a "generalization adding up to socialism without the word."[50]

But the participative idea added a notion of both democratic and responsible citizenship absent from the socialist thinking of the Old Left. On the one hand, direct involvement by ordinary people rather than planning from the top would make self-development and individual empowerment more than just rhetoric, fulfilling the Port Huron statement's dream of true independence for all. And the idea of participation as a potent means of generating commitment to institutions, whether in the workplace or the town meeting, added a credible theory of moral obligation to Left thinking, which had up to this point often seemed to promise rights without corresponding responsibilities.

The New Left idea depended on creating a participative democratic community in all the corporations, governments, and other huge bureaucracies in the United States, not just inside the friendly small cadres of activists in the movement. Beyond the enormity of the political obstacles represented by ruling elites unwilling to give up their power, the concept of direct participation and painstaking consensus building among all the members of huge institutions had inherent problems. It might take, as George Bernard Shaw said of socialism generally, too many meetings and too many evenings. Many members of the New Left themselves, as their own movement grew, began to feel that participatory democracy was best suited for small groups or organizations. For larger institutions, they did not back away from the democratic idea, but some shifted toward a less participatory (and thus potentially less communitarian) notion. As Staughton Lynd argued, if we want to discuss vast organizations or "a mass movement then we are talking about representative government and voting. This doesn't mean . . . that small groups taking direct action after consensual discussion must disappear. On the contrary. But there has got to be a way for hundreds and thousands of people to set policy together regarding fundamental issues, and consensus is not it."[51]

This concession to reality pointed to one of the constraints on democracy as a communitarian process. Even more painful for the New Left was the failure of participatory democracy as a guarantor of community even in its own ranks. The New Left was rarely the loving and cooperative community of its rhetoric, and it all too often became a bruising struggle of competitive (and usually male) egos for power. This gap between theory and practice reflected the ease with which even participatory democracy can succumb to competitive individualism. It also revealed the serious problems of a New Left that swept under the table the deep tensions between its individualistic impulses and its communitarian conscience.

Many of the individualistic impulses of the New Left were liberating. The bureaucratic soul of the university and the larger gray-suited corporate world made a mockery of American ideals of freedom and individuality. Self-expression, which sociologist Richard Flacks found to be a core value of radical student culture, fueled a life-affirming New Left cultural war on careerist conformity and bureaucratic repression—whether of free speech or free sex. Their privilege made these students idealistic and passionate champions of expressive individuality; economically they were secure enough to risk everything to be free and true to themselves.

The ideal of expressive individuality is not inherently contradictory to the spirit of communitarianism. A Left communitarianism cherishes community partly to nurture individual personality and "let a thousand flowers bloom." But expressive individuality can degenerate into the 1970s countercultural ethos expressed by the psychotherapist guru Fritz Perls: "I'm me and you're you. If we should meet, that's fine. But you do your own thing and I'll do mine." In the larger context of American individualism, the struggle for individuality degrades easily into the culture of narcissism.

Because of its intense sense of moral commitment to the oppressed of the world, the New Left never succumbed to the privatized idea of individuality embraced by some sectors of the counterculture. But it was plagued by its own debilitating forms of individualism. New Left meetings often degenerated into nasty ideological and personality conflicts, and Left activists (including most prominently its male leadership but many others as well) proved no freer of selfishness, overweening ambition, power lust, and abusiveness in sexual and other personal relations than other Americans. The contradiction between communitarian ideals and actual behavior disenchanted many activists, drove recruits away, and ultimately contributed to the factional suicide of the New Left itself.

These competitive individualistic propensities were the predictable legacy of the larger culture and the upper-middle-class position of the student activists. Raised to compete in business and the professions, student radicals could not magically transform themselves into paragons of cooperation. Admitted to the most elite universities, New Left activists were the most promising children of professional class culture, carrying its cosmopolitan version of individualism and the American Dream. After the decline of their movement, many New Leftists, while sustaining progressive political values and commitments, returned to graduate school and made names for themselves in law, medicine, and academic life, demonstrating that revolutionaries rarely fully renounce the heritage of their class.

The individualism of its own class legacy infected the New Left's entire political vision and practice, compromising its ability not only to create internal community but solidarity with less privileged groups off the campus. Flamboyant expressive individuality in hair, dress, sex, and personal style hampered students' ability to connect with working-class and poor people. New Left disdain for church, ethnicity, and traditional families—all seen as parochial and personally confining forms of "blood ties"—actually put the New Left in the position of opposing the most important communities giving meaning to the lives of ordinary Americans.

The limitations of participatory democracy as a communitarian vision are poignantly apparent in this contradiction. Participatory democracy was inevitably an attack on the hierarchal communities that managed to survive in the lives of working people. On campus and in poor neighborhoods, student radicals struggled to create alternative participatory communities for social change, but they rarely generated long-term commitments. Participatory democracy can unite people for collective action, but it does not by itself create the dense solidarity and long-term obligations necessary to create sustainable community. In the context of the fierce individualism at work both on and off the campus, participatory

## A Postcommunist Left Agenda

democracy bonded activists for short-term projects but could not override the fractious and fragmenting forces in most people's lives that eventually took each on his or her own life path. Participatory democracy was a necessary but insufficient vehicle for creating long-term commitments and caring communities.

# 7

# The Value(s) of the Left:

## TOWARD DEMOCRATIC COMMUNITY

During the 1992 presidential campaign, when Vice-President Dan Quayle hammered away at the television character and single mother Murphy Brown, he was talking what had become the standard Republican road to the White House. Tell the American people that we have lost our sense of values. Let them know that Republicans understand real "family values" and will work to restore them.

Liberals and leftists—and ultimately much of the population—dismissed this as exploitative campaign rhetoric and were eager to get the conversation back to economic reality. But the Republicans had seen something real about our current plight. Social breakdown ultimately reflects a crisis of values, which can have several faces. One is moral decline among both elites and the public. Another is the breakdown of the minimal normative consensus necessary to bind competing groups together. As the great sociologist Emile Durkheim argued, shared values are the "glue" of community. "Shared values" are rarely as consensual as Durkheim implied, for class, race, gender, and other identity groups typically struggle to advance competing moral orders. But, as Durkheim implied, in the absence of viable moral codes, communities dissolve into disassociated individuals preoccupied only with self.

The erosion of the social fabric in the United States reflects the kind of crisis that Durkheim feared. In the 1980s, led by its political and business leadership, the country descended into a moral morass of hyperindividualism. The savings and loan scandal, the BCCI scandal, Department of Defense payoff schemes, the Housing and Urban Development bribery scam, Iran-contra, Iraq-gate, and other moral nightmares set the tone. New cultural icons like Donald Trump and Michael Milken taught the upcoming generation that anything goes in the pursuit of money. In the process, the American Dream degenerated into a species of "wilding," the pursuit of profit or pleasure through acts that hurt others and weaken the social fabric.[1]

It is ironic that the Republicans appropriated values as their issue, since they carry such a heavy onus for this degraded individualism. Convicted Wall Street arbitrageur Ivan Boesky's phrase "greed is good" became the appropriate historical epitaph for the Reagan and Bush presidencies. Reaganomics turned selfishness into the national religion, enshrining the myth that the way to promote the common good was to encourage everyone to go out for "number one."

A politics of community in the United States has to start by addressing the question of moral decline that now haunts the country. In an era of social decay, values inevitably come to the fore, as people seek a moral foundation for rebuilding their lives and communities. The Left will find a receptive audience if it can offer a clear diagnosis of the moral malaise and who is responsible. That is preparation for a more difficult task: nourishing the morality and politics that can mobilize commitments beyond the self and guide social reconstruction.

The terms "morality" and "moral order" have a conservative tinge, reflecting the Right's monopoly over the discourse on values. Many leftists reject a politics of values, partly out of revulsion against the degraded conception of the issues that conservatives have exploited. Yet the entire history of the Left suggests a commitment to a moral tradition of justice and solidarity that is essential medicine for the West's plight. Articulating a "Left morality" as well as structural solutions that put it to work is the key to fashioning a new democratic community.

## Beyond Individualism: A Left Prescription

The task of social reconstruction is beyond the reach both of conservatives and liberals. Conservatives are wedded to a free-market gospel that is irrevocably individualistic. Conservatives see themselves as stewards of traditional community and family values, but they are unwilling to infringe on the market or challenge market values that are now contributing decisively to the erosion of the social fabric.

While conservatives have traditionally spoken for God, country, and family—the presumed pillars of community life—the image of community that they now espouse is so far out of touch with the realities of

## The Value(s) of the Left

American life that it is neither achievable nor palatable to the average citizen. Conservatives look backward to a community held together by coercion rather than consent and based on paternal authority rather than cooperation and sharing. Whether on abortion, sexuality, parenting, or the mores of family and neighborhood, conservatives appeal to Americans' nostalgia, but they are far more restrictive, authoritarian, and intolerant than the majority.

Why then were Republicans like Ronald Reagan and George Bush able to win campaigns based on the advocacy of "traditional values"? Not, as Congressman Barney Frank has written, because they were so in synch with middle Americans' values; does anyone really believe that most found George Bush or Dan Quayle moral beacons? Rather, the Republicans were, until the coming of the Clintons, the only politicians explicitly talking about values in an age of moral crisis. In an influential book on the decline of the Democratic Party in the 1980s, Tom and Mary Edsall show that Americans voted their morality as well as their pocketbooks, electing and reelecting Republicans because they openly and skillfully addressed the moral decline that haunted the country. U.S. citizens want to hear about values, and Republicans have more or less monopolized the conversation.

Liberals have also spoken ineffectively to America's values crisis, ultimately because, even more than conservatives, they are incapable of generating a compelling vision and vocabulary of community. This seems odd since liberals speak for public rather than purely privatized life and advocate modest public investment for community purposes. Even a reformed or "neo" liberal like Bill Clinton, an unexpected deficit hawk, has championed the costly communitarian proposition of health care for all.

But if liberals are prepared to infringe on the market to protect community values, they cannot generate a positive vision of the community they want to protect. Simplifying history, modern liberalism was born in the mind of John Locke, whose image of community was negative or restrictive: for Locke community existed to defend the liberty and property of the privatized individual against encroachments from others. In political terms, liberalism is at root more individualistic than conservatism.

In the nineteenth century, liberals like John Stuart Mill moved beyond Locke to lay out a rationale for limiting the free market. As Philip Green writes, Mill established the basis for "a complete theory of the modern welfare state." But Mill's concern was less the defense of community

## A Postcommunist Left Agenda

than advancing what Green calls liberalism's central project: creating "a social order in which individual liberty will be able to flourish equally for all to the limit of their capacities." Contemporary economic liberals who champion massive government intervention still do so to protect equal opportunity for each individual rather than to bolster community.

Liberals, limited by their fundamental individualism, see government as the embodiment of community. But while the state is essential in nourishing community, it should not be confused with community itself. Community arises in families, neighborhoods, workplaces, and other social sectors outside the state—in the realm of civil society. Government cannot legislate community, and as Eastern European and Soviet communism made painfully clear, it can become the enemy of civil society.

Liberalism offers an impoverished discourse about the social glue that helps constitute communities in civil society. The production of such cohesiveness—central to a politics of community—is a concern of the state, but it ultimately arises from structural conditions and moral forces that can be shaped but not imposed by government.

Can the Left step into the void left by liberals to address the values crisis? The idea would strike conservatives and liberals—and perhaps many leftists themselves—as bizarre. For years, Republicans have proclaimed that the Left is to blame for our moral decline. When Dan Quayle attacked what he called the "cultural elite," he was following the well-rehearsed conservative argument that America's values problem started with the indulgence and permissiveness of the 1960s, which decisively unhinged the moral restraints preserving American families and communities.

Liberals have not had a much more sanguine view of Left values. Indeed, Barney Frank, the liberal Democratic congressman from Massachusetts, wrote in 1992 that the Democratic Party owed its electoral failures to its association in the public mind with Left values that undermine community. According to Frank, "For most of the last twenty-five years, it has been on questions of values" that the Democrats have badly stumbled. "Democrats have come to be perceived as insufficiently pro-American, both internationally and at home; unenthusiastic about free enterprise . . . unprepared to move harshly against criminals; and disrespectful of the way average Americans live their lives." Such unsavory values, Frank argued, are those not of the party but of its left wing, led by George McGovern in the 1970s and Jesse Jackson in the 1980s. And while the Left does not control the party, Frank said, it has managed historically to hold Democratic presidential candidates hostage to its "politically correct" (PC) rhetoric, effectively undermining them as defenders of the American way.[2]

Blaming the Left for moral decline in the United States is something akin to blaming poverty on poverty programs. Nonetheless, both Quayle and Frank point to weaknesses in the value orientation of the Left that are real and to which we shall return shortly. Left values, as currently understood, cannot be a mobilizing force for large sectors of the American population. But the key story ignored by both Quayle and Frank is that the Left has the potential to address our moral dilemmas in ways that neither conservatives nor liberals can. The Left has always been at core a passionately moral movement, born out of the hunger for justice. Deep in the Left tradition—which rejects the economic individualism of conservatives and the political individualism of liberalism—are two insights about values that Americans now need to hear.

The first, a story about markets and morals, tells what has gone wrong. Since Marx, the Left has seen the side of capitalism that threatened to destroy the moral fabric and reduce human relations to the naked cash nexus. After 1980, the Reagan-Bush era unleashed that side of capitalism in full force. Far more morally consequential than "welfare cheats" or inner-city rioters has been the spectacle of wholesale looting at the top of the system. The conservatives' willingness to abandon the poor and weaken the entire social and economic infrastructure while offering "welfare" in the form of tax breaks, deregulation, subsidies, and bailouts to America's rich is the real moral story of the 1980s, and the Left's entire history is a preparation for telling that story.

The Left's historical role has been to show how capitalist market systems are, by their nature, profoundly morally compromised. Conventional markets, the Left has traditionally argued, inevitably inspire a religion of fevered self-interest, a moral climate plagued by deadly avarice, ambition, competitiveness, calculated indifference, and self-interested exploitation of others, all eroding the possibility of civility and community. The 1980s is a storybook parable of that basic Left message, and now more than ever the Left has a compelling mission to ensure that it is widely heard.

Americans need also to hear a second story, one about the possibility of a new ethos of solidarity. Here, the Left has its most compelling advantage over liberals, whose moral agenda is simply a more enlightened form of individualism. We need a moral vision of solidarity and community that no individualistic philosophy can offer.

# A Postcommunist Left Agenda

The idea of social solidarity and the values that make it possible have been at the heart of the Left as a historical tradition, as the last chapter showed. This is partly the pragmatism of the weak and marginalized, recognizing that change cannot come from the action of isolated individuals. But there is a deeper root of the Left's idea of solidarity: its pinpointing of capitalist individualism as critically morally flawed. Market capitalism liberated the individual from the bonds of feudalism, but in the process of destroying tyrannical communities and enshrining a new liberal code of individual rights, it uprooted the seeds of all community.

The Left has argued that ensuring freedom and opportunity for the privatized self, which guides liberal practice, is a morally incomplete vision. The sociologist in Marx understood people as constituted and fulfilled through their social connections. A central moral problem of capitalism was that it atomized the individual, turning increasingly weakened relations into means (for survival and self-aggrandizement) rather than ends. It was only in the process of shaping new authentic communities, often communities of struggle against oppressive conditions, that a morality transcending naked self-interest could be forged and society itself preserved.

The Left has thus joined the liberal defense of individual rights with a moral fervor for the sanctity of connection. The values of union and brotherhood or sisterhood were always at the core of the labor movement, which tried to offer workers the sense of belonging and community that the larger society could not deliver. The Left's historic defense of the poor, unemployed, and disenfranchised in the United States and throughout the Third World is also a manifesto of moral solidarity, asserting that nobody can be rightfully deprived of a place at the table.

## Making Civil Society Civil: Left Community Values

The Left's moral task requires an encounter with the entire tradition of American individualism, infusing it with a morality of community. But what kind of community, or community values, does the country need and does the Left offer?

To raise this question is to recognize that community is no less morally problematic than individualism. Historically, every form of crime has been committed in the name of community. The Catholic church burned infidels at the stake to protect Christian community, and Hitler slaughtered the Jews to defend his vision of Aryan community. Today,

## The Value(s) of the Left

whole countries in Eastern Europe are "ethnically cleansed" to defend the territory or honor of one ethnic community against another.

The traditional communities of the United States, romanticized in the lore of small towns and idealized by politicians from Ronald Reagan to Bill Clinton, had their own profound moral shortcomings. The cohesiveness of such communities often contained very large elements of coercion, represented by the family patriarch who enforced discipline by trips to the woodshed or the boss who ruled his small business as his own kingdom. Such traditional authority was reinforced by the moral sanctions of racism and a host of other "traditional values" that have helped make community more of a prison than a haven through much of history.

Civil society, then, has not proved very civil, a matter conveniently ignored by neoconservatives who preach moral revitalization through a return to traditional communities and values. The morality of communities has traditionally been tailored to those who control them and the civility of civil society largely denied to those not among the ruling elites.

In light of this history, many on the left will be tempted to respond to the erosion of civil society with a sigh of "good riddance." Like most Americans, they have good reason to reject the community of the past and to doubt whether any in the future will be much better. But the Left, like the country as a whole, has little choice but to struggle for its own vision of community, since continuing in the present direction is suicidal. Moreover, the Left has a special potential to envision a civil society that is truly civil and a community morality that is not tyrannical.

The marriage of democracy and community, the two values arguably most central to the Left, is a new starting point. The moral limits of communities, as just noted, have historically been linked to their inequalities of power. The racism, sexism, and authoritarianism that bound premodern communities were firmly rooted in traditional political and economic hierarchies. Democratic communities offer the hope of a nonauthoritarian basis for unity that does not trade justice for solidarity.

The Left has a vision of democratic communities not only in civil society but in the market and the state: democratic families, neighborhoods, social clubs, workplaces, professions, and industrial councils as well as participatory governments from the local to national level. Differing fundamentally from traditional communities, such modern democratic communities are based on three moral principles: inclusion, universalism, and participation.

## A Postcommunist Left Agenda

Exclusion was central to traditional communities, which typically built their solidarity around the threat of an enemy, either outsiders defined as dangerous heathen or, in their absence, insiders deemed barbaric. The urge to build solidarity on such grounds remains powerful in modern times. The Soviet threat was the most potent source of national solidarity in Cold War America, and with the Soviet Union's collapse, the frenzied search by conservative elites for new, homegrown enemies looms as one of the great dangers of the post–Cold War era.

The Left first and foremost seeks a democratic community that is inclusive. This implies a solidarity arising out of something quite different from fear and distrust of outsiders (or marginalized insiders). The ties that bind the inclusive community can embrace the stranger, affirming something common to both insiders and outsiders. Such inclusiveness is not always displayed in democratic cultures, but it has a natural affinity with the democratic ethos, for it is rooted in the notion that we all share, as citizens and human beings, certain rights and a common inheritance.

Is such inclusiveness utopian? Many sociologists have concluded from the historical record that it is, but the conditions that made exclusion tolerable or functional in earlier times have disappeared. Modern communications, technology, and economic exchange have made the boundaries of every modern community highly permeable and its fate mercilessly interdependent with that of others. Receptivity to outsiders—and defining one's common ground in terms of what links one to the outside world—is increasingly a condition for a community's survival. A barricaded, fortified, and exclusionary community bespeaks a premodern moral sensibility and a medieval world.

The inclusive community that the Left seeks, symbolized by Jesse Jackson's idea of a rainbow embracing all races and creeds, implies a looser set of connections than the gemeinschaft of the past, with greater freedom and choice and membership in multiple communities encouraged. This points to more fluid connections with access and exit options denied by traditional communities. Such openness adds a measure of risk and insecurity to people's lives, but it also erodes the in-group–out-group mentality that produced the xenophobia of earlier gemeinschafts.

The inclusive spirit helps to define a Left idea of community radically different from that now championed by conservatives. The Left communitarian idea of "family values," captured in the proverb "it takes a whole village to raise one child," envisions open and expansive kinship groups. In contrast to the Right's desire to return all authority and responsibility to parents, Left communitarianism recognizes that families

## The Value(s) of the Left

cannot survive without support from relatives, neighbors, teachers, and day-care providers—and without being embedded in secure economic communities. "Saving" the family means ending the myth of each family as an island haven unto itself; the real family crisis is rooted in the increasing isolation of the nuclear unit from the larger communities necessary to support it.

Similarly, no labor local or worker cooperative can stand alone as an insular community; each depends on solidaristic ties with local neighborhood groups as well as larger labor, industrial, and governmental associations. Such expansive community building requires the inclusive idea of solidarity advanced by the Knights of Labor, who, as the last chapter discussed, envisioned a national economy of interdependent cooperative associations and opened membership in their worker assemblies to almost everyone in the community.

Ironically, identity politics, the dominant force on the Left today, is reverting to an exclusionary vision, creating closed communities segregated by race, gender, and sexual orientation. The Left needs to recover the wisdom of the old Hasidic proverb: "How does one know when the night is over? When it becomes light enough to see the faces of the persons next to you and recognize that they are your brother and sister." In the daylight of Left communitarianism, they are your sister or brother whatever their race, gender, or sexual orientation.

Martin Luther King, Jr., a prophet of inclusive communitarianism, preached to civil rights activists in Montgomery, Alabama, that "the tension in this city is not between white people and Negro people. The tension is, at bottom between justice and injustice, between the forces of light and the forces of darkness. And if there is a victory, it will be a victory not merely for fifty thousand Negroes, but a victory for justice and the forces of light. We are out to defeat injustice and not white persons who may be unjust." King's "beloved community" was rooted in the black and civil rights movement, but it transcended race and held out the possibility of solidarity even with those whites who clung to segregation and racism.[3]

The Left needs to recover other voices of inclusiveness in its history. Black feminists, sensing that white middle-class sisterhood excludes not only men but themselves, have long called for a feminist movement of men and women battling all forms of injustice. A hundred years ago, Josephine St. Pierre Ruffin called for a feminist movement of women and men "directed by women for the good of women and men, for the benefit of all humanity."[4]

Today, leading black feminist bell hooks affirms that the feminist movement needs "to have a liberatory ideology that can be shared with everyone." Hooks explicitly denounces the breed of feminism that antagonizes and excludes by "identifying men as the villains, the 'enemy.'" Hooks calls for a feminist movement of men and women together "committed to feminist struggle" and to "the establishment of a new social order" free of class and race as well as gender oppression.[5]

Hooks's critique of exclusionary feminism has profound importance for the Left as a whole. The Left is always vulnerable to an exclusionary politics fueled by hatred of oppressor groups. But as Susan Griffin writes, "a deeply political knowledge of the world does not lead to a creation (and thus exclusion) of an enemy.... When a movement for liberation inspires itself chiefly by a hatred for an enemy ... it begins to defeat itself." Communities based on the exclusionary dualism of oppressed and oppressor are inevitably diminished in spirit and vision, ironically reproducing a version of the uncivil communities of tradition that created solidarity by demonizing outsiders.[6]

Identity politics and the Left as a whole have a dim future if they do not embrace a more generous and inclusive politics. "To create monsters," Griffin adds, "is to forget the political vision which above all explains behavior as emanating from circumstance, a vision which believes in a capacity born to all human beings for creation, joys, and kindness, in a human nature which, under the right circumstances can bloom." Left communitarianism recognizes that everyone is scarred by the current social order and is a potential recruit to the cause of human liberation; it aims not to crush oppressors but to change the social structures giving rise to their oppressive behavior.[7]

Overcoming the segregation of men and women, blacks and white, gays and straights within the Left is a first step in healing the deeper cleavages of the larger society. A national communitarian movement must unite suburban whites and inner-city blacks and Hispanics and also heal the rifts among the inner-city groups themselves, who are being forced to compete mercilessly for scarce jobs. Bill Clinton, saying "there is no they, only we," has begun the process of creating a national language of reconciliation and solidarity. The Left will have to struggle to ensure that such language offers an authentically inclusive vision and that it is backed up with the universal social policies that can give it substance.

Universalism is a second, closely related core value of a Left politics of community. Traditional communities typically cultivate a parochial morality favoring local people over strangers and the powerful over the

## The Value(s) of the Left

weak. While a certain local bias is inevitable, traditional communities are often excessively parochial, manifesting bias in the ugly forms described above of militaristic territoriality, racism, ethnic "cleansing," savage religious intolerance, and class domination—all of which legitimate not only community exploitation of outsiders but repression of community members by its own elites.

The Left seeks to balance parochialism with a universalism that can help build community rather than weaken it. Communities, as the Left itself demonstrates, can create solidarity on the basis of shared commitment to universal values: democracy, equality, and justice. The commitment to social justice, which rivets attention on the weakest and most vulnerable members of the community, can be an enormously powerful social glue, since it draws on our deepest moral sensibilities. Democratic communities have a special affinity for such universalistic cohesion, since democracy is rooted in the recognition of the rights of every member of the community to representation and dignity.

Nonetheless, even democratic communities, as we know from the American experience, can lapse into horrific parochialism, often expressed in majority decisions that neglect or brutalize the minority. How would the Left "civilize" such errant democratic communities? It supports, as do liberals, constitutional protections for minorities, restraining the majority from unjust uses of democratic power. But the Left's main strategy is to nurture universalistic social movements that struggle to deepen democracy while defending justice for all. As communities democratize more deeply, parochial hierarchies weaken and citizens absorb more fully the universalist ethos of democratic culture. But even radical democracy is no surefire or permanent recipe for justice, whose defense will always require social movements committed to moral universalism.

As discussed in previous chapters, the commitment to universalism emphatically does not imply a rejection of particularistic communities, whether they are the traditional blood ties of kinship, ethnicity, and religion or the postmodern identity communities of race and gender. The current task of the Left is to help connect these communities to larger universal ideals. One model discussed in the last chapter is the Jewish socialists, who taught that commitment to a Jewish identity meant a commitment as well to universal brotherhood and sisterhood. Here, the particularity of Jewishness deepened the sense of solidarity with and commitment to justice for all peoples.

Jewish socialism eventually became more Jewish than socialist, mirroring the tendency of race and gender movements today to lose sight of the universal. The women's, black, and gay movements have raised linguistic and philosophical obstacles to common ground even more profound than those of traditional ethnic and religious community. Leading theorists within these movements, most being postmodernist champions of both moral relativism and social constructionism, argue that all worldviews have their own inevitable particularities. Arguing that the "universality" of the past was nothing but the hegemony of Western white, male, and capitalist mindsets, they have insisted that women and racial minorities will never again subscribe to such damaging and illusory universalisms.

But identity movements have another side, offering a potential to coalesce in a new universalistic agenda. Left intellectuals within these movements, such as Cornel West and bell hooks, have persuasively argued that movements for sexual and racial equality are linked by common values and a shared imperative to transform the larger economic and political system. Feminist and antiracist movements were born out of a common resistance to oppression, and the systems of domination giving rise to their struggle—patriarchy, capitalism, racism—are themselves thoroughly intermeshed. The intricate and systemic interpenetration of class, race, and gender power means that the labor, feminist, and antiracist movements will have to coalesce in common cause not only to wage successful resistance but to perceive accurately the source of their own oppression.[8]

The women's, black, and gay movements—despite their radical challenge to the very idea of universality—are the most vital forces on the Left today. The communitarian solution is not to impose a false universalism but to celebrate their most authentically universalistic features, for all of them carry their own transcendent ideals of freedom and justice. There is no going back to a universalism that is blind to the uniqueness of female, black, and gay realities and to the importance of sustaining communities of resistance with their own particularisms. Re-creating a universal movement thus does not imply subordinating racial or gender movements to the Old Left's struggle for socialism or to the New Left's battle for participatory democracy. It means rather that the most fundamental moral impulses that helped unite women, blacks, and gays into their own political communities are precisely the same values—democracy, equality, and justice—that can call into being a larger and more universal civil society in the nation as a whole. The current task of the Left is to forge that new common ground, starting with the bridging politics that can bring together its own fragmented movements.

The third core value of the Left politics of community is democratic participation. The authoritarianism of traditional communities has led many to doubt whether a participatory democratic community is possible. Conservatives have argued that communities require hierarchical authority to hold things together and enforce the collective will. But while there is no flawless model, many historical examples, including New England town meetings, suggest that democratic participation can create a solidarity more durable and robust than any arising through hierarchy or coercion.

De Tocqueville was one of the first observers of American life to see democratic participation as the cement of community. De Tocqueville wrote that involvement in town meetings, and civil affairs generally, "remind every citizen, and in a thousand ways, that he lives in society." Participation was the means by which Americans were constantly connecting and spontaneously creating the bonds of friendship, trust, and cooperation that are the glue of civil society.[9]

De Tocqueville's observations have been borne out by extensive modern research. Studies in families, schools, and workplaces suggest that participation is a powerful tool for generating solidarity and collective commitments. Workers who participate in job-related decisions feel greater commitment to their work and company because they have invested their own ideas and feel a sense of ownership. The same is true in participatory classrooms, where students are far more likely to feel connected to other students than in lecture courses.

The rise of democratic participation as a basis of solidarity is profoundly threatening to contemporary elites, leading them to decry "excess democracy" as undermining community. Too much participation, writes neoconservative political scientist Samuel Huntington, "overloads" the system with demands for entitlements from greedy citizens. It is true that participation can degrade into the pure pursuit of self-interest in highly individualistic cultures like the United States. But Huntington, fearful of the democratic mobilization of ordinary citizens, chooses to ignore the importance of participation as a catalyst of community. The task of the Left is to mobilize a form of participation that can transcend market logic and nourish the social fabric.

## Left Myopias: Changing Left Values

With the opportunity and responsibility that the Left now inherits comes the need for self-criticism and change. While it can draw on a tradition of great moral force and relevance, the Left needs to renew its thinking on a wide range of issues from family to crime. To move from "moral witness" to moral voice of the majority, the Left will have to resolve contradictions that cloud its vision and weaken its credibility—especially those that concern unresolved and critical tensions between its communitarian and individualistic values—and enter new terrain now effectively monopolized by the Right.

Many conservatives and liberals believe that the Left is simply too deviant in its positions on such pivotal moral issues as crime, family, drugs, authority, and patriotism to have a credible voice. Surveys of the values of U.S. citizens suggest that this view, at least as it is expressed by a Dan Quayle or Barney Frank, is false. Ronald Inglehart, who has carried out the most extensive public-opinion research, particularly among youth, reports that Americans are increasingly tolerant, open-minded, and progressive on social and moral issues ranging from abortion to homosexuality, from women's rights to concern for the environment.[10]

Nonetheless, there is an element of truth to the idea that the Left is out of step with American moral sensibilities, and it starts with the issue of community itself. The American Dream is a paean to individualism, and one might well conclude that Americans are die-hard individualists who have no interest in the Left idea of community or any other stripe of anti-individualism. But virtually all Americans have hungered for some idea of community, traditionally embodied in the romance with the American small town. When Bill Clinton tried to counter the charge that he lacked "family values," he reached to Al Gore, another Southerner who could credibly claim roots in the small-town community culture that still symbolizes America's moral fiber. In the 1980s, the communitarian side of the American tradition expired in the roaring heat of Reaganesque individualism, and Americans are now seeking a way to restore the balance.

The Left, moreover, is itself a balance of individualistic and communitarian values, and, with the exception of some of its utopian offshoots, has never embraced a pure communitarianism that would place it off the American political map. Indeed, the principal charge of both liberals and conservatives has been that the Left's problem is its ultra-individualism. As the last chapter discussed, the Left is typically seen as the embodiment of the 1960s principle, "do your own thing." At minimum, this suggests that the Left is not so anti-individualistic as to render itself incapable of speaking to ordinary Americans.

But the Left faces problems in its effort to reconcile an undeniably

## The Value(s) of the Left

fierce individualistic streak with its community values. To skeptics, the Left is seeking to have its cake and eat it too. Leftists idealize solidarity and community, but many are disinclined to accept collective constraints on their own behavior. To critics, this undermines the credibility of the commitment to community, since the very essence of community implies acceptance of responsibilities and obligations to the collectivity that inevitably restrict individual freedom.

In fact, the Left's thinking on individualism and community may need revising in several fundamental ways. First, the Left needs to be fully authentic, that is, true to its own personal commitments. The reality is that many leftists are intensely individualistic and are prepared to accept in their own lives only limited forms of community. As the 1960s made painfully apparent, leftists have all too often set up moral standards for others that they cannot fulfill themselves. This leads, at best, to utopianism and, at worst, to the kind of official political correctness, hypocrisy, and sham moralism that helped turn Eastern Europeans against their communist leaders.

Moral purity about community, or any other issue, should have no place on the left, which needs to affirm the healthy aspects of individualism. Leftists have never been able to purge themselves of competitiveness and ambition, a sign not of weakness but of human imperfection and the inevitable importance of self-interest in human affairs. It is folly to advocate a new communal order that seeks to dispense altogether with self-orientation. Leftists need to clearly define, partly through an honest assessment of their own lives, the forms of self-interest that should be protected and the forms that are pathological and subversive of civil society.

Eastern Europe has some lessons to offer here. Eastern European leftists now speak of the need for private property and market incentives, as institutional forms that protect individual liberty and the kinds of self-interest that cannot and should not be purged from social life. Ironically, when Eastern European regimes abolished property and markets in the name of communist community and the "new man," they produced a culture of distrust, competitiveness, and self-interest that ruined civil society. To survive and defend a private self, Eastern Europeans under communist governments became as sociopathic in their own way as their counterparts in Western capitalist countries.

The Left needs to critique the degraded individualism of greed and sociopathy that is the legacy of the Reagan-Bush era while defending the individualism that underpins personal freedom, tolerance, self-fulfillment, and healthy self-interest. A Left that totally repudiates individualism is not only inauthentic and self-mutilating, but it divorces itself falsely from the American tradition. The Left shares with American culture the individualistic heritage that respects the inalienable rights of the individual to life, liberty, and the pursuit of happiness.

Left communitarianism, which seeks a community nourishing the individuality of each member, embraces the historical Left struggle against state tyranny, bureaucratic repression, and the deadening conformity of contemporary capitalist culture. The Left's fight to preserve communities threatened by the market goes hand and hand with the struggle for individual freedom and self-development in a corporate world. Capitalism endangers both community and individuality, and the Left historically has struggled for both causes, differentiating itself from mainstream and conservative communitarian movements that seek to preserve community by restraining personal expression.

The most robust communitarian movements in Left history often have also been champions of expressive individualism. The early-twentieth-century International Workers of the World, or "Wobblies," were a communitarian brotherhood of thousands of hoboes and itinerant workers; the organization provided halls and houses, as Richard Flacks writes, where "itinerants could find comradeship and a place to crash . . . enabling [them] to obtain brotherly protection from police and toughs who hassled or preyed upon the hoboes." But Flacks notes that the Wobblies also championed a remarkable expressive individuality among its members: "Wobbly publications were filled with the stories, poems and drawings of hundreds of working stiffs; Wobbly streetcorner rallies featured the songs of its numbers of troubadours and provided platforms for an army of homegrown orators. And for the majority of Wobblies, who might not have had aspirations to artistic or intellectual expression, the movement in its heyday provided daily opportunities for members to test their courage in combat and in jail." The Wobblies provided an inspiring model of working-class communitarianism at the same time that they encouraged the "framework for self-development" that Flacks implies is the positive form of Left individualism.[11]

The Wobblies embodied the spirit of the anarcho-socialist tradition, which since the mid-nineteenth century in both Europe and the United States has been the Left tradition most explicitly reconciling communitarianism with expressive individuality. Pierre-Joseph Proudhon and Mikhail Bukanin, the intellectual pioneers of anarcho-socialism, defended the freedom of the individual to "seek no other sanctions for his actions than his own conscience," and if he or she so desires to "go and live in the deserts or the forests among the wild beasts." But they also rejected the bourgeois individualism that, as Bakunin wrote, "drives the individual to conquest . . . on the backs of others," or the pure individualism of anarchist Max Stirner, who wrote, "We do not aspire to a communal life but a life apart. The People is dead. Good day Self." In opposition to Stirner, Proudhon and Bakunin viewed the individual as the foundation for an authentic community of free association, which humans needed to fulfill their essentially social nature. Bakunin wrote that "man is both the most individual and the most social of animals," and American anarchist Adolph Fisher, one of the martyrs of the Chicago Haymarket debacle, proclaimed that "every anarchist is a socialist."[12]

The anarcho-socialist Left has spawned historic communitarian movements—including the Paris Commune of 1871, the radical worker self-management movements in Germany and Italy after World War I, and the Spanish anarchists of Barcelona in 1936—all championing individual rights and expressiveness through free association and democratic community. Running counter to the more centralized, authoritarian, and statist Left of the official communist movements, such movements have advocated a cooperativist, decentralized, and democratic version of a postcapitalist world. Their vision—which as we show in the next chapter must inform the economic agenda of Left communitarianism—has involved self-governing workplaces and local communities linked in larger associations of democratic industrial and political councils.

The radical student movement of the 1960s is an American model of a Left communitarian movement deeply committed to expressive individualism. As the last chapter discussed, the movement mushroomed by meeting the authentic hunger of students for community and commitment to the world, as well as for self-development and personal expressiveness. But despite its successes, the ultimate failures and decline of the student movement dramatize the need for clearer thinking on the left about the unavoidable tensions between its communitarian and individualistic souls. Part of this means responding to the hard questions raised by conservatives about what limits on individual freedom leftists are prepared to accept in the service of community, questions that the radicals of the 1960s did more to aggravate than to resolve. Leftists are often accused by conservatives and liberals of ducking tough choices, and the Left bears the burden of spelling out its vision of communal obligations and the sacrifices in individual freedom that these entail.

At the heart of any community is a set of obligations and responsibilities that limit the individual. While the Left has always championed responsibility to society, whether by recycling one's own garbage or fighting for justice, its political agenda, especially in recent years, has sought to expand rights without giving equal time to obligations. The proponents of communal obligation have been conservatives and, more recently, neoliberals such as Bill Clinton, whose pragmatic communitarianism is an effort to emphasize the reciprocity of rights and responsibilities. As the Left, in the wake of Eastern European revolutions, has started to focus on civil society, it has only begun the process of talking about a code of civic obligation and a theory of individual responsibility.

Entering the debate about responsibility is a perilous enterprise for the Left, because the Right has scurrilously appropriated the term for its own uses. Michael Katz shows that conservatives have historically exploited a moral discourse of responsibility to blame the victim. Framing the poverty debate in moral terms has long permitted elites to divert attention from economic inequities to myths about the deficient values of the poor. Since at least the beginning of the Reagan years, "responsibility" has been a political codeword for neoconservatives trying to brand single mothers, welfare recipients, and inner-city minorities as undeserving. The Reagan-Bush politics of responsibility, part of an effort to destroy the welfare state, offered a tenuous but seductive argument that the public dole undermined people's characters; "responsibility" itself was adopted as a buzzword that catered to the underlying racism and self-interest of economically squeezed voters. The whole debate was framed to focus on the values of the poor, thereby conveniently distracting attention from the morality of the elites, ultimately a far more consequential matter.[13]

But while this suggests caution in any use of the term "responsibility," the idea behind it needs to be addressed. The Left has often appeared to dismiss individual responsibility altogether, particularly in its discourse on major public issues like crime. Focusing on structural causes of crime such as poverty or racism, the Left in the eyes of the public absolves criminals of personal responsibility. As we show shortly, a concern with personal responsibility can reinforce the Left's structural analysis of social problems and can help undermine the "blame the victim" ideology that permeates the public discussion of poverty and welfare.

The Left has to address pressing moral dilemmas about responsibility that help define what community means. Are the economically dispossessed bound by the same set of civic obligations, and held to the same standard of personal responsibility, as other citizens? And what is the more general set of responsibilities and obligations that the Left views as incumbent on all citizens?

The Left has also had little to say about authority, discipline, sacrifice, and other conservative-sounding values. Such values, however, must come into play in any sustainable community; they are perceived by the majority of Americans as vital to solving our moral crisis. With such slogans as the 1960s' "Question Authority," the Left has allowed itself to be caricatured as opposed to all forms of authority and hostile to any mode of discipline, not just the brutal forms meted out by militaristic states or repressive bosses. To the public, this seems a recipe for more social disintegration, not reconstruction.

As social breakdown deepens, a frightened public will drift toward authoritarian solutions if there is no alternative view of how to restore civil society. The Left speaks broadly of just, democratic authority, but such abstractions have to be concretized in ways that speak directly to a teacher confronting one of the more than three hundred thousand kids who brings a gun into the classroom every day, or a parent who can't motivate his or her kids to stay in school. The Left's long-term structural solutions can help guide public policy, but they do not offer practical solutions for people struggling to survive in desperate here-and-now circumstances. Nor do they paint more than a schematic picture of how to revive the moral virtues that could strengthen families and communities and energize citizens to accept sacrifice for collective ends.

As the Left builds a politics of community and civil society, it will have to advance its own version of what Bill Clinton in his campaign for the presidency called a "new covenant." If the Left's version seeks a more comprehensive set of personal and social rights than Bill Clinton's, as it should, it must also embrace a more demanding set of obligations and responsibilities. Clinton proposed that welfare rights should be conditional and linked to the obligation to accept training and work. There has been justifiable reaction on the left against any curtailment of welfare rights because it appears punitive to the poor and because it is doubtful that decent opportunities for work can be made available. But the issue of welfare versus work, and the question of obligations to work, need a fuller airing on the left than they have received. A job is the strongest thread tying individuals to society, and a politics of civil society should seek to enhance not only the right and opportunity to work but the incentives to do so for those seeking state support. If the Left advocates more unconditional welfare rights than Clinton supports, what are the concomitant civic obligations that it is willing to fight for?

The Left has sometimes backed away from such discussions, assuming that they blame the victim. Instead, it should be a crusader for civic obligations that, in a community-oriented society, have to be embraced as part of the good life.

In his national-service legislation, Clinton offered a powerful example of "covenant" politics. He proposed initially that everyone was entitled to a college education but that such an expensive entitlement was only possible if graduates repaid their debt to society through several years of community service. The National Service program, while scaled back and severely underfunded, speaks effectively to the needs of a society in social breakdown and embodies the win-win logic of a civil society politics. Individuals get an education and become connected to communities. Society is strengthened in numerous ways, including the enhanced skills of the population, the mobilization of a new labor pool for community reconstruction, and the legitimation of a new ethos of giving. A Left politics in the next stage should be advancing such politics beyond the level that conservative or neoliberal politicians are prepared to move.

## Morals and Politics: The Pitfalls

Commitment to social justice and compassion for the downtrodden have always helped define the Left. But our argument for a renewed leftist focus on values implies a more explicit marriage between morality and politics than many leftist may be comfortable with. While we are arguing for a "politics of values"—a position now advanced by such diverse leftist thinkers and activists as Jesse Jackson, Cornel West, and Michael Lerner (who calls for a "politics of meaning")—the pitfalls and limits of any effort to inject morality into politics are real and need explicit attention.

Many on the left may question the reality of a values crisis, believing that the issue has been fabricated by the Right to distract attention from economic and other systemic inequities. As we just noted, the history of the Reagan-Bush years offers generous support for this notion. Talking about values has been a conscious strategy for blaming the victim, discrediting social programs, and distracting attention from the power and self-serving policies of the elites themselves.

The idea of a generalized crisis of values in the United States is, indeed, not to be taken for granted, as there are millions of ordinary citizens who live their lives according to moral principles and have strong commitments to families, neighborhoods, and indeed a national or global community. Nor is there evidence of a distinctive moral crisis among the poor, who according to surveys share the values of the rest of the population and differ mainly in the opportunities available to them. The task of the Left, then, is to turn the focus of the moral debate where it belongs: to the elites and the institutions they control.

This is not to say that the Left should ignore more general moral problems, since rebuilding the social fabric requires change in the hyperindividualistic values that permeate the entire society. But the first task is to shift the values debate into a prolonged public examination of morality at the top, where the moral decline with the greatest impact on civil society is concentrated. The elites, as we have argued, are the principal source of the moral rot leeching into the rest of the culture. A cynical public now expects to hear about the crimes of the rich and powerful and must be weaned from the media focus on scandals and personal corruption to an understanding of the institutionalized corrupt policy that is the elites' main contribution to the undoing of the social fabric. Such a shift must go beyond examining the morality of specific government initiatives like the tax and regulatory policies of the Reagan and Bush administrations, which constituted an outrageous corporate welfare system. The Left must also spotlight systemic immorality, such as the new corporate strategies in a global economy that, through capital flight and disinvestment, made the junking of workers and neighborhoods a routine tool of making money.

A second caution concerns the distinction between moral politics and moralism. Instructive is the Right's failure in the 1992 presidential campaign, when the initial focus by Bush and Quayle on "family values" had to be abandoned because it boomeranged against them. Surveys showed that people turned against the Republicans on the values issue because they resented public officials lecturing them about their conduct in the bedroom and elsewhere. Bush's and Quayle's problems partly proved the old adage that people living in glass houses should not throw stones, but, more important, they demonstrated that moralism from any quarter is unwelcome and indeed counterproductive.

Humility and tolerance, not to mention the willingness to own up to one's own moral weaknesses, must permeate the discourse of any politics of values. The Christian fundamentalist right led by preachers such as Pat Robertson, and now a vital force in the Republican Party, illustrates the dangers of moral zealousness in politics and the ease with which a politics of morality can slide into absolutism. One need only

## A Postcommunist Left Agenda

look at the Inquisition and other manifestations of religion in politics to recognize that one of the greatest historic dangers to civil society can be the moralization of politics itself.

The lesson here of Eastern European and Soviet communism should not escape the Western Left. Eastern bloc communist regimes cloaked themselves in the moral rhetoric of class equality and social justice. Never before has a ruling class so thoroughly sought to legitimate itself in the values discourse of the Left—nor imposed its moral regimen on its own population with greater dogmatism and intolerance. This not only helped undermine civil society in the communist world but created extraordinary hatred of the leaders, whose hypocrisy engendered an unprecedented sense of public betrayal. As the corruption and privileges of the communist elite became fully apparent, a population schooled in the official morality became revolted, seeking a Western capitalist "normality" that made a virtue of its amorality.

In the Western Left, the problem has cropped up in a different form: recurrent tendencies toward doctrinal or moral purity that have wreaked havoc on the Left's internal solidarity as well as undermined its credibility with the public. In the 1960s, the problem became terminal when splinter groups, such as the Progressive Labor Party, brought to the student movement a dogmatic sectarianism that helped destroy it. In the current era, it has reemerged in the incarnation of "political correctness." The Right helped create the PC myth, greatly exaggerating the Left's dogmatism while obscuring its own more consequential PC doctrine—the free-market religion that straitjackets the teaching of economics and political science in many universities and sets the limits of debate on television and in legislatures around the country. But the Left, while struggling to open the minds closed by the Right's economic dogma, *does* have its own problem of political correctness. Discussions on the left of race, class, and gender, inevitably difficult because they are so emotionally charged, are too often subjected to an orthodoxy that perversely mirrors the dogmas they have arisen to challenge.

Any movement arising out of the moral passion to combat injustice is vulnerable to moralism, and the moral sensitivities that make the Left possible can easily turn into zealotry. As the Left enters the national debate on values, it must remain hypervigilant to its own weaknesses, tolerating its own imperfectibility as well as everyone else's. The Left's greatest strength is that it is a moral movement that is not fundamentalist: the looming specter of the fundamentalist Right should remain a compelling model of what not to be.

Finally, our approach should not be mistaken as a call for a culturalist politics, which preaches morality but has no real economic agenda or political program. A politics of democratic community starts with values but can hardly end there. The purpose of the moral debate is only to lay the foundation for change in the material world. The nature of that change is our next subject.

# 8

# If Not Socialism, What?

## THE SOCIAL MARKET AND ECONOMIC DEMOCRACY

The sun has set on the prospects for socialism after the Cold War. As Paul Starr proclaimed in a funeral oratory, "it is evidently harder to enter the kingdom of socialism than for a camel to pass through the eye of a needle." But the "death of socialism," a tragedy for many on the left, may be a blessing in disguise, opening the door to more promising and pragmatic economic alternatives. The most important of these, which has been emerging quietly in the shadow of the socialism-vs.-capitalism debate, is the "social market."

While very different from each other, the two most attractive social-market models are the remarkable Mondragon cooperative economy in the Basque region of Spain and the social democracies of central Europe, especially Sweden and Austria. In a tough-minded postcommunist world, they offer hope and direction to those seeking to reconcile the ideals of democracy, community, and equality with prosperity and political realism. Defying the Reaganomic wisdom of the 1980s, they are viable economic alternatives to the "free market"; disproving leftist common sense in the 1960s, they show that a market system can operate in the social interest.

But both Mondragon cooperativism and European social democracy are imperfect models, as the severe economic and political crisis in mid-1990s Sweden most clearly attests. When the Swedish population voted out the social democrats in 1991, even many liberals pronounced it a failed experiment. Fortunately, the most serious flaws of social democracy—and of cooperativism, which has never been implemented in a large country—can be remedied by a selective marriage of the two approaches. This will take bold new thinking and action, since social democracy and cooperativism, while both important parts of the Left tradition, have been viewed as antithetical and have not been understood as the common basis for a new economic order.

The economic challenge of the post–Cold War era is to envision this new social-market economy, which has been discussed on the left mostly in the language of economic democracy, and put it to work. Building a new economic vision is critical to the Left's future, particularly in the United States, not only to help bring together the currently fragmented movements of labor, women, and racial minorities in common cause, but to ensure that the Left speaks to the national crisis of economy and community that seems certain to haunt the 1990s and beyond.

## Beyond Socialism: The Legacy of Eastern Europe

The collapse of the communist Eastern bloc has killed socialist economics for the foreseeable future. While the socialism of the Soviet Union and Eastern Europe may have been very different from the real thing, as conceived by Marx or most American leftists, it was by far the most important self-identified Marxist alternative to Western capitalism. Fairly or not, communism's abject failures have, as chapter 5 noted, thoroughly undermined whatever political credibility the socialist idea had in both East and West.

This may mainly constitute a victory for the propagandists and spin doctors of capitalism, but it is not an entirely unwarranted conclusion. Soviet and Eastern European regimes did incorporate two of the central features of traditional socialist economics: public ownership of the means of production and central government planning of the entire economy. While these helped fuel an earlier period of rapid industrialization, few economists, whether capitalist or Marxist, now defend either public ownership or central planning on the basis of the Eastern European record. Indeed, a large number of socialists have themselves turned against state-led socialism in part because of the Eastern Europe debacle.

The toxic authoritarianism of Eastern European regimes was their fatal flaw. But this scarcely implies that we can resurrect the socialist ideal by simply mixing public ownership and central planning with a healthy dose of democracy. Socialist authoritarianism was inevitable given the extraordinary centralization of power in the state that sweeping government ownership and central planning require. It is difficult to avoid the conclusion advanced now by many East European leftists that a market order is necessary not only to ensure economic viability but to protect democracy itself.

The voice of the Eastern European Left deserves a thorough hearing by the Western Left. In a trip to Eastern Europe in 1990, I found that many envisioned a new "third way" but thought it could come only after the foundations of a Western market order had been securely laid. It is easy to dismiss the East European Left as the dupe of Western propaganda, for some talked of privatization as an almost magical elixir. But few were smitten by Ronald Reagan and George Bush's free-market religion, looking rather toward Austria, Germany, or Scandinavia. Moreover, they spoke with the authority of experience about the tragedy of socialism in practice. The misty romanticism that some Western leftists have maintained about industrial development or expansive social welfare programs in state socialism could not be sustained by those who have lived the dream and found only a nightmare.

## The Social Market

The post–Cold War economic debate will not be about whether to embrace markets but what kinds of markets to embrace. The Left cannot advance a credible socialist agenda, but it has a major role to play in conceiving a market system that nurtures democracy and community.

While the emerging contest is, at the most obvious level, between U.S., Japanese, and European variants of the market economy, the deeper and more interesting competition is between two fundamentally different structural models. The "free-market" model is best exemplified by the U.S. economy under Reagan and Bush. The "social-market" model is imperfectly illustrated by both Japan and the social democratic economies of Western Europe, as well as by cooperative economies such as Mondragon. There is no pure, real-world incarnation of either model, but, as ideal types, the free market and social market define the emerging debate about the post–Cold War economic future.

Conservative and Marxist economists alike have joined in the consensus that markets are fundamentally individualistic, but this is true only of the free-market model. The idealized free market is a sophisticated accounting system for registering individual preferences and balancing supply and demand among millions of disconnected buyers and sellers. It is no accident that Robinson Crusoe is the favorite example

## If Not Socialism, What?

of free-market theorists, for he perfectly symbolizes the premise of detached, self-interested individuals acting to fill their own stomachs.

While the free market registers the desires of each individual, it is largely indifferent to the spillover effects that transactions have on the rest of society. When a factory decides to pollute, the social cost of bad air and lung disease is what economists call an "externality," a real cost but one that the owner can ignore, since society rather than the factory pays the ultimate bill. In the pure free-market model, there is no economic incentive to protect society nor any market disincentive to be antisocial; the market simply does not discriminate, operating with what passes as "benign neglect." As such neglect accumulates, with the market turning a blind eye to the millions of small and large "externalities" that affect society every day, it becomes a catastrophic social blindness that places civil society in jeopardy.

The Achilles' heel of the free market is its sociological obtuseness. Its view of human beings, as economist Herman Daly says, "is profoundly erroneous. We come into being in and through relationships and have no identity apart from them." We are not Robinson Crusoes and act like him only at great peril to the society that makes us human. A market system that is blind to social costs and benefits can produce explosive short-term growth and profits, but ultimately it shreds the social fabric that, as Adam Smith acknowledged, makes markets possible in the first place.[1]

Despite his faith in the "invisible hand," which presumably translates the greedy ambition of each individual into the good of all, Smith saw the danger in the free market's reliance on selfishness. Societies would disintegrate if everyone always acted in the egoistic mode prescribed by free-market economics. Fortunately, in Smith's late-eighteenth-century world, there were strong communities that sustained values of loyalty, altruism, and social obligation. Smith wrote that such communities cultivated "a natural sympathy" that allowed people in economic competition to live peaceably and harmoniously with one another.

Nonetheless, Smith alerted us to the basic free-market paradox. The free market requires trust and solidarity in order for buyer and seller to sit down at the same table, but its religion of self-interest relentlessly chips away at all forms of social solidarity. In Smith's day, civil society (with all its incivilities) constantly regenerated social values, but now, with the erosion of community, there is no restorative force to prevent the free market from sabotaging the conditions of its own survival.

# A Postcommunist Left Agenda

As modern free-market societies, such as the United States, succumb to violence, homelessness, and environmental and urban decay, the attractions of the social market alternative become palpable. Social-market systems, such as Japan, Sweden, and Mondragon—with far less violence and social decay than in the United States—tackle the basic free-market problem by rejecting wholesale its individualistic assumptions. Social markets presume that economic actors include communities as well as individuals, that social costs and benefits can be registered and measured, that cooperation, like competition, is essential to productivity and growth, and that there are a wide array of possible market incentives that can better preserve the social fabric while sustaining economic viability than those offered by the free market.

The social market writes social costs and benefits back into the business equation—among other ways, by internalizing the externalities. The social market gives social stakeholders—including workers, consumers, neighbors, and "public interest" representatives—a voice in corporate decisions, and it structures incentives to guarantee that the direct parties to any transaction cannot ignore the consequences of their decisions for the larger community.

The "ideal type" social market is defined by unique structures including, (1) a social accounting system for measuring and factoring social costs and benefits into economic decisions; (2) social accountability mechanisms ensuring that businesses and other economic actors are responsive to community interests; (3) distribution mechanisms that ensure a high level of equality in income and wealth; and (4) forms of economic participation and governance that institutionalize the logic of democratic community inside business itself. While existing social-market economies such as Sweden, Austria, or Mondragon differ radically in their approaches to these shared imperatives, all reject both laissez-faire and statism, neither of which is compatible with the social-market strategy. Instead, they rely on their own combinations of government intervention, employee and community representation, and self-disciplining social business practice.

Like the free market, the social market rejects government ownership of the means of production and comprehensive central planning. It is thus not a veiled reintroduction of classical socialist economics. But it reconfigures markets to promote traditionalist socialist values such as community and social justice. Social democracies rely on the tax, regulatory, and social-policy mechanisms of an activist state. Cooperativist economies do it differently, through, for example, democratic ownership arrangements that allow workers or consumers to speak up directly for the needs of their communities.[2]

Joining the fight for the social market will require new thinking on the left. The very word "market" is alien to traditional Left sensibilities. Those wedded to socialist ideals and the Marxist tradition will have to reject some of their most cherished assumptions in order to accept the idea of a market order consistent with community, equality, and justice. It will take new categories to describe innovative economic arrangements, as in Mondragon, which are market based but neither capitalist nor socialist. It will also require a deeper receptivity to communitarian economic thinking: extending the traditional Left concern with economic power and inequality to the impact of the economy on values, community (including the full and shared participation of women and racial minorities), and the social bond itself.

Nonetheless, the social-market idea has deep roots in leftist tradition, and just as the Right will champion the cause of the free market, the Left will have to lead the battle for the social-market alternative. As the Clinton administration demonstrates, even the most liberal economic and political elites in Western capitalism resist a radical break from the free-market model. Both social democracy and cooperativism arose from the Left tradition and came into being only through the struggles of Left groups committed to alternative economic values. Marxism and the Left generally has been the leading opponent of the economic individualism of the free market, implicitly carrying the seeds of a new communitarian tradition. While the social market is not socialism by another name, it enshrines values of social solidarity, cooperation, and democratic association for which the Left has always stood.

The Left needs to rediscover and reconcile in a new paradigm parts of its past that have been deeply in conflict. Social democracy arises from the socialist, state-oriented Left historically at odds with the decentralized, community-oriented Left. The Left is just beginning to find a way to reconcile these two traditions around the ideas of economic democracy and the social market.

## Social-Market Alternatives 1: European Social Democracy

The best-known examples of social-market systems are the social democracies of central Europe, including Sweden, Norway, Holland, Austria, and Germany. During the Cold War, they were lumped with the United States and Japan as free-market economies opposed to Eastern bloc socialism. But European market systems are as different from the American free market as they are from socialism.

After World War II, West Germany explicitly identified itself as a "social-market economy." Alfred Muller-Armak, a minister of state under Ludwig Erhard, coined the term in 1949 to describe his own blueprint for a modest welfare state. Erhard put this very limited social-market vision into practice in the 1950s, introducing an elaborate national pension and health scheme, as well as the state-mandated codetermination system, which put workers on the boards of directors of large German industrial concerns. The German version of the social market, ultimately a blend of Christian Democratic politics, social democratic trade unionism, and Catholic reformism, relied on state interventionism to preserve and nurture a semblance of community values and civil society in the postwar economic wreckage.

The European social marketeers—particularly in Scandinavia—envisioned government as the social conscience of market economics. Social democracy reflected the socialist dreams of the labor unions and parties that helped bring it into being; in 1928, the Swedish socialist leader Per Albin Hansson conceived social democracy as a "peoples' home" in which government would help reshape society in the spirit of "equality, concern, cooperation and helpfulness." But the power of the capitalist classes throughout Western Europe and Scandinavia prevented the social democrats from realizing their boldest aspirations. Social democracy was a compromise between socialist and free-market economics, leading to the state-guided social market that reached its most advanced form in Sweden in the 1970s and early 1980s. A political and economic crisis has engulfed Sweden since then, pointing to very significant flaws in social democracy. But the earlier accomplishments point to arrangements that need to be part of a new social-market synthesis, embodying the promise of a Left tradition that takes politics seriously and understands the potential of enlightened government to help preserve the social fabric.

Sweden's greatest accomplishment was its extensive and enlightened social-welfare system, embracing the principle of universal social rights to employment, health care, education, and housing. Swedish universalism brilliantly created a progressive social common ground, politically uniting the population in support of solidaristic and egalitarian programs. The Swedish model demonstrates that targeting the poor or any disadvantaged group is a less politically expedient strategy than the universalistic approach, perhaps the most important "Left" political insight

## If Not Socialism, What?

that President Clinton has recognized in his struggle for health care in the United States.

While justly famous for its social-welfare vision, Sweden's ingeniously designed social markets for both labor and capital also deserve close attention. The Swedes recognize that employment is the umbilical cord connecting the individual to society and that to tolerate unemployment is the fastest way to put civil society at risk. Through most of the Cold War period, the Swedish system of economic governance—bringing together national business, labor, and government in a unique social compact—kept unemployment under 2 percent while sustaining low inflation and high productivity growth. National and local boards tracked job-market trends, coordinated job training and research, and intervened early, with the help of other state agencies, to help revitalize lagging regions or industrial sectors. Full employment, viewed by free-market economists as inflationary and unachievable, helped produce not only social harmony but decades of high growth matching the best performances in the developed world.

The "solidarity-wage" policy exemplifies Swedish social-market logic. In national collective bargaining, Swedish unions fought to keep wage differentials low; notably between high-skilled and low-skilled employees as well as between blue-collar and white-collar workers and men and women. By narrowing the acceptable wage spread, the Swedes created wage inflexibilities within industries that may have contributed to recent problems in the supply of skilled labor. However, it not only helped Sweden achieve one of the most egalitarian income distributions in the world, but also created compensatory efficiencies described by Robert Kuttner: "By taking wages out of competition the system allows more productive companies to keep profits that otherwise would be bargained away in wage increases. By the same token, inefficient producers are no longer able to compete by making their workers bear the costs of their inefficiency through lower wages."[3]

Swedes pay about 50 percent of their incomes in taxes to support the education, health, child-rearing, housing, and other social needs of the entire population. A massive market distortion in free-market terms, Swedish policy has nevertheless averted the catastrophic damage to the social infrastructure now being suffered by the United States and other free-market societies. Like the United States, Sweden faces daunting challenges in the new global economy. But the Swedes can still boast of having some of the lowest rates of violence, crime, infant mortality, and homelessness in the world and health care, education and training, housing, and day care that are among the world's best. At least they do not have to rebuild their schools or cities and have spared themselves the terrible costs now burdening the United States of reconstructing the entire social fabric.

The fall of the Swedish labor government in 1991 points to newly visible limits of the Swedish social-market model. Swedish economic growth collapsed in the mid-1980s, as many of its major industries, such as shipbuilding and automaking, succumbed to foreign competition. The Swedish unemployment rate in 1992 skyrocketed to a startling 14 percent.

Swedish labor costs are too high to maintain global competitiveness, and Swedish taxes are proving higher than many Swedes want to pay. Social-market systems, like free-market ones, face enormous challenges in adapting to globalism. Social-market systems are better prepared to manage the social costs of transition and can draw on their social cohesion and tradition of government intervention to plan a national strategy of revitalization. But solutions will also require new social-market arrangements at the "macro" international level—preventing international trade from degenerating into a competition to see who can shred wages and social standards more rapidly—and also at the "micro" level of the community and workplace, where the maximum flexibility and responsiveness to change needs to be institutionalized.

Sweden's new economic problems hint at surprising weaknesses in the capacity of the Swedish model to sustain civil society itself, a potentially fatal flaw apparent to some observers even before the current crisis. After spending several years in Sweden, Alan Wolfe made the case that the Swedish welfare state both builds and erodes community. Wolfe acknowledges the contributions to equality of Sweden's enlightened system of universal health care and family and other welfare policies, and he also seems to appreciate that when everyone sends their children to the same schools and is tended in the same hospitals and clinics, cohesion and the sense of a "common fate" increase. But, like other observers, Wolfe is disturbed by indications of eroding family ties, declining volunteerism, increasing tax evasion, greater use of bicycle locks, and other telltale symptoms of the fraying of community.

It may be the very success of the welfare state that is contributing to the problem. The Swedish state symbolizes community and caring, cradling its infants in well-appointed public day-care centers and humanely tending to its elderly with personalized "meals on wheels" and expensive geriatric counseling programs. But as the state learns how to carry out these caring functions better, ordinary citizens may be shedding responsibility for them. As the state social worker becomes the old person's best friend—and in some Swedish programs, where the social worker visits every day, this is exactly what happens—family and neighbors may see less need to drop by. Likewise, as children get enlightened "surrogate parenting" in government day-care centers, parents may take the opportunity to focus more on their own lives.

Wolfe concludes that "the new welfare state increasingly enables middle class people to buy the labor of others who will perform their moral obligations for them. . . . By intervening in civil society to an extent that no one could have anticipated," Wolfe continues, the state has led to "a decline in a sense of individual moral responsibility that threatens the ability of Scandinavian societies to find new sources of moral energy."[4]

A related problem is the rise of a professionalized class of economic apparatchiks and social-service providers. The governmental "new class" that figured so prominently in Eastern bloc socialist authoritarianism has emerged with a more benign and enlightened face in Scandinavia. As the power of the new class increases, the democratic impulse declines and ordinary citizens become passive and apathetic. Particularly disturbing are reports about bored and anomic Swedish youth who seem unmotivated in schools and display little interest in politics or community affairs. Throughout the population, there are indications of growing political alienation.

The data is still out regarding Swedish civil society. But Wolfe has undoubtedly hit upon the great problematic of the welfare-state version of the social market. Governments have undeniable limits as champions of morality and community, which must ultimately be sustained in the hearts and actions of ordinary citizens. States help make democratic communities possible, but they can sabotage them when they become the primary guardians of morality or the main purveyors of affection. The ideal balance between state intervention and restraint is unclear, but the excesses of statism in the social democratic model point to the value of the cooperativist alternative, where the state plays scarcely any role at all.

## Social-Market Alternatives 2: Cooperativism and Mondragon

Mondragon is not a household name, but it should be and may soon become so. The most successful cooperative economy in modern history, it consists of a remarkable group of worker-owned and -managed

## A Postcommunist Left Agenda

companies in the Basque region of Spain. Having developed into a world-class manufacturing giant, Mondragon is the most impressive symbol of the cooperativist type of social-market economy. It has its own serious limitations, but without any dependence on "big government," it may be the most attractive existing model for an alternative economic future in the United States.

Mondragon reflects a cooperativist impulse that has a long but largely forgotten history on the left. Cooperativism involves a vision of an alternative to capitalism based not on government but on new forms of community and cooperation within society and business itself; as such, it seems antithetical to the emphasis on the state that gave rise to social democracy and largely defined the Left during the communist era. But if we go back to the earliest traditions of socialism—emerging in France after the Revolution of 1789 in the thinking of visionaries like Robert Owen, Charles Fourier, and Henri de Saint-Simon—we find a movement that, as Martin Buber wrote, sought "to substitute society for State to the greatest degree possible, moreover a society that is 'genuine' and not a State in disguise." This socialism envisioned, as the St. Simonians proclaimed, an "association of workers" bonding ordinary employees together to control their own workplaces and industries. It also understood that building new egalitarian bonds of solidarity in civil society was the road to economic health.[5]

Michael Harrington describes this first socialist vision as an essentially communitarian idea based on the self-organization of workers and the initiatives of family, neighborhood, and civic associations rather than the dictates of the government. "A striking word," Harrington writes, "had come into play, one that echoes throughout the history of French socialism: *association*." This original socialism, Harrington adds, "was concerned with morality, community and feminism," a mixture of utopian and pragmatic visions of cooperative work and living. It recognized social solidarity and the struggle for gender and racial as well as economic equality as central to the Left mission.

Karl Marx embraced in his early and most philosophical work this original socialist view of a humanistic and communitarian alternative to capitalism. While Marx wrote relatively little about the shape of socialism, he always insisted that it meant the "withering away of the state." This makes clear, as Harrington argues, that socialism "is the transformation of society, not of the government." While Marx denounced the utopians who rejected labor organizing within capitalist industries in favor of communal alternatives in the here and now, he remained a lifelong critic of economic individualism and fully embraced in his long-term vision the concept of society controlled from the bottom through self-organized communities of workers and citizens.

The anarcho-syndicalist tradition of the Left also helped spawn cooperativism. Anarchist Max Stirner wrote that "Every state is a tyranny, be it the tyranny of a single man or a group," and Pierre-Joseph Proudhon proclaimed that "To be governed is to be watched over, inspected, spied on, directed, legislated, regimented, closed in, indoctrinated, preached at, controlled, assessed, evaluated, censored, commanded; all by creatures that have neither the right, nor wisdom, nor virtue." Like the early French socialists and in radical opposition to the statist Left of communism, the anarcho-syndicalists advanced an essentially communitarian economic vision based on self-administered forms of worker and citizen cooperation. As Mikhail Bukanin pronounced: "Anarcho-syndicalists are convinced that a Socialist economic order cannot be created by the decrees and statutes of government, but only by the solidaric collaboration of the workers . . . that is, through the taking over of the management of all plants by the producers" who "carry on production and the distribution of the products in the interest of the community." This cooperativist vision gave rise to the movements for worker control in Germany and Italy after World War I and during the Spanish Civil War.[6]

Cooperativism has a long history even in the United States, whose first national labor movement, the Knights of Labor, rallied to the cooperativist banner, as chapter 6 discussed. In recent years American environmentalists, feminists, and racial minority movements are helping rekindle interest in economic cooperativism, based on the recognition that neither the free market nor the state has served their interests. Thus Herman E. Daly and John B. Cobb, in a leading environmentalist manifesto, *For the Common Ground,* call for "rethinking economics on the basis of a new concept of *Homo economicus* as person-in-community" and argue that ecological sanity depends on a new communitarian economic vision rooted in rebuilding nurturant social bonds at every level of society. An economics of consideration for the environment, they argue, must start with consideration for other people, and economic development cannot be separated from community development—the central premise of cooperativism.[7]

Likewise, Left feminists have recognized that the liberation of women requires ending their economic subordination and dependency, which in turn requires central attention to families and communities as pivots of the economy. This helps refocus economic thinking toward civil society, reawakening the central cooperativist insight that economic success depends on the quality of community both at home and work. The state can help create the proper incentives but cannot manufacture the underlying social solidarity on which the social market ultimately depends.

Mondragon, the most promising of all global cooperativist models, started as a daring effort by one Catholic priest and five of his followers to create a small, cooperatively owned manufacturing enterprise known as ULGOR. But Mondragon has since expanded into a complex of over one hundred industrial cooperatives linked to a cooperative banking system and cooperative farming enterprises, schools and universities, supermarkets and other consumer stores, hospitals, and even a cooperative social welfare system. With a base in all four provinces of the Basque region, Mondragon has evolved into a breathtaking model of how to organize a regional—and increasingly national—economy on cooperativist principles.[8]

Started in the 1940s by José María Arizmendi, a priest deeply influenced by the cooperativist tradition, Mondragon demonstrates how markets, without any state intervention, can operate on democratic, communitarian, and egalitarian principles. Part of the secret is the design of Mondragon's cooperative enterprises, which solved fatal flaws in pre-Mondragon coops. In the famous nineteenth-century British Rochdale consumer coops, which helped launch the coop movement, nonworker investors were accorded ownership rights including the vote. In the Pacific Northwest plywood producer coops, the longest-surviving coops in the United States, coop members hired employees who were not considered part of the community and could not vote. In many worker-owned firms, different employees had different degrees of voting power, depending on the amount of money they had invested. In all cases, these led to deformations in the coops' functioning as communities and to their eventual failure.

As David Ellerman has pointed out, pre-Mondragon coops still linked ownership partially to capital. Every member was vested with a voting share in the cooperative, but this involved a tacit acceptance of the capitalist principle tying capital to control. This logic still prevails in most employee stock-ownership programs (ESOPs), the dominant form of worker ownership in the United States, where more shares entitle a worker to more votes.[9]

Mondragon reconceived ownership as a social right attached to membership in the cooperative community rather than a right connected to capital possession or investment. Each Mondragon worker has one, and only one, vote for the same reason that each citizen in a democracy does: all have the same human stake in the community and therefore are entitled to the same degree of representation. Cooperative members invest money in the coop and receive interest on their contribution, but the biggest investor has the same vote as the smallest. Mondragon's ownership rules prevent outside investors from taking control of the firm, keep insiders from employing nonvoting wage workers, and help to account for the communitarian and egalitarian ethos that keeps the highest coop salary only six times that of the lowest.[10]

As a community member, a Mondragon employee's moral claims on the enterprise are radically different from that of a free-market wage worker. Firing a worker is something akin to disowning a son or daughter—as in Japan a mortal wound to the corporate family. British journalist and cooperativist advocate Robert Oakeshott, who has done the most to bring Mondragon to the attention of the rest of the world, reports that there has not been a single involuntary layoff in Mondragon's history. Cooperative bylaws stipulate that in case of unavoidable stoppage or downsizing, affected employees are assured of employment in other cooperatives. If an emergency dictates layoffs, worker-members are assured payment of 80 percent of their salary until they are brought back to work, which Oakeshott characterizes as the equivalent of "an employment guarantee."[11]

In return, Mondragon coops expect and generate unusually high levels of employee responsibility, the flip side of the communitarian bargain struck by worker-owned companies. Mondragon's coop members are among the world's most motivated and self-disciplined employees and have imposed on themselves, as Oakeshott reports, a formidably "tough regime of labor and work discipline." They upbraid—and penalize through pay cuts—fellow employees who do not live up to their collective codes of commitment and hard work. They commit heavily to the governance and communal life of the firm: electing the board members who run the firm, participating directly in governance and strategic planning as members of the General Assembly, self-managing themselves in work teams and other shop floor and social councils, and helping supervise fellow workers. They invest the great proportion of their dividends, profit shares, and life savings back into the firm, reciprocating the long-term commitment the firm has made to them.

The uniqueness of Mondragon cooperativism, however, is not only the unbreakable social-market covenant binding the coop to its members, but the relations of the base coops, such as ULGOR, with each other and with the entire cluster of "secondary coops," especially the Caja Laboral Populaire or coop bank. Mondragon proves that market firms can extensively cooperate and by doing so enhance their prospects for economic viability and prosperity.

Base and secondary coops are intertwined, as in the case between Japanese firms and their bankers and suppliers, through overlapping ownership. Mondragon's secondary coops, such as the bank, are owned partly by their own workers, but also by each of the base coops that they service. The governing board of the Caja is selected in equal numbers from the bank's employees and representatives of ULGOR and the other producer coops. This ensures extensive social interaction and community building among members of different enterprises, transforming the anonymity of free-market relations to the highly personalized relations of the social market.

As in Japan, firms in Mondragon blend competition with mutual aid and extensive joint consultation and planning. A contract of association among all the base coops mandates that each one "will respect the principle of intergroup loyalty and mutual assistance when formulating future plans concerning production, selection of personnel," and related matters. Other things being equal, coops will order supplies preferentially from each other, avoid business directly harmful to another coop's interests, and offer mutual help, as when an expanding coop "borrows" or permanently takes on members of a downsizing coop. Formal cooperative associations have emerged among coops working in the same sector, such as the ULARCO network in manufacturing. The member coops cooperate on matters of finance, personnel, and market planning, and pool their profits for the purpose of calculating individual member annual dividends.

The bank is the nerve center of Mondragon's expansive nongovernmental form of planning. Pre-Mondragon coops usually failed because they were starved of capital by hostile financiers. ULGOR and other base coops avoided this fate by mandating that as much as 85 to 90 percent of annual profits, including dividends paid to individual members, be plowed back into the firm, ensuring a healthy internal supply of funds for expansion. But the bank also pays a critical role in financing, initially capitalizing a new coop, tiding it through hard times, and funding new research and technology.

The bank is a pioneer in "social entrepreneurship." A large entrepreneurial section of the bank works closely with any community members who want to start a new coop. It provides capital and technical assistance

## If Not Socialism, What?

for the market analysis as well as a "godfather" who mentors the entrepreneurs until the firm is securely underway. The bank midwifed scores of new coops in the last two decades, and it is the secret to Mondragon's status as one of the world's most prolific job creators.

Many of the left have dismissed coops because while they are unarguably more accountable to their worker-owners, there is no reason to believe that they will better serve community needs than the traditional capitalist firm. In Mondragon, however, this is clearly not the case. The most visible sign of social accountability is the constitutional provision that each coop distribute 10 percent of its profits to the local community. Mondragon also mandates that all business decisions must explicitly take into account the needs of the community. The coops contribute extensively to educational, social, and cultural clubs and activities in Mondragon and surrounding cities while also directly providing jobs, services, and goods.

The base coops and bank study the impact of their decisions on the community and modify their business plans accordingly. In this spirit, the bank "instead of being guided by principles of profit maximization . . . looks upon profits as a limiting factor . . . investment decisions are based upon judgments of the social and economic needs and interests of the people directly involved and in terms of long-range plans for the development of the region."[12]

An intimate and mutually sustaining relation between coops and the community dates from the founding of ULGOR. In 1956, when its original five founders started to raise money for their new venture, they went first to their own savings and then to friends and neighbors. As in Japan, where late-night drinking in restaurants and geisha houses builds community within and between firms, drinking clubs played a surprisingly pivotal role in creating Mondragon and keeping it going. ULGOR's founders were all members in good standing of the *chiquitos,* the Basque drinking clubs of between ten and twenty members that are part of the secret of Basque solidarity. The starting capital for ULGOR came heavily from drinking club associates, a factor of such importance that Oakeshott implies that anyone hoping to replicate Mondragon will have to start by discovering their own local form of chiquito life.[13]

The ultimate reason for Mondragon's success is its sustained financial and moral support by the community. The coop bank, with local branches throughout the Basque region, has grown rapidly, reflecting not only the 1 percent higher interest rate that, by Spanish law, it is entitled to pay depositors but the genuine community desire to support the coops. A high percentage of both coop employees and outsiders bank at the Caja, ensuring the secure capital base whose absence doomed pre-Mondragon coops.

Ethnic homogeneity and long-standing Basque solidarity help explain the coops' success, and many observers note that the Basques had a rich communitarian life long before the rise of the coops. But their new economic system has provided a more stable employment base and transformed their communal life. A new set of cooperative social institutions—each jointly owned and managed by employees, clients, and the larger community—now knits Mondragon together, including cooperative hospitals and clinics, kindergartens, schools and technical colleges, day-care centers, insurance companies, and retail stores, as well as the coop factories. This nontraditional communitarian infrastructure services the social needs of the population, undergirds the stability of families and neighborhoods, and sustains Mondragon's tangible warmth and morality.

The coops are a departure from the traditional Basque economy, which did not embody democratic, employee, or community ownership. The new cooperative economy, while consistent with Mondragon's traditional communitarian values, was grafted onto a very different agrarian and craft economy; it is not "organic to" the Basque region nor suited only to traditional societies (which Mondragon, a high-tech giant, no longer is). Oakeshott argues that Mondragon's economic model can be adapted successfully to more heterogeneous and less communal cultures such as Great Britain and the United States, offering not only economic renewal but powerful communitarian medicine for ailing civil societies.

Mondragon has proved that a cooperativist social market can become a world-class competitor, drawing on its deep roots in a local community and an ingenious system of nonstatist planning and cooperation. Nonetheless, as a purely private-sector, nongovernmental model, it has its own limits. Mondragon has brought prosperity to its members but does not provide an answer for those not lucky enough to work in one of the coops. If it is to be a model for entire countries such as the United States, Mondragon has to address the underclass tragedy and the general problem of unemployment and underemployment. While it offers a sterling example of job creation, Mondragon's magic dims for those mismatched for the job market and unable or unwilling to work. Their problems almost certainly require some form of public education and national welfare system in addition to the training programs and charities offered by coops in a local community.

Government is also necessary to protect the rights of coop members. Researchers in the 1980s found that Mondragon's female employees endured harassment from fellow workers, as well as obstacles to promotion and underrepresentation in coop decision-making bodies. Such discrimination, which Mondragon has begun to rectify, reflects parochialisms in the community that cannot assuredly be eliminated by the community itself. Just as the federal government in the United States had to intervene to eliminate legalized racism in Southern states, the rights of minorities in any cooperativist system require governmental protection. Enlightened coops and communities can go a long way by themselves to protect minorities by educating members and enforcing internal codes of ethics and nondiscrimination. But the historical record—and the current explosion of communitarian racism and violence from Serbia and Bosnia to Armenia and Azerbaijan—does not support those who believe that these kinds of initiatives eliminate the need for public regulation and legal safeguards.

The problem of rich and poor communities—leading to radical inequalities among coops that are widely dispersed geographically—is another potentially intractable problem for those envisioning Mondragon as a national model. The Mondragon social market is exquisitely structured to build solidarity within and across coops in a given community; as noted earlier, coops restrict income inequality to a six-to-one ratio—lower than any other system in the industrialized world—while also maintaining mechanisms for partially redistributing income from better-off to poor coops. But just as Mondragon does not substantially redistribute income or wealth from workers to the unemployed, it does not offer a clear strategy for equalizing wealth among communities with vastly different resources. Theoretically, solidarity extending across entire regions of the country could lead prosperous areas to subsidize poor ones, but such solidarity exists, if at all, only in far more localized communities. The social-welfare states of Europe arose to provide public remedies to this problem, and it is difficult to imagine any strategy for national equality that does not depend partly on government.

## Toward Synthesis: Economic Democracy and the Social Market

The limits of Sweden and Mondragon as models are formidable, but each offers partial solutions to the shortcomings of the other. In the emerging postcommunist economic competition, social-market systems will prevail only if they evolve toward a new synthesis of social democracy and cooperativism.

Historically, as we have emphasized, social democracy and cooperativism have seemed contradictory, since one relies on a centralized national government and the other is voluntaristic and rooted in decentralized communities. But there is an underlying convergence in philosophy and practice. Both view the social costs of the free market, now so transparent in the crumbling social fabric of the United States, as unacceptable and avoidable. Both look to a market alternative that is guided by the principles of community, democracy, and social justice. In very different ways, both institutionalize market-based systems of social accountability that are intended to reconcile prosperity with equality and civil society.

Moreover, both offer the right medicine for the problems of the other. Social democracy has developed the governmental apparatus that can help solve the problems of minority rights, inequality, and large-scale poverty and unemployment for which cooperativism has no proven answers. Cooperativism offers the participatory foundation, both in the community and the workplace, to nourish the civil society and economic dynamism that a statist social democracy is not able to sustain.

The theoretical foundations for this new synthesis have begun to emerge on the left, particularly in the United States. Well before the crumbling of the Berlin Wall in 1989, the New Left of the 1960s had denounced the authoritarianism of Eastern bloc state socialism and had begun searching for democratic and community-oriented alternatives. There was no explicit rejection of socialism as a guiding concept but rather a gradual shift toward "economic democracy" as the new vision of the Left.

The new vision does not use the language of the social market (reflecting the traditional Left hostility to the market) nor does it explicitly seek to reconcile social democracy and cooperativism. As we argue below, the new democratic paradigm should acknowledge its embrace of social markets and adopt a more explicit communitarian language and perspective. But the idea of economic democracy has offered a felicitous umbrella under which both social democrats and cooperativists can mingle and begin to envision an agenda uniting the strongest features of both.

In the United States, the rise of the new paradigm was driven by increasing disenchantment with the communist model, the emergence of a New Left committed to "participatory democracy," and the increasing recognition that economic democracy not only embodied core Left values but was the secret to the reconstruction of the American economy in an era of fierce global competition. At the same time that American corporations were beginning to emulate the participatory practices of the Japanese, Left thinkers began to produce a flood of books on workplace and industrial democracy. With the publication in 1980 of *Economic Democracy* by Derek Shearer and Martin Carnoy, who defined the new vision in terms of both cooperative control by workers over their own companies and democratic control over national economic decision making, the ascendancy of the new paradigm was symbolically affirmed.

Economic democracy became a home for many partially contradictory visions on the left. Social democrats identified with the new paradigm (represented today by such thinkers as Robert Kuttner and the contributors to his journal, *The American Prospect*) see public regulation of markets as key to the democratic idea, with an activist government—as in Sweden and other Western European social democracies—as the central player. Economic democrats of the cooperativist variety, who seek to go "beyond the market and the state," as Severyn Bruyn and James Meehan titled their cooperativist manifesto, see cooperative projects in the workplace or community, linked nationally by Mondragon-like financial cooperatives and industrial federations, as the future of economic democracy. While they may quarrel about the relative value and importance of their various projects, the new paradigm gives them a common language and points to the possibilities of a new synthesis.[14]

In a series of publications in the 1980s, Left economist Samuel Bowles and his collaborators advanced the most systematic formulation of the new paradigm and the one with the most promising melding of social democratic and cooperativist ideas. Like Carnoy and Shearer, they envision economic democracy in terms of far-reaching new cooperative control by workers and communities from the "micro" realm of the shop floor to the "macro" realm of global governmental and financial institutions. Their cooperativism is rooted mainly in their emphatic embrace of worker and community control at the local level. Arguing for a fundamental "right to a democratic workplace," they advocate a vast network of "worker owned and managed cooperatives," basing the argument not only on traditional Left concerns for justice but on research showing that employee participation and ownership are the key to high productivity and global competitiveness. They also champion community-owned corporations and investment boards—not unlike the Mondragon cooperative bank—which help ensure that cooperative workplaces serve not just the parochial interests of the worker-owners but the common good of the local community.[15]

But such micro-level cooperativism, they argue, ultimately requires macro-level social democracy. Without employment security, workers will not develop the loyalty and commitment that make cooperation on the job possible. Bowles and his colleagues thus argue that "Direct intervention to promote the right to a job, to promote employment security, is the first requirement of any democratic alternative." Sounding very much like Swedish-style social democrats, they call for massive government intervention not only for full employment but for high-wage jobs, social welfare, a modernized public infrastructure, and environmental protection.[16]

A similar synthesis was offered by the late Michael Harrington, the influential Left thinker and leader of the Democratic Socialists of America, who died just before the collapse of communism. While Harrington wore the "democratic socialist" label, he agreed that economic democracy based on "control from below by people and their communities" was the essence of the Left vision. Like Bowles and his associates, he championed a new localist commitment to worker cooperatives and community-controlled enterprises, one tied to a national (and now globalist) Swedish-style strategy of public investment and government planning. Identifying himself with both the "communitarian-socialist" and social-democratic traditions, Harrington explicitly embraced markets, arguing that a combination of government regulation and cooperativism could make them function in the social interest.[17]

The economic-democracy paradigm is a major intellectual advance, a postsocialist vision around which all elements of a fragmented Left may be able to unite. But to succeed, it will have to embrace a more robust version of the cooperativist perspective. An element of the state-socialist tradition lingers in the tendency to see government as the main player in the macro realm and in the failure to apply cooperativist principles beyond the workplace and local community. The most important lesson of Mondragon is that micro-oriented cooperativism can prosper only when wedded to a macro cooperativism. This implies a vital role, now reserved largely for government in traditional Left thinking, for federations of worker cooperatives and intercommunity organizations at every level of industry and society. Macro-level cooperativism does not by any means end the need for government and social democratic commitments, for reasons discussed earlier. But it deserves a larger place in an emerging Left economics based on the communitarian insight that the health of the economy and civil society cannot be separated.

Paul Hirst, drawing on French associationism and British guild socialism (especially as advanced by the famous industrial theorist G. D. H. Cole), conceives a new macro-cooperativist political economy that he calls "associative democracy." Embracing "socially embedded" markets and the idea that "individual liberty and human welfare are both best served when as many of the affairs of society as possible are managed by voluntary and democratically self-governing associations," Hirst envisions social and economic planning carried out through a dense network of cooperating firms, labor organizations, and trade and civic associations, all working in partnership with regional and national governments. Rather than simply implementing plans hatched by central bureaucrats, each industry and region would build policy from the bottom up. Companies have powerful interests, he points out, in cooperating on everything from training and research to quality control and customer satisfaction. The secret is to help build the democratic associative structures that can define and implement this economic "common good." The preconditions, Hirst argues, are "to create sufficient levels of solidarity and trust between the members of economic associations, and between those associations" such that "trust both overcomes the pressures toward increasingly self-interested behavior in competitive markets and by doing so enables the market economy" to be both efficient and socially responsive.[18]

A small number of left thinkers are beginning to highlight empirically the importance of macro-cooperativist strategies in Europe, Japan, and the United States. For example, Michael Piore and Charles Sabel have helped identify the crucial role of cooperation among competing businesses, showing that particular communities of firms succeed or fail as a group, reflecting the strength of underlying bonds of kinship and civic association in the region. In studies of world-class economic performers in northern Italy, they have shown that economic innovation, job creation, and productivity all depend on firms' pooling resources and sharing training and research programs in a cooperative manner that defies the traditional view of the market. Piore and Sabel's work hints that planning among communally linked firms in the private sector is every bit as vital as state planning.

In a series of important books, sociologist Severyn Bruyn has expanded this macro-cooperativist view, showing the rich potential of regional, national, and global networks of industrial and civic associations. Bruyn highlights the potential of trade associations, which are embryonic cooperativist federations of businesses. He shows that when they represent democratic firms—as in the case of the Swiss, Dutch, and American federated dairy cooperatives which help regulate the quality, safety, and price of milk as well as provide social welfare for industry employees—they can carry out comprehensive social and industrial planning in the public interest. On another front, Bruyn also shows that unions, state governments, and other bodies, separately and together, are beginning to cooperate to wrest control from banks of the $3 trillion worth of American pension funds and invest them in affordable housing and community economic development. Along with the growing numbers of "social investment" brokerage houses, such as Franklin Research and Good Money, which work with many others to help direct billions of dollars toward socially responsible companies, these efforts constitute initial steps toward a cooperativist, nonstatist strategy to transform the capital market into what Bruyn explicitly calls a social market.[19]

Macro-cooperativism is important for Left economic thinkers in another sense: it offers an economic vision that may help unite women, African Americans, and other racial minorities. Macro-cooperativists understand that government alone cannot ensure either the equality of women and racial minorities or broader economic justice and health. By rooting economics in the social relations of civil society—including family, neighborhood, and ethnic and racial communities—cooperativism (and social-market thinking more generally) tightly links economic change and the remaking of civil society.

In cooperativist thinking, family and community relations are not marginalized to the sphere of reproduction but are seen as constitutive of the market itself. Real economic change will have to involve more egalitarian families and more enlightened race relations, for this is the only way to create the solidarity across race and gender necessary for both micro and macro levels of economic cooperation. A truly social market, moreover, is one in which all segments of the community participate directly and on equal terms: in the workplace, in trade associations and industrial federations, and, of course, in government itself.

Left thinkers face the challenge of more fully synthesizing economic democracy and economic communitarianism. The cooperativist tradition and the language of the social market can light the way.

If Not Socialism, What?

## Unexpected Opportunities: Social-Market Politics in the United States

A theoretical synthesis may be emerging, but in practice can the institutions of cooperativism be reconciled with those of social democracy? Could the Swedes, for example, sustain the basic framework of their social-democratic system while embracing the model of Mondragon cooperative production? History offers some encouraging clues. In the early 1980s, when social democracy in Sweden was prospering, many Swedes were already arguing that social democracy could not long flourish without kindling a new participatory spirit at the grass roots. The Swedish labor movement, and some Swedish industrialists, began implementing workplace democracy and innovative forms of employee stock ownership, recognizing that if the workers themselves were not more highly motivated and involved, no amount of state action could solve the emerging problems of global competition or the eroding sense of community. Before succumbing to the global "free market" mania of the 1980s, Sweden had already begun the journey toward a cooperativist social democracy.

The United States under Bill Clinton emerged, quite unexpectedly, as the most interesting laboratory for a new social-market synthesis. This is ironic, since the United States has been the most hostile of all the Western industrialized nations to the welfare state and remains among the least communitarian of all societies. But in his initial call for a "new covenant," Clinton signaled a break with free-market thinking and a shift to a new, more community-oriented economic vision integrating elements of both social democracy and cooperativism.

After he became president, Clinton abandoned his new-covenant language and retreated significantly from the communitarian promise of his campaign. The task of the Left in the Clinton years is to help mobilize a grassroots movement that will hold him to (and push him beyond) his early rhetoric. At the time of this writing, in the second year of the Clinton administration, there remains the possibility of Clinton's moving the country in a new economic direction, but only if intense pressure is mobilized from the grass roots.

Bill Clinton has always distanced himself from "big government" and traditional liberalism. Yet, during the campaign and throughout his presidency, he remained committed in rhetoric to an expansive social agenda—including universal health care, minority and women's rights, affordable housing, public and private child care, revitalized public education, and environmental protection—all of which require an activist government. Moreover, Clinton embraced, notably in his health-care legislation, a Swedish-style universalism, targeting social programs not to the poor but to the entire population. Such universalism is the strongest part of the social democratic tradition, not only disproportionately helping the poor and minorities but uniting the entire society in a progressive common interest.

Clinton's rejection of "tax and spend" approaches to social problems and his budget-cutting passions, driven by the politics of the deficit, clearly mark him as different from the European social democrat. But precisely because financial and ideological straitjackets prevent him from depending on a central government in the European fashion, he has to rely on states, communities, and empowered citizens to help conceive and administer his programs. Clinton has a modest social-democratic agenda that can only be implemented through activism at the grass roots. This may help explain his embrace of national service and a community-oriented agenda, including community development block grants, community development banks, and "community empowerment."

Like the European social democrats, candidate Clinton proposed major public investment to rebuild the infrastructure, revitalize education and job training, and stimulate growth. But the deficit, the weakness of labor, and the influence of his corporate patrons turned Clinton into a militant deficit hawk who spent less on domestic social programs in his first year in office than his predecessor, George Bush. This reversal, deeply disappointing to Left social democrats, had, however, a potential silver lining; it created a powerful incentive for Clinton to marry his governmental activism with a cooperativist approach, one that "grows" the economy by tapping the power of community to increase productivity and competitiveness.

Clinton's turn away from public investment was associated with a more general regressive shift toward the free-market economics of his Republican predecessors in the White House, visible in his embrace of the North American Free Trade Agreement (NAFTA) and associated free-trade initiatives with Asian and other international trading partners. But despite the rightward turn of his economic policies, Clinton did not reject his pragmatic communitarian dreams of rebuilding the social fabric, nor his social-democratic ideals of economic and social security. As Clinton reduced government spending further, cooperativist strategies increasingly became the only way that he could implement his economic and social aims. Beyond seeking to restore Clinton's commitment to public investment, the Left needs to push him toward the ambitious cooperativism that could help sustain both his presidency and the fragile national social fabric.[20]

Employee participation and worker ownership, two cornerstones of cooperativism, are potentially of great importance, since Clinton has rhetorically embraced both. In his campaign, he explicitly recognized the importance of a "New Covenant for labor and management based on participation, cooperation and teamwork," claiming that "such an approach to working smarter will have to be adopted if America is to regain its competitive edge." Clinton has also explicitly endorsed employee ownership, understanding that, along with shop-floor participation, it can increase worker motivation and productivity without bleeding the public budget. Since at least half of the largest American corporations have already introduced limited forms of worker participation, and over ten thousand companies have started employee stock-ownership plans (ESOPS), the seeds of Clinton's tentative cooperativism preceded him and continue to grow.[21]

Knowledgeable observers know that most forms of labor-management cooperation are "shotgun marriages with corporations holding the shotgun" and that ESOPS have emerged mainly as financial gimmicks to help companies avoid takeovers and exploit tax breaks. Bill Clinton also seems to understand this, and he has gone on record in support of more promising forms of employee involvement and ESOPS, including a proposal that would encourage full democratic labor participation in America's corporate boardrooms. While maintaining his distance from the labor movement, he has also recognized that worker participation is more likely to bear fruit if shaped jointly by strong unions, and he has made tentative steps toward labor-law reform that would catalyze the growth of democratic unions—a very high Left priority from both the social democratic and cooperativist perspectives.

Moreover, Clinton appears to support a wide spectrum of other Mondragon-style initiatives. These include using corporate and public pension funds for social ends such as affordable housing, encouraging other forms of private "social capital" that can be invested in communities through community development credit unions or the Community Re-investment Act, and promoting a new agenda of community and national service. The Clinton administration has signed on to a modest social-democratic agenda centered on universal health care, along with

## A Postcommunist Left Agenda

an embryonic cooperativist agenda of economic democracy and community empowerment. While the commitment is cautious and limited, it is a first step toward the new social market that could ultimately replace the free market in the United States and much of the rest of the world.

Clinton's words will remain mostly rhetoric unless social movements mobilize to make them a reality. Clinton is beholden to many entrenched interests, including the hundreds of large corporations that helped fund his campaign. To overcome their resistance and bring to fruition even the modest version of the "new covenant" that candidate Clinton proposed will require organizing the constituencies, including workers and the labor movement, women, and inner-city minorities, who potentially have the most to gain. The larger political task is to move Clinton beyond his own cautious dreams and help build a grass-roots tide for the more ambitious and comprehensive social-market vision and program that could finally put the failed free-market idea to rest.

The Left has criticized Clinton for abandoning his commitment to public investment and defunding social programs, seeking to turn him into a partner for social democracy. Much of Clinton's "economic security" agenda can only be realized by government spending on job creation and training, affordable housing, child care, and other social democratic programs, and the Left should take the lead in mobilizing support for these initiatives. But the Left's primary opportunity (other than universal health care, a very high Left priority) during the Clinton years may be cooperativist strategies that do not bleed the federal budget and that can win some support among the moderate Democrats and Republicans who are Clinton's political base. Worker ownership, pension reform, employee participation, community development, labor law reform, and social investment are prime examples of such strategies, and Clinton has verbally endorsed them. The role of the Left is to hold him to his words and help him envision comprehensive, democratic initiatives in each area rather than opportunistic changes that reinforce existing power relations. Left social democrats should join Left cooperativists in this struggle for cooperativist alternatives, recognizing that the political prospects for massive public investment are dim and that the cooperativist moment may be closer at hand.

The disappointments of Clinton's early economic initiatives are not surprising. No president can break significantly from the corporate agenda without an enormous groundswell of public support for a new economic direction. Despite his retreat from the language and practice of economic communitarianism, Clinton remains the most receptive president to such new thinking that we are likely to see for some time. It is the task of the Left to mobilize grassroots communities and social movements that, in any case, must be the prime movers for economic democracy and the social market. The president cannot in the end create the social market but only help provide a supportive institutional environment. The rest is up to us.

# 9

## Coming Glued:

### LEFT COMMUNITARIANISM VS. COMMUNITARIANISM OF THE PROFESSIONAL MIDDLE CLASS

In his early 1990s film hit *Falling Down,* Michael Douglas has "double trouble." He has been laid off from his solidly middle-class job as an engineer, and his wife has left him. There is no neighborhood or friendship network to help him get through the day. Douglas is a man with no community and nothing left to lose. Feeling abandoned by society, he strikes back in a torrent of senseless violence.

Most middle-class Americans don't have such serious double trouble, but they feel threatened. Few can assume that their jobs or their marriages are secure for the long term. And as the foundations of their own lives seem more shaky, Americans can see all around them the signs of a spreading social and moral breakdown. There is more violence on the streets and in the home, greed in the corporate boardroom, corruption in government, frightening fragmentation of races and ethnic groups, and the growing sense that it's everyone for himself and herself.

When community begins to erode, communitarian movements sometimes arise to offer solutions. Recognizing the fragility of society, communitarians are centrally concerned with the "social glue" that binds people together. Communitarians understand that personal fulfillment and social order depend on the secure attachments and moral frameworks that only communities offer. In periods of great social dislocation, a communitarian politics may be the only viable alternative to less attractive movements—including nativism and fascism—that also commonly spring up to offer people seductive but dangerous medicine for their economic and spiritual pain. Taking that pain as its own touchstone, communitarianism speaks centrally to our need for belonging and purpose; at its best, it offers new values and institutions that can bring us together with greater civility and humanity.

In 1990, sociologist Amitai Etzioni and policy analyst William Galston, who became a Clinton administration official, called together a group of fifteen influential academics to discuss the moral malaise of America. In January 1991, this group went public with the first edition of a new communitarian journal, eliciting a flood of favorable comment from *Business Week, Time,* and the *Chronicle of Higher Education.* In November 1991, the group organized a communitarian teach-in whose participants included not only notable academics but Democratic Senators Bill Bradley and Daniel Patrick Moynihan, Republican Senators Dave Durenberger and Alan Simpson, and then-Senator, now Vice-President, Al Gore. Early in 1993, Etzioni published a new book, *The Spirit of Community,* the group's public manifesto and call to arms. Thus has a new communitarian movement burst onto the American scene from a surprising birthplace, the ivy-covered halls and professional minds of our elite and highly individualistic universities.[1]

In his new manifesto, Etzioni makes an eloquent case for the potential of a new American communitarianism. His communitarian movement, he tells us, is a harbinger of a new American politics, one that has the potential to transcend old Left-Right divisions, bring together the classes, and heal the moral decay of a civil society in disarray. Americans should read Etzioni's remarkably accessible volume, which succeeds in pinpointing the problems of morality and social commitment that are gnawing at the American soul. But Etzioni's readers will find a remarkably limited perspective on solutions, for his is what I shall call "PMC communitarianism," the communitarianism of the professional middle class. PMC communitarianism has new and important insights, but it is not a communitarianism that can speak to the needs of all Americans.

Because of the considerable publicity that Etzioni and Galston have won for their movement and their close links to the Clinton administration, much of the public, as well as many on the left, have come to identify communitarian ideas with the Etzioni formulation. Indeed, because it is helping shape President Clinton's own brand of communitarianism, it needs to be taken seriously. We view the communitarian movement, despite its significant contributions, as a flawed beginning. We treat it here both to show the dangerous implications of a communitarianism divorced from an analysis of class and power and to illuminate, by contrast, the very different assumptions of the Left communitarian tradition.

## Moral Medicine: Diagnosis and Prescription

In his diagnosis, Etzioni speaks to the social and spiritual anguish of Americans across the class spectrum. We confront, he suggests, a collective crisis of morality and social responsibility. Our spiraling rates of violent crime, greed, divorce, child neglect, elderly abuse, and "me-firstism" are all symptoms of the same underlying moral malady. We are losing our sense of what binds us together and what we owe one another as we compulsively pursue our individual needs and dreams. Personal conscience and social solidarity are yielding to the nightmare of unregulated self-aggrandizement and the ethos of instant gratification.

Etzioni warns that society will not survive such degraded individualism, which I have described elsewhere as a national culture of "wilding." The slippery slope from civil society to the Hobbesian state of war is real, as bullets on the streets and guns in the schools attest. Etzioni concludes that we need a communitarian movement to catalyze a national moral revitalization and preserve civil society.[2]

Etzioni's diagnosis is flawed mainly by his inattention to the contribution of the elites to our moral crisis. After the experience of the 1980s, it is hard to ignore the spectacular corruption at the top—from the flamboyant white-collar crime of savings-and-loan outlaws to the rampant greed of government officials on the take—which has been the inspiration for so much of the wilding further down the social ladder. While he lambastes "special interests," including wealthy and powerful corporations, Etzioni locates the source of our moral decay in the millions of ordinary Americans who are obsessively pursuing their "rights" rather than respecting their obligations to others. This argument is not entirely misguided, but it is one of the first hints of a PMC communitarian analysis that is reluctant to make class distinctions or indict privileged elites.

The real limits of PMC communitarianism arise in Etzioni's solutions, which are largely cultural and "micro-institutional," involving family, school, and neighborhood. These measures are necessary—indeed crucial—but they are insufficient by themselves, for morality and civil society cannot be saved without deep changes in our underlying economic and political arrangements.

Etzioni's solutions begin with a call for a momentous cultural shift away from the exaggerated individualism of recent decades to a renewed concern for others. Etzioni is unapologetic for his focus on morality as a subject of politics, and he offers a reasoned view that while there always lurk the dangers of puritanism, coercion, and overzealousness, a politics that ignores morality cannot speak to our underlying crisis. In contrast to far-right and fundamentalist political moralists such as Pat Buchanan or the Moral Majority's Jerry Falwell, he proposes a tolerant public moralism, one that is respectful of difference but insistent on common standards that should help to unite us, such as avoiding stealing, lying, and violence. It is useful to remind us of these shared values, particularly in our current deeply fragmented and divisive condition. But communitarian politics must also insist, as we shall see, on values that are less consensual, related to equality and social justice.

Many civil libertarians have been properly concerned about the authoritarianism that creeps into Etzioni's discussion of consensual values. For example, assuming a consensus that drug use is bad and dangerous on the job, Etzioni advocates selective drug-testing—say of pilots or flight mechanics—to protect community interests, a position that is worthy of discussion and on which Etzioni's communitarianism offers useful insights. But a significant minority of Americans disagree that drug use should be either tested or banned and view the official "war on drugs" as ineffective, coercive, moralistic, and invasive of privacy, suggesting the extreme delicacy of making claims for any consensual values. In fact, in a healthy democracy, almost all major social values are contested and clash with other values, suggesting that "consensual" values are, in reality, the voice of one part of the community—usually the majority or an elite minority—against another. This is not an argument against the communitarian virtue of seeking shared values, but points to the need for greater sensitivity than Etzioni displays to the role of power (including professional expertise) in defining our "common ground."

Left communitarianism seeks common ground on the public values of democracy, equality, and justice—all integral to the American moral tradition. But while this objective requires changes in personal attitudes, it must begin with change in elite behavior and the structure of American institutions. The problem is less that ordinary Americans do not believe enough in such values but that elites and the institutions they run enforce a different moral regime, suggesting the need for less PMC preaching about personal morality and more focus on structural change.

This hardly means that Left communitarians are unconcerned with the morality of individuals, for they also seek to encourage the sense of social obligation and the highest moral ideals. But, recognizing the coercive potential of all communities, the Left is less ready to curb expressive behavior unless it is blatantly injurious to others. Left communitarians, as discussed in chapter 7, value expressive individualism and are critical mainly of the competitive individualism (including greed, selfishness, and excessive competitiveness) that undermine the possibility of community itself.

## Are Rights Wrong? Social Rights and Responsibility

Central to Etzioni's cultural politics is a new discourse about rights and responsibilities. We subscribe to a culture of entitlement, Etzioni writes, that underlies a national obsession with individual rights at the expense of obligations. Increasingly, all of us feel entitled to a well-paid job even if we haven't studied for it, generous public services that we are unwilling to pay for, and civil and nondiscriminatory treatment by friends, strangers, or authorities that we are not prepared to reciprocate. This inflationary riot of rights is reinforced not only by the culture of greed but by the individualistic bent of our entire legal apparatus and political discourse, an argument that Etzioni has borrowed from Mary Ann Glendon, his communitarian colleague at the Harvard Law School and the author of *Rights Talk*. All of this leads Etzioni to propose a "tight lid on the manufacturing of new rights" and a new focus instead on what we owe each other.[3]

There is great merit in the concern with the decline of an ethos of obligation, for a politics of rights without obligations is, in fact, an individualistic seduction that will end in social collapse. And, yes, many Americans are infected with entitlement fever, threatening to weaken our most cherished rights by claiming frivolous or unwarranted ones, although this is as much the legacy of the capitalist culture of consumerism as it is the liberal pursuit of rights. But if there is good reason to assess the impact of individual rights (such as the right to carry guns, smoke, or drive at high speeds) on the community—and to recognize explicitly the social obligations that inhere in each new right—Etzioni's critique is profoundly flawed by his focus on personal rights at the expense of property rights. Our culture is a battleground between these two opposing sets of rights, and individual rights are far from ascendant and certainly not the greater threat to community. The expansion and abuse of property rights, now exercised by multinational corporations on a global scale, has created shuttered plants and ghost communities all over America, yet Etzioni makes scant reference either to property rights or to corporate social obligations. Nor does he explain that the struggle for expanded personal or social rights, such as health care or day care, is partly a survival response to new corporate arrangements, such as low-wage, part-time, and temporary labor, that are undermining earlier forms of security and community.

The tone of the new communitarians' critique of rights sometimes harkens back to the neoconservative politics of the 1970s, when Harvard political scientist Samuel Huntington wrote of the dangers of "excess democracy," decrying the participatory movements that were "overloading" the system with their demands. While Etzioni advocates responsive citizen action, he shares with Huntington the visceral fear of grassroots democratic activism that burdens the system and its elites with unruly new claims. This is another hint of a PMC communitarianism that is profoundly ambivalent about participatory democracy and predisposed toward consensual management by experts.

Left communitarianism inverts the PMC understanding of the relation between rights and social responsibility, recognizing that as individuals acquire rights that ensure security and freedom, they increasingly gain the capacity and desire to act responsibly. Society grants rights partly as a means of giving each individual a "stake in the system." In return, it can expect a greater measure of social commitment.

American managers are beginning to understand this principle, not as communitarians but as bottom-line pragmatists with their eyes on Japan. The Japanese miracle arose from the remarkable loyalty and motivation of Japanese workers, whose employers extended rights of security and participation for this purpose. American corporations are slowly learning that by denying workers the rights to security, benefits, and participation, they sabotage the worker commitment to the enterprise that can make it globally competitive.

Left communitarians seek to expand the realm of "social rights"—including those to housing, health care, day care, and, most of all, a job. It takes no special expertise to recognize that those denied such rights (as in the case, notably, of the American underclass) will feel minimal loyalty to society and more disposed toward violence, crime, and other socially irresponsible behavior. It is not coincidental that such behavior is at an epidemic level in the United States relative to Japan and Western Europe, societies that guarantee their citizens health care, housing allowances, public day care, and a panoply of other rights repudiated only in America.

Left communitarians embrace rights because they ultimately guarantee rather than erode both justice and social responsibility. Rights are nothing but responsibilities imposed on the state, corporations, or citizens to treat all individuals as full members of the community. The struggle for rights reflects the communitarian philosophy, as Wendy Kaminer notes, that "Americans don't just take care of themselves; they also take care of each other, partly through their common government. That's the message requiring the embrace, not the abandonment of individual rights."[4]

## Family Values: Save the Children, but How?

The "micro-institutional" solutions of the PMC communitarians stress the revitalization of family, school, and neighborhood. Etzioni powerfully communicates the sociological perspective that individual conscience is largely a social creation of these key civil-society institutions; when they break down, so do people. The majority of Americans will agree that a moral politics starts at home and will find much instructive in Etzioni's approach to rebuilding the family, particularly his passionate call for a new personal and national commitment to children. Etzioni argues that children are the ultimate victims of our new culture of entitlement, for it has led adults to place a higher value on their own careers and personal fulfillment than on the needs of their offspring. Parents, he argues, have cut the time they spend with their children over the last generation from thirty-five to seventeen hours a week on average—an abandonment magnified by high rates of divorce and single parenting. All this, Etzioni believes, yields a family system that is ill-suited to the intensive love and discipline that produces moral fiber.

Etzioni calls for a new communitarian family that can regenerate meaningful parent-child "bonding." This means, in his view, national policy favoring two-parent families, laws making divorce more difficult, and family-leave policies and other incentives that favor parental care over day care or other forms of child "institutionalization"—especially for infants and toddlers under the age of two. Most of all we need a "change of heart," in which parents recommit themselves to parenting.

But if the call for new inner commitments strikes a resonant nerve and deserves to be mediated upon in living rooms across the country, the policy framework is again deeply flawed. The concept of bonding that underlies it is problematic, perpetuating such highly debatable notions that day care for infants undermines character formation and that the nontraditional family (lacking two parents of the opposite sex) tends to inhibit moral development. Etzioni disregards the reality that through most of human history, children were raised in hugely diverse extended kinship systems, many resembling a form of tribal day care and socialized parenting, that did not demonstrably injure the souls of the young. In her recent book, *Mother-Infant Bonding,* Diane E. Eyer concludes that the bonding concept—one of the most ideological and controversial in the history of science—has now been broadened "to describe the successful development of babies being raised by multiple caretakers—a situation originally thought to cause maternal deprivation."[5]

The class bias of PMC communitarianism emerges clearly in the economics of Etzioni's family policy. On the one hand, there is little discussion of the job and financial pressures that have sliced into parental time, making problematic for many ordinary Americans the generous parenting that Etzioni rightly values. As the one-wage family yields to the two-, three-, or four-job family, with parents shuttling from one part-time job to another just to pay the bills, the "change of heart" that Etzioni prescribes becomes a cruel illusion. At least sixty million Americans—the poor and the working poor, the unemployed and underemployed from the working and lower-middle classes—do not have the luxury of the trade-offs that Etzioni envisions. When he argues for six months of paid parental leave and another year and a half of unpaid leave to ensure that every child under two can have a parent at home, he is speaking to his professional and social peers and obviously not to the vast majority of Americans whose wallets are far too thin to entertain the fantasy of eighteen months without pay.

Left communitarianism approaches "family values" with the philosophy of the old African proverb: "It takes a whole village to raise one child." Even the most committed parents need help from relatives, neighbors, teachers, and other support communities to do their job responsibly. Through most of human history, as just noted, children have been raised in extended kinship groups, with many adults taking responsibility for their care. The current crisis of the family reflects less the disinterest of parents in caring for children (although that is too often a serious problem) than the erosion of the lifelines between the family and the larger society—burdening of parents, especially mothers, with too much to do in too little time. In an influential study of work and family life, economist Juliet Schor shows that mothers "*average* over eighty hours [per week] of housework, child care, and employment."[6]

Repairing the ecology of family support systems is thus the leading edge of a Left communitarian family policy. This means, first, ensuring a viable economic foundation for the family—that is, a job for every adult with high enough wages and short enough hours to permit the generous parenting that Etzioni seeks. Second, since both parents in most families must work, guaranteeing affordable, high-quality day care is the sine qua non of any politics concerned with "saving our children." Third, since our central cities are too poor and dangerous to permit parents, relatives, and neighbors to congregate and cooperate safely, an amply-funded urban and community development program is a major priority.

Left communitarianism does not dismiss the concern with parental commitment and responsibility. But it challenges the unproven consensus that the most responsible and effective parents are those living out the 1950s Ozzie and Harriet model. We do not know whether children suffer less in households of unhappily married couples or in single-parent households after divorce; in the absence of such understanding, the emphasis should be not on the form of the household (single, divorced or married, gay or straight) but on the quality of the parenting.

## Capitalism and Community: Toward a Communitarian Economics

Professional middle-class communitarianism is startlingly blind to the economic and political transformations that are necessary to create a real option of community for ordinary Americans. Ultimately, the unraveling of the social fabric is rooted in the radically individualistic market system that reached its unholy apotheosis in the Reagan-Bush years. Except possibly for the PMC and other elites, there can be no communitarian haven until we rebuild that system on a radically new, "kinder and gentler" foundation.

The PMC communitarians recognize a need for national political change, but their vision is astonishingly narrow, focusing mainly on campaign-finance reform and curbing the influence of lobbyists and other "special interests." Limiting the role of money in politics would certainly help clean up Washington and empower new voices, and it can potentially contribute to a broader vision of the common good. But it is only one of a host of structural changes in our capitalist system that demand urgent attention, and while campaign finance reform is currently a hot issue, it will not happen meaningfully without a broad-based assault on the entrenched powers whom the lobbyists and special interests represent.

Etzioni devotes lengthy chapters to family and school, but there is not a single chapter on the economy and no mention of the "C" word: capitalism. Etzioni, an accomplished sociologist, is fully aware that morals and values are anchored in the economic and political arrangements that determine how we make and distribute our daily bread. Indeed, *The Moral Dimension,* Etzioni's earlier book on economics, forcefully argues that our communities are in peril precisely because of the radical individualism of our economic thought and practice. But if he earlier portrayed our free-market logic as almost frighteningly sociopathic, Etzioni seems now to suggest that if we simply resolve to recharge our moral sensibilities and reform our families, schools, and political campaigns, we will not have to attend to the explosively divisive issues of economic transformation.

Virtually all PMC communitarians share Etzioni's astonishing predisposition to detach the problem of community from the basic realities of capitalism, conveying the remarkable impression that the decline of community can be understood and reversed without any change in our economic arrangements. Mary Ann Glendon, in her influential book *Rights Talk,* shows that our legal thinking is radically individualistic, reflecting the traditional doctrine that each man is the king of his own castle. While pinpointing the corrosive impact of this ethic on our morality and communities, Glendon, like Etzioni, never discusses capitalism or the vital role of business in shaping legal individualism. Neither does she explain how a more communitarian legal framework might be useful in binding corporations as well as individuals to a new standard of social responsibility.[7]

A. Lawrence Chickering, a conservative communitarianism, explicitly rejects the view that capitalism is responsible for our crisis of values and community, declaring that "any effort to explain the breakdown of values in terms of systems—in terms of economic, social or political structures—will fail." Chickering argues that the level of selfishness and materialism in the former socialist societies was no less than in Western capitalist societies, a clear indication, in his view, that the transformation of capitalism will not solve our crisis of values and community. Indeed, he argues that free markets are consistent with whatever values we choose and are entirely compatible with nonmaterialist communitarian ideals.[8]

The communitarianism of Japanese capitalism leads some observers to support the view that we can't entirely blame our crisis of community on the capitalist system. Different models of capitalism can clearly accommodate different cultures and values orientations, but that is quite different from the argument that capitalism (or the various national capitalisms) are "value-neutral." American capitalism is the great atomizer, throwing us on our own resources to sink or swim. If it does not always cultivate greed and narcissism, as it did in the 1980s, capitalism binds most of us to a morality of dedicated self-interest. Market values penetrate private life, and while they do not reduce all family, work, and friendship ties to the icy calculations of the cash nexus, as Marx described it, they certainly undermine the trust and cooperation on which civil society, and the market itself, ultimately depend.

In the context of shuttered manufacturing plants and deindustrialized ghost towns across America, it is stupefying that PMC communitarians can suggest that economic systems are unrelated to our crisis of community. Ever since the British enclosures that threw the peasantry off the land, the history of capitalism has meant never-ending social dislocation, with the restless drive for profit always leaving a trail of uprooted workers and broken communities. This is true even when capitalists are committed to social responsibility, as in the case of Arnold Hiatt, former CEO of Stride Rite, the shoe manufacturer, who invested in inner-city communities during the 1970s and then disinvested and relocated Stride Rite plants overseas in the 1980s. Hiatt fought against the plant closings with his board of directors and ultimately resigned, but his personal commitment to helping poor communities could not counter the systemic forces leading his corporation ultimately to betray those communities.

In their disregard of capitalism, we see the political essence of PMC communitarianism laid bare. Class conflict is off the agenda, as is any discourse that initiates confrontational politics about power hierarchies or income distribution. These issues are part of the old left-right politics that the new PMC communitarianism claims to transcend. Professional middle-class communitarianism invites us to a new politics of the common ground, where the intelligentsia and enlightened policy experts elicit consensus and manage the country in the interests of everyone.

But while there is much attractive about such a "new politics," it is not quite as new as it seems. A similar politics of consensus characterized the Progressive movement in the first decades of this century and reemerged among the professorial advisers who helped manage and administer the New Deal of the 1930s. Both are earlier manifestations of PMC politics, dominated by privileged professional elites, and both shared with the New Communitarianism the vision of a consensual common good that could unite all the classes and preserve capitalism. Not surprisingly, Etzioni identifies himself as a "neo-Progressive," claiming that the New Communitarianism is like the earlier Progressive movement, which "appealed to all classes, since its emphasis was on formulating the proper rules of the game rather than serving the interests of one class."[9]

There is something soothing and, indeed, healing in our troubled, antagonistic society about such a consensual, conflict-free vision. Communitarians of any stripe should strongly affirm the merits of a politics of common ground as long as it does not bury divisions that have to be confronted in order to achieve a just community. Etzioni has forcefully articulated the virtues of a less polarized politics and is wise not to, a priori, read anyone in or out of the communitarian cause. But PMC communitarians, by shunning an analysis of the market forces that are eroding community, are defeating the aims they embrace.

Communitarianism must propose a structural politics that forthrightly addresses the economic foundations of our problems. It must, for example, challenge the system of income distribution that in recent years has promoted an extreme division of rich and poor incompatible with community. A number of communitarians, such as Mickey Kauss, a *New Republic* editor and author, have proposed the irrelevancy of money and its distribution to community, and Etzioni, remarkably, ignores the issue completely. Kauss argues that it is far more important to mix the classes in common public institutions, such as schools and hospitals, than to try to level their incomes. But it is hard to imagine a consensual civil society that will happily unite multimillionaires such as Donald Trump with the homeless sleeping on the grates in front of the Trump Tower.[10]

Closely related to the question of income redistribution is the need for a wholehearted assault on the dreadful problems of our central cities, something—particularly after the explosion in Los Angeles—that would seem to be an obvious priority for any communitarian. Again, Etzioni is virtually silent about the linked crises of race and urban poverty, saying simply that the communitarian perspective on social justice is that "first, people have a moral responsibility to help themselves as best they can" and that "the second line of responsibility lies with those closest to the person, including kin, friends, neighbors and other community members." Etzioni recognizes the need for government aid as a source of support when other resources fail or don't exist, and his perspective on self-help would make a great deal of sense if it were linked to a larger economic and political vision of empowering local, particularly poor, communities. At this point, Left communitarianism steps in and offers a way to wrestle capital and power away from multinational corporations and federal bureaucracies into the bosom of the community.[11]

Left communitarianism is ultimately rooted in a bold agenda on capitalism and the market system. It offers a communitarian economics seeking to integrate the class perspectives of Marx with Durkheim's analysis of social solidarity and leading toward a social market and economic democracy. As the last chapter elaborated, the social market offers a practical communitarian alternative to the free-market model, incorporating in varying degrees and in different ways (1) a social accounting system by which a growing number of corporations seek to measure the human costs of their policy and to factor social costs and benefits into economic decisions; (2) accountability mechanisms to ensure that businesses are responsive to community interests; (3) distribution mechanisms that ensure a high level of equality in income and wealth; (4) social investment strategies, such as the use of pension funds to build affordable housing and promote community development; and (5) forms of economic participation and governance, such as employee ownership, that institutionalize the logic of democratic community inside business itself.

No country has fully developed the social market, but the vision is hardly utopian, since it is being partially implemented in many different countries and is spreading, driven by moral and bottom-line arguments that speak to the concerns of both liberals and conservatives. For liberals, the payoff is more equality, power sharing, and social responsibility; for conservatives, it is greater productivity, stability, and economic yield. But communitarians see the most profound virtue: a moral economics that links individual enterprise and profit-seeking with the common good. Since the social market does not require the end of private enterprise, communitarian economics is not necessarily anticapitalist. But Left communitarian economics pushes toward a radically different capitalism than currently practiced in the United States, and it will likely synthesize elements of the Western European social democracies with elements of the worker-owned and community-based economies represented by Mondragon, as well as new American forms of worker participation, commitment to quality, and corporate social responsibility.

The social market is, at root, a project for social solidarity, molding economic institutions that can help manufacture responsibility and community as well as profitable commodities. But this is more than idle idealism or "do-goodism." For an economy to prosper, it must respect and nourish the social bonds and moral concerns that make civil commerce possible. Indeed, social organization and solidarity are the great intangible ingredients of economic success. Japan, a relatively authoritarian form of the social market, has created its economic miracle by successfully melding the communitarian values of Confucianism with the market values of accumulation and profit. Social-market systems in the West will unfold differently, infused by more democratic Western visions of community. This cannot happen fully without a clearer vision of the democratic community we seek, pointing to the constant and profound dependence of economics on our moral discourse and sensibilities.

## Politics: Prospects for Professional Middle Class and Left Communitarianism

The communitarian language and sensibilities of the elites, including the professional middle class, will never square fully with those of ordinary Americans, whose lives are built around different forms of community at work and in local neighborhoods. But even if PMC communitarians have articulated cultural and moral issues that reverberate across the class spectrum, their words are not likely to be widely attended outside their own group. Less privileged Americans have always been distrustful of the words of elites, looking instead to their actions. In addition to all the barriers of concept and program already discussed, a principal obstacle limiting the spread of PMC communitarianism is that ordinary folk understand that whatever they say, members of the professional middle class live by the rules of the radically individualistic professional career model. Indeed, there is hardly any more consensual finding in sociology than the notion that the professions have been principal definers and carriers of the American dream of individualism and are among its most privileged beneficiaries. Ordinary Americans both admire and resent the freedoms and rights that the professional middle class enjoys and propagates; many feel shackled by their more traditional lifestyles, which, ironically, tend to be far less individualistic than those of the PMC communitarians themselves. Thus, potentially one of the most powerful means by which Etzioni and his fellow PMC communitarians could spread the word would be by helping to model the new ethos in their own lives and professional institutions. Developing a more communitarian model of the professions and reducing the individualistic fever of academic careerism would be a powerful signal that PMC communitarianism is serious. And when the professional middle class demonstrate through their own personal lifestyles that they are prepared to limit their personal rights and assume more social obligations, this would be the most convincing argument that others should heed their words.

PMC communitarianism ultimately reflects its proponents' own self-victimization and pain. No other class bought more fully into individualistic models of success and now suffers as deeply the consequences. Thus the adage "Physician, heal thyself" is particularly apt. If the professional middle class can wean itself from its own addictions to career, ego, money, and status, it will not only speak to its own deepest needs but offer through example the embryo of the new culture that can inspire others and model a less self-oriented version of the American Dream.

Communitarian politics must ultimately move from the halls of academe to bowling alleys, pubs, and street corners if it is going to do more than absorb volumes of printer's ink. This is not likely to be the path of PMC communitarianism, despite Etzioni's explicit call for social movements and citizen action. The real test of any communitarianism is whether it can engage the hearts and minds of ordinary people, and it will take a more populist communitarianism to take the movement beyond the academic conference rooms.

Left communitarianism addresses the practical and often desperate economic problems of survival and powerlessness that ordinary Americans confront every day, along with many of their pressing problems of human dignity and connection. But it also offers its own cultural politics that speaks directly to the problems of values and community that cannot be resolved purely through economic change. PMC communitarianism has powerfully introduced many of these cultural themes, but they will have to be reasserted by ordinary Americans in a language and spirit that reflect their own experiences.

The United States has periodically bred populist movements that articulated ordinary Americans' longings for community. These included turn-of-the-century populism reflecting prairie state and rural farm visions of community and the 1930s labor movements that evoked a vision of solidarity compelling to the new industrial workers dislocated during the Great Depression. The seedbeds of Left communitarian visions in the 1990s may come from surprising quarters, including rehabilitated gang leaders in the inner cities, self-help recovery groups now proliferating throughout the country, women in the community organizing to stem the epidemic of male violence against their sisters, and grassroots citizen groups organizing themselves for safe streets through crime-watch groups or for lower water and utility bills in neighborhood associations.

Communitarian social movements will be operating in a new and potentially fertile larger context. In the United States, global capitalism is so rapidly undermining the security and community traditionally enjoyed by the middle class that powerful counteractive forces are bub-

## Coming Glued

bling up that could steer our political economy in a Left communitarian direction. On the one hand, corporate management is dimly recognizing that productivity requires committed employees and that the mushrooming class of "disposable workers" it has created to cut costs is undermining labor-management cooperation and the flexible production system it needs to engage and mobilize skilled labor. High on the Left communitarian economic agenda should be a national program to help resolve this managerial schizophrenia by using governmental incentives and financing to encourage high-commitment systems of worker participation, such as those at Saturn, the GM auto subsidiary in Springhill, Tennessee. Saturn vests employees with a version of lifetime employment and empowers workers to comanage and share decision-making power from the top to the bottom of the company, while also making an unequivocal commitment to quality that gives employees a sense of meaning and social responsibility to customers.

As the last chapter discussed, a closely related Left communitarian economic priority is the massive expansion and reform of employee ownership, an unsung strategy for countering capital flight and building community both in and out of the workplace. Coops and properly structured ESOPs (employee stock-ownership companies) redefine ownership in exquisitely communitarian terms, basing rights to control and profits on membership in a work community rather than on capital investment. Beyond the merits of bonding workers in a common venture that offers them substantial material and spiritual returns, workers are also far more likely to accept lower profits to preserve local jobs and to reduce pollution or other "externalities" inflicted on their local communities. Employee ownership, as the experience of Mondragon shows, can nourish a sense of broader community responsibility; in Mondragon, coops cooperate extensively with each other and invest a significant fraction of their profits and volunteer time in the community. Left communitarians should press energetically for more attractive public financing and tax incentives for a Mondragon-like sector of coops and ESOPs, but only for ESOPs that make a genuine commitment to worker involvement and empowerment, including the right of workers to vote their stock on all corporate decisions and to define the mission and social responsibility of the company. President Clinton has endorsed both worker participation and employee ownership, and Labor Secretary Robert Reich is opening up opportunities to grassroots, labor, and ESOP or coop activists who can espouse a credible agenda of workplace communitarianism speaking both to the American worker's soul and pocketbook.

## A Postcommunist Left Agenda

As Clinton's push for national health care suggests, the surprising communitarian impulse emerging in American politics goes well beyond the workplace itself. The beleaguered middle class is now insisting that the government step in to protect its own standard of living and quality of life. In an era of tax revolts and deficit politics, Clinton has rhetorically embraced a remarkably expansive social agenda including universal health care, environmental activism, the physical and psychological health of children, expanded worker training and higher education, and urban and community development support, including block grants and a new community banking system. Left communitarians should hold Clinton to these early promises as baby steps toward a meaningful "new covenant"—Clinton's initial political slogan—that goes beyond the provision of material benefits to address our needs for civility, connection, and enhanced quality of personal and social life.

The political prospects of a communitarian social democratic agenda are enhanced by the new support that may be offered by some sectors of the corporate world. The breakdown of civil society has become prohibitively costly to corporations in both familiar and surprising ways. Many corporations are converts to the cause of national health care, recognizing that only the state can relieve them of the devastating burden of escalating health costs. The same logic could conceivably lead corporations toward a reluctant support of some version of the Western European welfare state not only in regard to health care, but child care, pensions, and training and education. While some on the left may viscerally reject alliances with such "class enemies," the communitarian movement may be better attuned to the new forces that could turn sectors of corporate America into partial comrades in struggle.

But while communitarians should be prepared to ally with corporations that become champions of social democracy or worker participation, it remains likely that elites will militantly resist much of the agenda of the Left communitarian movement we need. The structural agenda, after all, involves not only a new vision of corporate social responsibility but transferring the enormous concentrated power now resting in corporations and top management toward employees and local communities. Even the most enlightened corporations are likely to accede to such changes at a snail's pace—and only under pressure from below. Moreover, in the new global economy, corporations can readily exploit the exit option and flee abroad to escape social responsibility at home. Thus, Left communitarian politics will have to come up with innovative solutions to capital flight, including not only widespread employee ownership but international initiatives that will bind companies worldwide to communitarian standards. The NAFTA side agreements to protect labor and the environment as well as initiatives in the European Common Market to promote common social standards may ultimately prove to be fruitful models.

Left communitarianism offers a politics exquisitely tailored to the crisis of our times. In the service of its progressive legacy and of humanity, the Left should seize the moment.

# Notes

## Introduction

1. Robert Pear, "In a Final Draft, Democrats Reject a Part of Their Past," *New York Times*, June 16, 1992, A13.
2. Ralf Dahrendorf, *Reflections on the Revolution in Europe* [New York: Times Books, 1990), 42, 73.
3. Seymour Martin Lipset, "No Third Way: A Comparative Perspective on the Left," in *The Crisis of Leninism and the Decline of the Left: The Revolution of 1989*, ed. Daniel Chirot (Seattle: University of Washington Press, 1991), 183.
4. Michael Lowy, "Twelve Theses on the Crisis of 'Really Existing Socialism,'" *Monthly Review* 43 (May 1991): 33.
5. Ibid., 33–34.
6. Victor Wallis, "Marxism and the US Left: Thoughts for the 1990s," *Monthly Review* 43 (May 1991): 6–7.
7. Manning Marable, "Remaking American Marxism," *Monthly Review* 43 (May 1991): 53.
8. For relevant economic data, see Lawrence Mishel and David M. Frankel, *The State of Working America, 1993–94* (Armonk, N.Y.: M.E. Sharpe, 1994).
9. Dahrendorf, *Reflections*, 21.
10. For relevant social data and interpretation see Charles Derber, *Money, Murder and the American Dream: Wilding from Wall Street to Main Street* (Boston: Faber and Faber, 1993), especially chapter 6.
11. Ibid.
12. On postmodern capitalism, see David Harvey, *The Condition of Post-Modernity* (Cambridge, Mass.: Blackwell Publishers, 1990). See also the classic exposition in Karl Polanyi, *The Great Transformation* (Boston: Beacon Press, 1944).
13. Richard Flacks, *Making History: The American Left and the American Mind* (New York: Columbia University Press, 1988), 100ff.

## 1. Deconstructing the Death of the Left

1. Barbara Kantrowitz, "In Berlin, a World Turned Upside Down," *Newsweek*, December 7, 1992, 32.
2. E. P. Thompson, "Liberal Complacence," *Dissent* (Summer 1991): 426–28;

Seymour Martin Lipset, "No Third Way: A Comparative Perspective on the Left," in *The Crisis of Leninism and the Decline of the Left: The Revolutions of 1989,* ed. Daniel Chirot (Seattle: University of Washington Press, 1991).

3. Paul Starr, "Liberalism After Socialism," *The American Prospect* (Fall 1991).
4. Ibid., 73.
5. Ibid., 76.
6. Ibid., 80.
7. Ibid.
8. Ibid., 79.
9. Ralf Dahrendorf, *Reflections on the Revolution in Europe* (New York: Times Books, 1990).
10. Ibid., 50, 52.
11. Ibid., 18, 19.
12. Ibid., 60.
13. Ibid., 66.
14. Francis Fukuyama, "End of History?" *The National Interest* (Summer 1989): 3, 4.
15. Ibid., 8.
16. Ibid., 9.
17. Ibid., 13.
18. Ibid., 5, 8.
19. Ibid., 9.
20. Michael Walzer, "The Idea of Civil Society: A Path to Social Reconstruction," *Dissent* (Spring 1991): 293.
21. Alan Wolfe, *Whose Keeper? Social Science and Moral Obligation* (Berkeley: University of California Press, 1989), 18–19.
22. Ibid., 19.
23. Emile Durkheim, *The Division of Labor in Society* (New York: Free Press, 1984), 317.
24. Wolfe, *Whose Keeper?* 30.
25. Durkheim, *The Division of Labor,* 76.
26. Wolfe, *Whose Keeper?* 168, 30.
27. Walzer, "The Idea of Civil Society," 301.
28. Wolfe, *Whose Keeper?* 5.
29. Starr, "Liberalism After Socialism," 80.
30. Dahrendorf, *Reflections on the Revolution in Europe,* 102.
31. Jean Cohen and Andrew Arato, *Civil Society and Political Theory* (Cambridge: MIT Press, 1992), xii; Richard Flacks, *Making History: The American Left and the American Mind* (New York: Columbia University Press, 1988), 288.

## 2: Beyond Socialism and Identity Politics

I wish to thank the following people for their helpful comments on this paper: Charles Derber and all the other contributors to this volume, members of the Media Research Action Project (especially William Hoynes, Sharon Kurtz, David Meyer), Jonathan Kozol, Jennifer Schmidt, Jody Lester, Marta Rose, and Nancy, Steve, and Greta Schwerner, and all of my respondents.

1. Manning Marable and others point out that much of the reason for the

distinction between a new and old Left is a direct result of McCarthyism. For example, Marable argues that before McCarthy, Black radicals and the socialist Left were starting to work in a more united fashion and that in fact what we call the civil rights movement might have started much earlier had it not been for the absolute discrediting of the socialist and communist Left. Manning Marable, *Race, Reform, and Rebellion* (Jackson: University Press of Mississippi, 1991).

2. See Jean L. Cohen, "Strategy of Identity: New Theoretical Paradigms and Contemporary Social Movements," *Social Research* 52 (1985): 663–716; J. C. Jenkins, "Resource Mobilization Theory and the Study of Social Movements," *Annual Review of Sociology* 9 (1983); Alberto Melucci, *Nomads of the Present* (Philadelphia: Temple University Press, 1988).

3. Here the reader should note that I am not arguing that traditional Marxist-oriented groups no longer existed in U.S. culture but that in the 1970s and 1980s they were significantly more marginal than the populist identity-oriented movements; and for the purposes of this chapter I am focusing on these more populist struggles for social change. It is also worth noting, however, that throughout the mid-1970s and early 1980s there was a highly contested debate among the more Marxist-oriented Left over how best to be revolutionary—that is, how one works within mass movements and still brings to these movements a more revolutionary position. These debates were hotly disputed and at times so devastating that many activists simply chose to become inactive rather than participate in the painful discourse.

4. This cannot be considered a representative sample of the U.S. Left; rather, speaking with these ten leftists served as a sensitizing tool. I did not want to rely solely on what Left academics were saying but instead examine what "everyday Left folks" were thinking—seeing how and when it matched with academic thinking on the subject. Since the time of writing this chapter in the fall of 1992 these interviews were enriched and validated for me by my continuing research with other Left activists. Furthermore, as a "red-diaper grandbaby," I travel among a wide range of people who identify as leftists and have had numerous informal conversations on these topics that echo the voices of my ten respondents.

5. I did not speak with people who are members of what might be called the organized Left—members of the CPUSA, Socialist Worker's Party, or even Democratic Socialists of America (DSA). I felt that these groups would not be as productive for exploring the tension between the Left's identity and socialism because of their own formalized and somewhat dogmatic relationship with socialism. My hunch was that the events of Eastern Europe had not created a theoretical crisis for them; whereas for other Left movements, ones not so intrinsically connected to socialism, I was not so sure. Not interviewing members of DSA is a decision I now regret. Many of the insights of Cornel West, who is on the national board of DSA, reflect my own analysis, which I offer at the end of this chapter, and it would have been interesting to me if other DSA members share West's vision.

6. Michael Lowy, "Twelve Theses on the Crisis of 'Really Existing Socialism,'" *Monthly Review* 43, no. 1 (May 1991): 33.

7. I should note that many camps of leftists have long pointed to the failure of socialism in Eastern Europe. Some have argued that there are inherent flaws

in statist or Stalinist Marxism (a position taken by Marxists like Nikos Poulantzas, members of the Frankfurt School, anarchists, postmodernists, Marxist-feminists, and activist laypeople) and that this led to the failure of Eastern European societies. In a now-famous statement Rosa Luxemburg declared, "Without general elections, without unrestricted freedom of the press and assembly, without a free struggle of opinion, life dies out in every public institution." See David Held, *Political Theory and the Modern State* (Stanford, Calif.: Stanford University Press, 1989), 178. It is critical to note that because Eastern Europe did not represent the socialist vision of various individuals on the left, *many* abandoned these societies long ago—some during the "Moscow purge trials," others during or soon after the Khrushchev revelations. Here see Vivian Gornick, *The Romance of American Communism* (New York: Basic Books, 1977), Martin Jay, *The Dialectical Imagination* (Boston: Little, Brown, 1973), and Richard Flacks, *Making History: The American Left and the American Mind* (New York: Columbia University Press, 1988). Thus, according to many leftists, the failure of these societies was established long before the revolutions of 1989.

8. See Doug McAdam, *Freedom Summer* (Oxford: Oxford University Press, 1988) as an excellent source to back up this claim.

9. Galbraith cited in Eric Hobsbawm, "Out of the Ashes," *Marxism Today* (April 1991): 20.

10. From this organization's statement of purpose.

11. Flacks, *Making History*, 104.

12. Ibid., 222, 224.

13. Ibid., 87, 8.

14. Ibid., 101.

15. Race was also a highly visible component of these movements, and one could point to numerous African Americans who were part of these struggles because they believed in the link between class and race oppression. But class was still the primary mobilizing agent. And, in fact, many Black leftists (both leaders and "ordinary citizens") gave up on this Left and later shifted to a politics that allowed them to express a more race-oriented identity. Of course there were also several Pan-Africanist movements, such as Garvey's, but these were not directly connected to the Left.

16. In the social movement literature, peace and environment movements are considered part of the "identity-oriented paradigm."

17. See Stanley Aronowitz, *The Politics of Identity: Class, Culture, Social Movements* (New York: Routledge, 1992).

18. Much of the sociological literature on "new" social movements addresses this point.

19. This point is crucial. The tendency to slip into what Sharon Kurtz refers to as the "lowest common denominator" syndrome will be tremendous—the third stage of Left activism will only be successful if a truly multicultural experience is reflected in our politics.

## 3. Reflections on the Death of Marxism

1. Although a number of my respondents used the terms "America" and "American," there is much controversy regarding their usage. My preference is

to use the more precise terms of "United States" and "U.S." The former pair of terms reflect a bias or, more truthfully, a prejudice on the part of those from the United States, in that it serves to exclude much of the hemisphere given the name "America." However, in order to respect the integrity of the interviews, the terminology has not been changed.

2. Before we delve into the "failings of Marxism," it is interesting to note that not everyone entirely agrees that it is theoretical Marxism which is challenged by the events in Eastern Europe and the Soviet Union. One somewhat surprising point of view—surprising in that it is has not been brought up in any other context, to my knowledge—comes from a more orthodox Marxist who is also familiar with Weberian theory:

> They challenge my conception of Weber more than they do of Marx. His theory can certainly be read to say that bureaucracy is eternal, there is a unidirectional motion toward increasing task rationality—increasing bureaucratization—and that this is irreversible except for occasional, irrational outbursts. So I think . . . the events in Eastern Europe challenge Weber, who I think ventured specific hypotheses about their irreversibility, more than they challenge Marx, who I think is basically silent about those issues.

3. Anselm L. Strauss, *Mirrors and Masks: The Search for Identity* (Glencoe, Ill.: The Free Press, 1959), 26–27.

4. Thomas S. Kuhn, *The Structure of Scientific Revolutions*, 2d ed. (Chicago: University of Chicago Press, 1970), 10, viii, 10. Kuhn himself would hesitate to apply his theory of scientific revolutions to anything but the natural sciences. He considered the social sciences to be "pre-paradigmatic" in that they have not developed a single theoretical paradigm to use for the study of society. However, it can be argued that the social sciences, such as sociology, are "multi-paradigmatic" in the sense that they have several coherent perspectives from which to understand society. It is in this sense which the following analysis will use the paradigmatic model. Kuhn's approach, while more relevant to the natural sciences, provides a useful framework or analogy for understanding the crisis within the Marxist paradigm.

5. Ibid., 5, 52–53, 64, 66.

6. Ibid., 70–71, 82, 92.

7. Diane Vaughan, *Uncoupling: Turning Points in Intimate Relationships* (New York: Oxford University Press, 1986).

8. Kuhn, *The Structure of Scientific Revolution*, 77, 145, 169, 151–52, 158; emphasis mine.

9. Ibid., 85.

10. Strauss, *Mirrors and Masks*, 26.

## 4. Reframing the Revolution

1. Eduardo Galeano, "In Defense of the Right to Dream," *Newstatesman Society*, 11 October 1991, 7.

2. Carlos Gabetta, "The Latin Left Takes a New Path," *Newstatesman Society*, 11 October 1991, 14.

3. Jill Smolowe, "The Hapless Peacemaker," *Time,* 5 March 1990, 32.

4. United Nations General Assembly, Security Council, A/46/846, S/23501 (English version), "Peace Agreement," 30 January 1992, 39.

5. Joaquín Villalobos, "A Democratic Revolution for El Salvador," *Foreign Policy* 74 (Spring 1989): 106; Thomas Long and Frank Smyth, "How the FMLN Won the Peace," *Village Voice,* February 18, 1992, 19; James LeMoyne, "Out of the Jungle: El Salvador's Guerrillas," *New York Times Magazine,* February 9, 1992, 27.

6. LeMoyne, "Out of the Jungle," 56; Long and Smyth, "How the FMLN Won the Peace," 22.

7. Villalobos, "A Democratic Revolution," 112, 117.

8. Ibid., 117, 118, 121.

9. United Nations General Assembly, "Peace Agreement," 37; Frente Farabundo Martí para la Liberación Nacional (FMLN), "Plan de Reconstrucción para el Desarrollo de la Nueva Sociedad Salvadoreña" (preliminary version) (San Salvador, El Savador: mimeographed document, February 1992), 2 (my translation).

10. "Plan de Reconstrucción," 3.

11. Ibid., 1.

12. Ibid., 7.

13. Ibid., 8.

14. Ibid., 1–2, 5.

15. Ibid., 2, 10, 3.

16. Ibid., 2.

17. It should be noted that I do not intend this analysis to apply to the Democratic Convergence (CD), presidential candidate Rubén Zamora's political party. In the March 1994 elections, the FMLN ran in coalition with the CD for the executive seat. The vice-presidential candidate associated with the Zamora ticket is, however, a member of the FMLN political party, and the FMLN officially supported this ticket. Nevertheless, this analysis is in no way intended to apply to the CD, but rather only to the FMLN as an autonomous political party. The FMLN did run its own candidates for legislative assembly and in several municipal and local elections, all of which took place on March 20, 1994.

18. Salvador Samayoa interviewed by Terry Karl, "El Salvador: Negotiations or Total War?" *World Policy Journal* (Spring 1989): 335; Inter-Institutional Coordination (CII), "The New Initiative for Popular Self-Development in El Salvador" (San Salvador, El Salvador; mimeographed document, 1991).

19. Inter-Institutional Coordination (CII), "The New Initiative."

20. Mario Lungo Ucles, *El Salvador en los 80: Contrainsurgencia y Revolución* (San Jose, Costa Rica: Editorial Universitaria Centroamericana, 1990), 152; Sara Gordon, *Crisis Política y Guerro en El Salvador* (Mexico, D.F.: Siglo Ventunio Editores, 1989), 13 (my translation); Samayoa, "El Salvador," 332; LeMoyne, "Out of the Jungle," 26.

21. Long and Smyth, "How the FMLN Won," 22; LeMoyne, "Out of the Jungle," 58.

22. "ONUSAL's Grim Assessment of the Peace Process," *Salpress* (San Salvador, El Salvador), April 9, 1992.

23. David R. Dye, "Right-Wing Retrenchment May Slow Peace Process," *In These Times,* April 1–7, 1992, 9; Committee in Solidarity with the People of El Salvador (CISPES), "Will Peace Process Advances Continue?" *El Salvador Peace Accords Watch* 5 (August 1, 1992): 2.

24. Oxfam America informational advertisement, *New York Times,* Sunday, January 16, 1994, op-ed page; Amnesty International, *The 1993 Report on Human Rights Around the World* (Alameda, Calif.: Hunter House, 1993), 122; Jack Spense and George Vickers, "Toward a Level Playing Field? A Report of the Post-War Salvadoran Electoral Process" (Cambridge, Mass.: Hemisphere Initiatives, January 1994): 21.

25. LeMoyne, "Out of the Jungle," 67.

26. For a detailed discussion of the Palace of Justice event, see Ramón Jimeno, *Noche de Lobos* (Bogotá: Siglo Ventiuno Editores, 1989).

27. James Brooke, "Ex-Guerrillas Favored in Colombia Vote," *New York Times,* December 9, 1990, 3; James Brooke, "Former Rebels in First Place in Colombia Elections," ibid., December 10, 1990, A11; Mark Chernick, "Is the Armed Struggle Still Relevant?" *NACLA Report on the Americas* 27, no. 4 (Jan.–Feb. 1994): 13.

28. James Brooke, "Colombian Guerrillas Forsake the Gun for Politics," *New York Times,* September 2, 1990, 14.

29. Tim Coone, "The Sandinistas Lose Office but Not Power," *World Press Review,* April 1990, 24.

30. Ibid., 23.

31. Ibid.

32. Margaret E. Keck, "Brazil's P: Socialism as Radical Democracy," *NACLA Report on the Americas* 25, no. 5 (May 1992): 24.

33. Ibid., 24, 26.

## 5. Four Futures of the Left

1. Eric Hobsbawm, "Out of the Ashes," *Marxism Today* (April 1991): 18–22.

2. Sharon Kurtz, "All Kinds of Justice: Labor and Identity Politics," unpublished manuscript, Boston College, 1993.

3. Richard Flacks, *Making History: The American Left and the American Mind* (New York: Columbia University Press, 1988), 101. See also Stanley Aronowitz, *The Politics of Identity: Class, Culture and Social Movements* (New York: Routledge, 1992), and Stanley Aronowitz, "Radical Democracy," *Socialist Review* (January 1994).

4. For a conservative critique, see Lawrence Mead, *Beyond Entitlement* (New York: Free Press, 1988). On the liberal side, see Paul Starr, "Liberalism after Socialism," *The American Prospect* (Fall 1992): 71–80.

5. Sara M. Evans and Harry Boyte, *Free Spaces: The Sources of Democratic Change in America* (New York: Harper and Row, 1986), 112.

6. Benjamin Barber, *Strong Democracy: Participatory Politics for a New Age* (Berkeley: University of California Press, 1984).

7. Ibid., 222.

8. Evans and Boyte, *Free Spaces,* 8–9.

## 6. Beloved Comrades

1. Philip Foner, *History of the Labor Movement in the United States* (New York: New World Publishers, 1955), 170.
2. Uriah Stephens, cited in Terence Powderly, *Thirty Years of Labor, 1859–1889* (Columbus, Ohio: Excelsior Publishing, 1889), 166.
3. Ibid., 162.
4. Ibid., 168.
5. Ibid., 168–69.
6. Cited in Leon Fink, *Workingmen's Democracy: The Knights of Labor and American Politics* (Champaign: University of Illinois Press, 1983), 34.
7. Louis Blanc, cited in Powderly, *Thirty Years of Labor*, 31.
8. Powderly, *Thirty Years of Labor*, 459.
9. Ibid., 453, 463.
10. Cited in Norman Ware, *The Labor Movement in the United States, 1860–1895: A Study in Democracy* (New York and London: D. Appleton and Co., 1929), 324.
11. Cited in Powderly, *Thirty Years of Labor*, 467.
12. Cited in ibid., 467, 469.
13. Foner, *History of the Labor Movement*, 77.
14. Ibid., 55.
15. Frederick Engels, *Conditions of the British Working Class in 1844* (London, 1887), preface. Also cited in Foner, *History of the Labor Movement*, 55.
16. Cited in Foner, *History of the Labor Movement*, 61.
17. Ibid., 61.
18. Ibid., 65.
19. Cited in ibid., 63.
20. Ibid., 69.
21. Ibid., 66.
22. *John Swinton's Paper*, May 13, 1886; cited in ibid., 69.
23. Cited in Foner, *History of the Labor Movement*, 70.
24. This account of the Knights in Richmond draws on Fink, *Workingmen's Democracy*, chapter 6; Sara M. Evans and Harry Boyte, *Free Spaces: The Sources of Democratic Change in America* (New York: Harper and Row, 1986), 122ff.; and Foner, *History of the Labor Movement*, 71ff.
25. Vivian Gornick, *The Romance of American Communism* (New York: Basic Books, 1977), 41, 43.
26. Ibid., 84–85.
27. Ibid., 9.
28. Richard Flacks, *Making History: The American Left and the American Mind* (New York: Columbia University Press, 1988), 138–39.
29. Evans and Boyte, *Free Spaces*, 140.
30. John Bodnar, *Immigration and Industrialization: Ethnicity in an American Mill Town* (Pittsburgh: University of Pennsylvania Press, 1977), 112.
31. Harvey Klehr and John Earl Haynes, *The American Communist Movement: Storming Heaven Itself* (New York: Macmillan, 1992), 86.
32. Lev Martov, cited in Arthur Liebman, *Jews and the Left* (New York: Wiley and Sons, 1978), 113.
33. Moissay J. Olgin, cited in ibid., 317.

## Notes to The Value(s) of the Left

34. Elsie Suller, cited in ibid., 323.
35. Abraham Cahan, cited in ibid., 337.
36. Ibid., 207.
37. "The Port Huron Statement," in Judith C. Albert and Stewart E. Albert, *The Sixties Papers* (New York: Praeger, 1984), 180–81.
38. "SNCC: Founding Statement," in Albert and Albert, *The Sixties Papers*, 113.
39. Wini Breines, *Community and Organization in the New Left, 1962–1968: The Great Refusal* (New Brunswick, N.J.: Rutgers University Press, 1988), 6–7.
40. Cited in ibid., 7, 26.
41. Cited in ibid., 48.
42. Cited in ibid.
43. Flacks, *Making History*, 132, 134.
44. Cited in Breines, *Community and Organization*, 22.
45. Cited in ibid., 48.
46. "The Port Huron Statement," 181.
47. Ibid., 180.
48. Ibid., 180–81.
49. Cited in Breines, *Community and Organization*, 56–57.
50. Cited in ibid., 57.
51. Cited in ibid., 64.

## 7: The Value(s) of the Left

1. See Charles Derber, *Money, Murder and the American Dream: Wilding From Wall Street to Main Street* (Boston: Faber and Faber, 1993).
2. Barney Frank, *Speaking Frankly* (New York: Times Books, 1992), 21.
3. Martin Luther King, Jr., "Pilgrimage to Nonviolence" in *Stride Toward Freedom: The Montgomery Story*, cited in Judith C. Albert and Steward E. Albert, *The Sixties Papers* (New York: Praeger, 1984), 109.
4. Josephine St. Pierre Ruffin, "Address to the First National Conference of Coloured Women," in *Black Women in White America: A Documentary History*, ed. Gerda Lerner (New York: Vintage, 1972).
5. bell hooks, *Feminist Theory: From Margin to Center* (Boston: South End Press, 1984), 158ff.
6. Susan Griffin, cited in ibid., 162.
7. Ibid.
8. Cornel West, *Prophetic Reflections: Notes on Race and Power in America* (Monroe, Maine: Common Courage Press, 1993); hooks, *Feminist Theory*. For an excellent discussion of the interpenetration of oppressions, see Sharon Kurtz, "All Kinds of Justice: Labor and Identity Politics" (Ph.D. thesis, Boston College, 1994).
9. Alexis de Tocqueville, *Democracy in America* (Cambridge: Sever and Francis, 1863), 3: 129.
10. Ronald Inglehart, *Cultural Shift in Advanced Industrial Society* (Princeton, N.J.: Princeton University Press, 1990).
11. Richard Flacks, *Making History: The American Left and the American Mind* (New York: Columbia University Press, 1988), 126–28.

12. Pierre-Joseph Proudhon, Mikhail Bukanin, Max Stirner, and Adolph Fisher, all cited in Daniel Guerin, *Anarchism* (New York: Monthly Review Press, 1970), 12, 31, 33.

13. Michael B. Katz, *The Undeserving Poor: From the War on Poverty to the War on Welfare* (New York: Pantheon, 1989).

## 8: If Not Socialism, What?

Portions of this chapter appeared in an essay by Charles Derber in *The Responsive Community* (forthcoming as of this writing).

1. Herman E. Daly and John B. Cobb, Jr., *For the Common Good: Redirecting the Economy toward Community, the Environment and a Sustainable Future* (Boston: Beacon Press, 1989).

2. Social democracy and cooperativism are so different—and in some respects antithetical—that many may question whether both can be analyzed as manifestations of the same species, the social market. But both are characterized by the four analytical dimensions described above, and both are clearly not manifestations of the free-market model.

3. This description of Sweden relies heavily on the account of Robert Kuttner, *The Economic Illusion* (Boston: Houghton Mifflin, 1984), 152.

4. Alan Wolfe, *Whose Keeper? Social Science and Moral Obligation* (Berkeley: University of California Press, 1989), part 2, 156, 181.

5. Martin Buber, cited in Michael Harrington, *Socialism: Past and Future* (New York: Penguin, 1990), 29.

6. Max Stirner and Pierre-Joseph Proudhon, cited in Daniel Guerin, *Anarchism* (New York: Monthly Review Press, 1970), 15. Mikhail Bukanin, cited by Noam Chomsky in Guerin, *Anarchism*, ix.

7. Daly and Cobb, *For the Common Good,* 164, 165ff.

8. This account of Mondragon draws most heavily on Robert Oakeshott, *The Case for Workers' Coops* (London: Routledge and Kegan Paul, 1978). See also Ana Gutierrez Johnson and William Foote Whyte, "The Mondragon System of Worker Production Cooperatives," in *Workplace Democracy and Social Change,* Frank Lindenfeld and Joyce Rothschild-Whitt, eds. (Boston: Porter Sargent, 1982), 177–98.

9. David Ellerman, "On the Legal Structure of Workers' Cooperatives," in Lindenfeld and Rothschild-Whitt, eds., *Workplace Democracy and Social Change,* 299–313.

10. The Mondragon firm is still, of course, a market actor, required to compete and generate surplus for reinvestment. Its economic success is startling, with almost no failures over forty years and consistently high levels of profit, productivity, and technological innovation. But with capital no longer the basis of ownership or control, and the elimination of labor and capital as antagonistic groups, the coop cannot be regarded as capitalist. It is a new breed of enterprise that internalizes the principle of democratic community within the market itself.

11. Oakeshott, *The Case for Workers' Coops,* 195.

12. Johnson and Whyte, "The Mondragon System of Worker Production

Cooperatives," in Lindenfeld and Rothschild-Whitt, eds., *Workplace Democracy and Social Change*, 194–95.

13. Oakeshott, *The Case for Workers' Coops*, 173ff.

14. Severyn Bruyn and James Meehan, *Beyond the Market and the State* (Philadelphia: Temple University Press, 1987).

15. Samuel Bowles, David M. Gordon, and Thomas E. Weisskopf, *After the Wasteland* (Armonk, N.Y.: M.E. Sharpe, 1990), 208. Samuel Bowles et al., *Beyond the Wasteland* (New York: Doubleday, 1983), 305.

16. Bowles et al., *Beyond the Wasteland*, 274ff.

17. Harrington, *Socialism*, 9, 218ff.

18. Paul Hirst, *Associative Democracy: New Forms of Economic and Social Governance* (Amherst, Mass.: University of Massachusetts Press, 1994), 99–100.

19. Severyn Bruyn, *A Future for the American Economy: The Social Market* (Stanford: Stanford University Press, 1991). See also Bruyn, *The Field of Social Investment* (Cambridge: Cambridge University Press, 1989). And see Hirst, *Associative Democracy*, for a helpful discussion of macro-cooperativist approaches.

20. For analysis of Clinton as a "pragmatic communitarian," see Charles Derber, "Clintonism: Beyond Left and Right?" in *Tikkun*, January–February 1994, 40–45.

21. Bill Clinton and Al Gore, *Putting People First* (New York: Times Books, 1992). Quotation is from Clinton, cited on jacket of Barry and Irving Bluestone, *Negotiating the Future* (New York: Basic Books, 1992).

## 9: Coming Glued

An earlier draft of this chapter appeared as Charles Derber, "Coming Glued," *Tikkun* (July/August 1993): 27ff.

1. Amitai Etzioni, *The Spirit of Community* (New York: Morrow, 1993).

2. Charles Derber, *Money, Murder and the American Dream: Wilding From Wall Street to Main Street* (Boston: Faber and Faber, 1993).

3. Mary Ann Glendon, *Rights Talk* (New York: Free Press, 1991).

4. Wendy Kaminer, "Morality—The Newest Deal," *Mirabella*, September 1993, 36.

5. Diane E. Eyer, *Mother-Infant Bonding* (New Haven: Yale University Press, 1992).

6. Juliet Schor, *The Overworked American* (New York: Basic Books, 1992), 21.

7. This paragraph and the three that follow are drawn from Charles Derber, "Clintonism: Beyond Left and Right?" *Tikkun* (January/February 1994): 42–43.

8. A. Lawrence Chickering, "A Conservative's View of the Politics of Meaning," *Tikkun* (November/December 1993): 26. See also Chickering's *Beyond Left and Right* (San Francisco: ICS Press, 1993).

9. Etzioni, *The Spirit of Community*, 232. For a discussion of the Progressives as a model of PMC politics, see Charles Derber, William A. Schwartz, and Yale Magrass, *Professionals in the Highest Degree: Professionals and the Rise of a New Mandarin Capitalism* (New York: Oxford University Press, 1990).

10. Mickey Kauss, *The End of Equality* (New York: Basic Books, 1992).

11. Etzioni, *The Spirit of Community*, 144.